Wilfred Cantwell Smith:
A Theology for the World

Wilfred Cantwell Smith:
A Theology for the World

Edward J. Hughes

SCM PRESS LTD

BL
43
.S65
H84
1986

British Library Cataloguing-in-Publication Data available

334 02333 5
First published 1986
by SCM Press Ltd
26–30 Tottenham Road London N1 4BZ

Phototypeset by Input Typesetting Ltd
and printed in Great Britain by
The Camelot Press Ltd, Southampton

*This work is dedicated to Mary
whose help was heroic and inestimable*

CONTENTS

PREFACE

During the last three decades Wilfred Cantwell Smith's thought has exerted a growing influence among those religious thinkers who are responding to the fact of religious pluralism. That there are a number of religious traditions has always been a fact; but throughout long periods and wide areas of history the fact has not been felt as a problem. For centuries Christendom, for example, was able to dismiss the wider religious life of humanity as pagan superstition. However, the modern explosion of information concerning the history of religions, the uniting of the world by electronic communications into a complex global city, and the many-directional migrations of millions of people since the Second World War, drawing members of the Eastern traditions into the Western societies of Europe and North America, have all contributed to a new awareness both of the continuing strength and of the immense diversity of the great religious traditions of the world. This recognition has stimulated interest in the practical and intellectual problems of religious pluralism. How should the people of the different traditions view one another and treat one another? How should they think of their apparently incompatible belief systems? In the past, and still sometimes today, religious differences have been the occasion of war, persecution, oppression and exploitation. Today there is a widespread, though still by no means universal, reaction against the old dogmatic intolerance. But the emerging sense of a universal human community, embracing a variety of different forms of religious experience and thought, still needs what Smith calls a world theology.

It is in this move towards an intellectual understanding of religious plurality that Wilfred Cantwell Smith's thought has been so influential. His seminal work *The Meaning and End of Religion* (1963), now a modern classic of religious studies, distinguished between, on the one hand, response to the transcendent, which Smith calls faith, and which is constitutive of human life in all places and times, and, on the other hand, the various religious traditions which have accumulated through the centuries as major ingredients in the formation of civilizations. Faith, or response to the transcendent, is thus the substance which has been given different historical forms by the cumulative traditions. In subsequent books Smith has studied in careful detail the key concepts of faith, belief, knowledge, history, tradition, showing their interconnections and opening the way for the development of a global religious consciousness in which faith within each tradition can accept its diverse expression within other traditions.

The features of Smith's books which have made them so influential within the scholarly community are their immense learning and their wealth of challenging insights. The notes to his books often occupy almost as many pages as the main text, and arise from studies over many years and in many languages. Starting from (and continuing within) Christianity, Smith became a front-rank authority on Islam and then extended his field to include the Jewish and then the Hindu and Buddhist traditions. The strength of his work is the rooting of bold theories of wide scope in a scholarship which is not only remarkably wide-ranging but always thorough and exact.

There has been an increasing need for a volume which could introduce Wilfred Cantwell Smith's work to a wider public, and Dr Edward Hughes' book now admirably meets this need.

Claremont Graduate School   John Hick
California

INTRODUCTION

The writings of Wilfred Cantwell Smith, especially *Islam in Modern History* (1957) and *The Meaning and End of Religion* (1961), have been recognized as classics in religious studies.[1] The former deals with the ferment of Islamic self-definition in the twentieth century, while the latter treats of problems that the ambiguous term 'religion' presents to the student of religious life. It analyses how this ambiguity distorts Western analysis of religious existence in non-Western cultures.

Smith's success with these works has established him as a giant among contemporary writers in the history of religions. What is perhaps less known is that he has written extensively on the nature of faith, belief and religious truth. In his analysis of these concepts Smith has much to contribute to the theology and philosophy of religion.

There are, however, obstacles in the way through the forest of Smith's writings. One is that his style is rhetorically rich and his grammatical convolutions can leave the reader dazed. There is also the problem that Smith addresses a variety of professions. The reader must have a sense for the scholarly concerns of several audiences. At moments Smith argues as a theologian for theologians, though usually he represents himself as an historian. He differs, however, from most historians in that his concerns focus on contemporary religious issues rather than on the past. In this he is akin to social scientists. On occasion he also addresses philosophical concerns that centre upon problems of linguistic analysis. Though Smith, as an historian, disclaims expertise in these other areas, his writings nonetheless raise important issues for all of them. In an age when many professionals are insulated from other fields both by the volume of material in their specializations and by group loyalty to the interests and methods of their disciplines, Smith is a maverick ranging outside the boundaries of accepted scholarship. This breadth reflects a creative concern for the unity of thought.

Yet other difficulties confront the reader. Smith's footnotes are many, elaborate and technical. In *Faith and Belief* the main body of text is 172 pages, while the footnotes cover 162 pages.[2] The main text of *The Meaning and End of Religion* in the Harper/SPCK paperback edition is 202 pages; yet footnotes consist of 129 pages of minuscule print. Added to this density of scholarship is the fact that Smith is a polyglot who quotes from a variety of sources in several languages. Few individuals exist who are competent to check his use of original sources and duplicate his ease with such disparate secondary material. This would, in fact, require a team of scholars. Further, his thought is spread throughout a number of volumes and many articles. Each of his major works treats of different themes; and the overall plan of his thinking is not readily discernible. This book organizes his thought according to central motifs that cut across his many writings and unify them as a whole. For this reason a good deal of it is expository, with the intention of enabling the reader to see the relations between Smith's concepts of 'faith', 'belief', 'truth', 'critical corporate self-consciousness' and 'global theology'. A chapter is devoted to each theme and evaluates the charges of critics.

If these remarks are not sufficient to make Smith's corpus appear difficult of access, there is also the fact that Smith is a language reformer, critical of the common academic use of terms like 'faith', 'belief', and 'religion'. He attempts to substitute more adequate ways of speaking about the phenomena to which these terms refer. The reader who is long accustomed to think within such terms may find him/herself confused as he/she acclimatizes to a new vocabulary. It is my hope to clarify Smith's positions, by removing unwarranted criticisms and pointing to the existence of actual problems. I hope to counter the essentially correct prediction by a reviewer of *The Meaning and End of Religion:*

> . . . he will be misunderstood by many. Some may admire the work for wrong reasons. And some may criticize it for wrong reasons. For there are not many who like Professor Smith have gone through the turmoils of comparative study with such thoroughness.[3]

Though Smith was originally acclaimed as an Islamicist, the present work does not attempt to evaluate his writings in this area, this being the task of Islamicists. Nevertheless, I have referred throughout to a number of Smith's contributions to the study of Islam in order to illustrate his wider philosophical and theological programme.

The overall position of this book is that Smith's understanding of the central concepts described and analysed in each chapter is coherent, cogent, and helpful for furthering an understanding of planetary religious existence. Though I have criticized his positions in a number of places, I am in substantial agreement with his analyses of faith, belief and truth. I also find his methodology appropriate for unearthing the faith dimension of others and agree with his new vision of the direction that a future theology should take.

1

AN UNDERSTANDING OF FAITH

In *The Meaning and End of Religion*, Wilfred Cantwell Smith separates faith from belief. He argues that faith is the foundation of a religious tradition, while belief is a secondary conceptual expression of the primary experience of faith.[4] This chapter explores the complex meaning that 'faith' has in Smith's writings.

The central aspects of faith

A practical purpose informs Smith's works. He believes that humanity is on the eve of a global civilization. He observes the external forces of science, economies and communications pressing in this direction, but argues that these are not sufficient to create global community, since community requires bonds of common interest and vision. He therefore turns to the world's religious traditions for aid. His task is to outline a programme that facilitates global religious inter-understanding. He is convinced that the effective creation of world community requires the intensity of a religious outlook, and that only such an outlook offers the possibility of overcoming tribal interest and individual self-centredness. Unlike those who find in secularism the cornerstone of a future inter-cultural community, Smith begins with the world religions as a place to weave a global web of understanding and co-operation.

Predicting dark possibilities for the world unless persons of different traditions cultivate loyalty to, and appreciation of, one another, Smith assumes that world fellowship will in large part be the task of religious persons. He holds that: 'From no other source than his faith, I believe, can man master the energy, devotion, vision, resolution, the capacity to survive disappointment, that will be necessary.'[5]

The Christian and Islamic religions have in the past hindered world community by denying authentic transcendence within other communities. Their exclusivist attitude has long obstructed trust and respect between the world's communities, for whoever denies the activity of transcendence in another tradition is, in effect, calling its participants deluded, ignorant, even deceitful or evil.

Christianity had generally little accurate awareness of other religions until the late twentieth century, when it now finds itself in tension between an exclusivist theology and a universalist morality. Its morality in agape-istic, calling for universal care, while its theology is particular and insular, dividing human beings into the classical camps of sheep and the goats, the saved and the damned.

Given these options, Smith has opted for universal openness. He insists that a twentieth-century church must reform its self-understanding to give an appropriate theological foundation to the ideal of universal service. The challenge offered is moral and intellectual. Morally, he avers that only a hypocrite can profess to love (including trust) another human being while viewing him/her as damned. Intellectually, he claims that the new-found knowledge of non-Christian traditions forces us to recognize in them ideas and values as cogent and as noble as those in Christianity. Further, as we study the lives of religious notables or personally encounter exemplary representatives from other traditions, we become aware of spiritual transformations as profound as any found in Christianity.[6]

Smith notes that the formation of a global community is not an ideal foreign to the religious traditions; for each contains within itself the dream of a unitary mankind, a dream that is experienced by the religious conscience as a sacred command. He even claims to recognize a providential hand behind the growing pressure upon faith communities to take each other seriously, a pressure that can move 'faith-ful' persons of all religions into greater cooperation.

> One of the tasks open to us today, and beckoning to us, is to participate in God's creative process of bringing into actual reality what has until now been an ideal reality only, that of the world-wide community.[7]

Smith views himself as an intellectual challenged to discover a unifying thread amidst the diversity of the world's faith. Yet he finds doctrinal divergence too vast to provide this unity. If one considers the doctrinal problems arising around images of ultimate reality, one immediately sees his point. In the Hindu tradition alone, ultimate reality is envisaged as one's liberated self (Jain), the absolute self (Vedantist), the cosmic personal self (Theist), and the no-self (Buddhist) – understood here historically as a Hindu reform movement. Such multiplicity resists unification. Recognizing, therefore, the fruitlessness of grounding global harmony in doctrinal similarity, Smith locates the thread of unification in what he calls 'faith'.

Smith has written a great deal about faith in books and articles that span more than thirty years of publication. Yet despite his voluminous efforts, he remains convinced that such delineations fail to capture the riches of its reality.

He does, however, attempt a number of approximately adequate formulations of the concept of faith; and I have included several in an appendix at the end of this work. Yet because of the variety of his depiction, readers may be confused as to his exact understanding. This is especially the case since Smith uses 'faith' to refer to several different but related aspects of religious life. It may be helpful, therefore, to differentiate four aspects of faith found in his writings. These are: 1. faith as a capacity for ultimate meaning; 2. faith as a response to transcendence; 3. faith as a quality of persons; 4. faith as an organizing pattern of meaning.

First, faith as a capacity for ultimate meaning refers to the ability of persons to orient their lives according to a symbolic vision of reality that transcends mundane facts.

Second, faith as a response to transcendence is the human capacity to react to a transcendent dimension of life. 'Transcendence' is Smith's term for ultimate reality, which includes values such as justice, beauty and truth. Transcendence may be understood as either imaginary or actual, so long as the reader recognizes that transcendence for one in a state of faith is a perceived reality. Smith normally assumes transcendence to be actual, i.e. to refer to the divine real.

Third, faith in its broadest characterization may be viewed as a human quality such as hope or charity. Faith as a capacity to discover meaning and as an openness to transcendence are illustrations of this quality. Those engaged in the activity of faith are faith-ing and may be described as faith-ful.

Fourth, faith refers to a pattern of meaning – a total way of seeing the world. This means that, once an individual has responded to transcendence and discovered meaning, he/she experiences a need to organize all of existence around the ultimate values that arise from that response. Such total ways of seeing are embodied in religious traditions and constitute world-views.

The relationship between the four aspects of faith may be briefly summarized. Faith as a capacity for meaning, when actualized, becomes faith as a realized quality. A person finding ultimate meaning has entered into a state of faithfulness through a response to transcendence. This process normally occurs when an individual is in contact with his/her religious tradition, which expresses the faith of earlier generations. The faithful person then organizes life into a pattern of meaning. In most instances, this pattern is given by one's tradition, though creative persons (and in some degree all persons) in turn modify their tradition. This brief description of 'faith' may be thought of as the skeleton upon which Smith hangs less central but nonetheless rewarding faith reflections.

Religion, faith and tradition

Let me now describe some further intricacies of Smith's analysis. In so doing I shall state what faith is *not* before developing an affirmative approach. This method follows Smith's own, in that he often describes the nature of faith in a *neti neti* fashion in order to dissolve the reader's previously held images. One thing we discover is that faith is not religion.

In *The Meaning and End of Religion* Smith investigates the history of the term 'religion' and shows how it has meant different things to different persons in different ages. Because of its long and complex history, 'religion' today refers to concepts that, for the sake of clarity, are best kept separate.

One usage finds religion to be synonymous with piety, a quality of persons valued in every tradition. When speaking of religion in this sense it is common to speak in the singular; for like charity or hope, piety is a unitary quality. One does not customarily speak of several pieties, though there may be numberless expressions of piety.

'Religion' also refers to an historical entity, to *a* religion, to a particular system of doctrine, ritual, ethics, etc. This may, of course, be spoken of in the plural. In this sense 'religion' is thought of as a depersonalized and outward something, as a reality that exists objectively apart from human involvement.

'Religion' may also refer to an ideal system rather than an actual historical entity. This usage is common among theologians who formulate their versions (visions) of true Christianity or true Islam by separating the ideal from actual historical embodiments. With the acumen of a referee aware of cross-cultural foul play, Smith notes that persons tend to speak of their own religion in ideal terms but of others' religions in empirical or sociological terms.

The last use of 'religion' is the most comprehensive. It refers to religion in a generic sense, religion in general, which includes all forms of piety (religiousness), and all religious systems, empirical or ideal. Given the ambiguity between these four separate meanings, Smith argues that the word 'religion' should be abandoned in scholarly discourse and replaced by two different terms, 'faith' and 'cumulative tradition'.

Faith refers to the inner, existential, and experiential dimension of religion. In this sense it is a synonym for the first usage given above – that is 'piety'. It is essentially adjectival, a quality of persons, and refers to a subject's involvement with transcendent value.

> By 'faith' I mean personal faith. . . . For the moment let it stand for an inner religious experience or involvement of a particular person; the impingement on him of the transcendent, putative or real.[8]

In contrast to this, the cumulative tradition refers to:

> . . . . the entire mass of overt objective data that constitute the historical deposit, . . . of the past religious life of the community in question: temples, scriptures, theological systems, dance patterns, legal and other social institutions, conventions, moral codes, myths, and so on; anything that can be and is transmitted from one person, one generation, to another, and that an historian can observe.[9]

By dividing 'religion' into the two hemispheres of 'faith' and 'tradition', Smith wants to clarify the study of both the inward dimension of faith and the objective data of the traditions. He finds that these two aspects have often been confused in past studies. John Hick lists the positive effects that Smith's reconceptualization of religion into 'faith' and 'cumulative tradition' would produce:

> (1) to release us from the notion of the religions as contraposed socio-theological entities, and so from the unprofitable question, Which of these is the true religion? (2) to identify the religiously all-important, and at a same time philosophically problematic, area of inner personal faith and experience; (3) to free study of the cumulative traditions from monolithic illusions, thus allowing the rich

detailed variety to show itself, not only between traditions, but also within each tradition.[10]

Hick's third point is important for anyone who wishes to understand the concept of cumulative tradition. Smith rejects the notion that a religion has an essence – an unchanging core. Rather, religions as cumulative traditions may be seen as constantly shifting processes. Doctrines, rituals, ecclesiastical institutions are all in movement. Even when certain elements of a tradition such as long-standing doctrines appear relatively stable, what they mean to the faithful shifts from generation to generation. The Christ of early Greek Christianity, the Christ-Son of Luther's severe Father-God, the Christ of nineteenth-century liberalism, all have Christ as the centre of devotion, but his meaning for the devotee has been transformed in each of these contexts. In a sense one may say that there is no one Christianity, but rather several; for Christianity has meant different things to different ages. This is not to say that there are not dominant or central themes that have persisted throughout a tradition's history. Liberation (*moksha*), for example, has been a constant motif in Indian life for millennia, though its exact understanding has altered with time. The primacy of love has likewise been relatively constant in Christianity, though love's requirements are reinterpreted in each age.[11]

The cumulative tradition is open to future redefinition. Once one rejects an essentialist definition, it is impossible to surmise what transformations Christianity, or any religion, may undergo in the future. The life of a tradition occurs in its members. And just as a person is open to change until his or her death, so too a tradition which is the creation of persons cannot be fully defined until it has expired. A theme that has been central to the life of a tradition may cease to be – as, for example, Christian exclusivism, which appears to be on the wane.

Elements that seemed alien to a tradition may also cease to be so. One thinks of the increasing Christian participation in the practice of yoga and zazen. Again, a tradition that has been other-worldly may become this-worldly in a different moment of its career.

A difficulty exists in this fluid understanding of tradition. One critic wonders if Smith has considered the elastic limits of a tradition. How does Smith account for the process of authority that exists in almost every tradition? 'How can there be internal discipline with regard to heresy when the cumulative tradition is as amorphous as he makes it out to be?[12] The answer lies in the fact that a tradition is only as amorphous as the faith of its constituents allows it to be. The community may well decide that an individual's interpretation of its religious life is peripheral, non-representative or distorted. Though communities vary in the ways they centralize religious authority, they nevertheless agree that certain representatives have spoken well for the faith that the majority have felt within them.

By analysing 'religion' into 'faith' and 'tradition', we now recognize why faith is not equivalent to religion. Faith corresponds to the inward manner in which a person makes sense of the world. This explains Smith's choice of wording in the title of his early work *The Faith of Other Men*, a work in which we see the world through the eyes of several types of faith.[13]

But if faith is not religion as a whole, because it excludes the cumulative tradition, it is also not belief. To understand why this is so, we must recognize that Smith also distinguishes several meanings in the term 'belief', two of which are important here.

The first form of belief consists of unconsciously held meanings and assumptions that one receives from one's tradition. This form of belief should not be confused with faith, for the holding of assumptions about the nature of reality or of humankind does not constitute an openness to transcendence. A person may accept the assumptions of his/her religious tradition without having a vital relationship with the ultimate reality to which these assumptions refer. Two individuals may hold the same world view with its many tacit beliefs; but the faith of one is strong, joyous and humble, while the faith of the other is dead, perverted and minor. In this sense it is possible to have belief without faith.

The second form of belief consists in a self-conscious holding to, or opting for, a set of propositionally stated doctrines. Emphasis upon this form of belief has arisen rather recently in the history of religious life with the Enlightenment's assumption that belief rather than faith is at the core of religious life – that *believing* is what religious people are primarily doing.[14]

Smith is not implying that prior to the Enlightenment persons did not concern themselves with an analyzing of propositional statements. One need only recall the mediaeval Hindu, Christian and Islamic scholastic traditions to remedy this misunderstanding. What he intends to prove is that prior to the Enlightenment, the term 'belief' referred to existential acts of trust, love and commitment rather than to a detached weighing of the truth or falsity of religious statements. It was the cultivation of love and trust that constituted the core of religious life. Only after the traditional doctrines of Western society became problematical, raising the question of whether persons of honest intellect could appropriate them, did Western intellectuals turn to the problem of belief in the modern sense. What was traditionally assumed now became an object of debate. Prior to this period, an analysis of religious propositions worked on clarifying what were assumed to be divine truths, not seriously open to debate.

Post-Enlightenment Westerners who understand religion as the holding of beliefs have naturally asked those with a different world-view 'What do you believe?' Smith suggests the question is misplaced and does not facilitate an acquaintance with the faith of others. More fruitful questions might be asked: How does their tradition mediate value? How do their symbols help members lead lives of purpose and serenity? How successful has a tradition been in helping persons contact the divine or in leading lives of integrity?[15]

Dimensions of faith

'Faith' does not refer to extraordinary phenomena. It does not primarily denote the visions of prophets or the illuminations of mystics. Faith is not a supernatural something added to human nature; it is rather a quality of human nature, a universal capacity for meaning. Even Western secularism, often narrowly thought of as faith-less and in opposition to faith, has a long faith-history. Persons living in accord with the ideals of secularism live by a form of faith, faith through ideals of reason, of justice, of human dignity.[16]

Smith prefers to speak (somewhat unusually) of faith *through* an ideal, rather than *in* an ideal. This is because he understands ideals to have transcendent properties which are never comprehended. Ideals lure persons with the force of an intrinsic attractiveness and demand. Through them, by means of them, by participating in them, persons are opened for growth in the direction of infinity. In Smith's writings one finds 'faith *through* God', or '*through* Dharma', or '*through* Christ' rather than the traditional 'faith *in* God', '*in* Dharma', or '*in* Christ'.[17] 'Through' preserves a sense of direction towards the divine which never presumes to contain the divine.

In a similar way Smith does not speak of the content of faith, since a container is larger than that which is contained. Persons of faith are unable to contain that which is limitless and greater than themselves.[18] He is even hesitant to speak of faith having a specific object, though he acknowledges that worshippers are naturally conditioned by a particular idea of reality. For Smith the idea is not the reality that worshippers open to in faith, but rather Reality itself. For this reason he speaks of faith 'in the shape of' an idea, rather than faith in an idea.[19]

Smith sees Western secularism at its most creative as a positive inheritance from the Graeco-Roman tradition. Yet, against this positive legacy, negative secularism has emerged in the modern period – a type of nihilism critical of all expression of positive value. Negative secularism is in essence a reaction against faith, and therefore against idealism and transcendence in all forms. This form of secularism, when viewed from the vantage of history, is a peculiar phenomenon – in that human beings in all recorded civilizations have lived by faith. The appearance of destructive secularism prompts Smith to speculate that the modern West may betray a spiritual bankruptcy and is entering a period of decline as it loses its faith.

Faith is not rare; persons have always lived by it, for most have sensed or held to a value that inspired and made claims upon them. Speaking from this broad view of faith, Smith affirms:

> Someone has remarked that the only true atheist is he who loves no one and whom no one loves; who does not care for truth, sees no beauty, strives for no justice; who knows no courage or no joy, finds no meaning, and has lost all hope.[20]

Though faith is a condition of normal persons, it is not arrived at automatically. There are those for whom the patrimony of the past has ceased to inspire or offer meaning. In the modern period many communities have failed to hold the interest of their members. To combat this drift towards faithlessness and meaninglessness, Smith points to the traditional significance that faith has had. He offers us descriptions of its many forms, hopeful that those unable to find meaning in its current forms may find clues to faith in its past expressions. This is urgent for well–being, since faith has been humankind's bastion of integrative stability.

> Faith then is a quality of human living. At its best it has taken the form of serenity and courage and loyalty and service; a quiet confidence and joy which enables one to feel at home in the universe, and to find meaning in the world and in one's own life, a meaning that is profound and ultimate, and is stable no matter what may happen to oneself at the level of the immediate event.[21]

Faith does not emerge from a mere scholastic acquaintance with the data of a tradition. Students of foreign traditions may know more about a religion than its devotees. Yet unless the student is equipped with sympathetic understanding, he/she will not sense, nor imaginatively orientate him/herself to, the participant's world, and will fail to apprehend faith.

The religious world of a participant includes the objective tradition in which he/she lives plus the ideals that lie inwards and spur the participant beyond his or her current state of spiritual development. For this reason Smith rejects those studies in the social sciences that focus upon present behaviour and neglect the transcendent aspects of existence as inadequate – a mistake Smith himself confesses to have made in his early historical work, *Modern Islam in India*.[22]

The locus of faith lies not in rituals, doctrines, or forms of organization: these are public items. The locus is in individuals who both find and give meaning to their cultural inheritance and who, in turn, are inspired by earlier generations. New generations turn to the inherited tradition but reinterpret its data and discover new meaning according to the psychological and historical demands of their situation. Through this ongoing interpretation a meaning world is constituted and kept vital. Yet it would not be correct to imply that persons seek the meaning of a tradition as their primary goal; instead, they seek the meaning of existence as illuminated by that tradition.

> We are concerned with meaning: not only the meaning that a person's tradition has for him or her, if they are involved, but more significantly the meaning that life and the universe have for them, in the light of their involvement.[23]

Meaning is not found chiefly in systems of doctrine or law. Legal codes and theologies are themselves reflections upon a more primary meaning that life and the cosmos have for the faithful. Codifications of doctrine or law are conceptualizations of a primary vision; it is vision which is foundational. Law and doctrine are simply its expression. Loss of vision is a failure of faith, and is synonymous with a collapse of meaning. In speaking of faith as vision and pattern Smith means to distance himself from historians and social scientists who conceive of faith as only an aspect of life, like economics or politics. As a pattern of meaning, faith may be thought of as the soul of a culture, as the organizing principle around which the whole of existence coheres. Discussing the Islamic pattern, Smith states:

> The system does not 'mean' something, so much as it confers meaning. It is in light of the total system that every word, every proposition, made within it has whatever meaning it has. And not only propositions, but things. . . . If a Muslim loses his faith nothing in his life may change; except that the various elements in it no longer cohere into a pattern, are no longer meaningful.[24]

Faith is accordingly not a category that describes a portion of human activity. It does not delimit a partial field or area, like geology or literature; rather, faith is the value that these activities or aspects of life take on. Faith is thus the pattern of basic loyalties that organizes the activities of life into a world-view. Smith is aware that this way of speaking is foreign to modern Westerners, who think of religious life as simply one social item among others. Smith, on the other hand, understands faith as the axis of meaning that provides unity for all life's activities, from economics to art.

> Faith is not a factor in a man's life, alongside others . . . yet once it has arisen in personal life . . . if it is authentic, it embraces, it colors, all. It is not one element in the total pattern of that person's life. . . .[25]

The fact that Americans and Europeans consider religious existence (faith) to delimit a portion of their world indicates that the West no longer finds in the Christian faith its primary focus of value. The United States, for example, has its primary meaning system in the American way of life, which includes within it, in sometimes uneasy suspension, elements of the Christian vision. It is statistically truer to say that the American (or Canadian) way of life is the faith of the majority of North Americans.

Though faith is a personal capacity for meaning, Smith does not conceive of faith in an individualist manner. Faith is personal; but the person is not isolated. For Smith the person is radically social. Personhood is constituted within the matrix of society. The opposite of personal is impersonal, not social. As a quality of persons, faith necessarily includes personal and social dimensions.

Though faith has a corporate dimension, Smith, unlike Durkheim, does not place the locus of faith in the community. Communities, unlike human beings, have no personal centre. In this sense, societies are not as ultimate as persons, who are able to demonstrate freedom over society. Hermits, prophets, founders, and rebels criticized and altered the values of their group. Smith is therefore able to say that society does not fully determine persons, but rather persons selectively interiorize, reject, or recreate the values available to them.

Contemporary faith also disproves any attempt to explain faith as a community phenomenon. Modern individualism has witnessed persons who have no membership in a religious community, yet have faith. Even members of specific communities often find their meaning in the insights of a variety of traditions. The number of Christians who find direction in the teaching of Gandhi or Buber illustrates this point.

Faith enables persons to attain self-transcendence by surrendering to ideals that they experience as making a claim upon them. Faith in this sense reveals the unique dignity of human freedom. Individuals reveal the ability either to embody value or to fall short of the mark. As an ideal, true personhood exists in each religion as a dream to be attained. A person may therefore be described as that creature who can be loyal to dreams. This way of speaking is uncommon among social scientists, who measure the actual rather than the lure of the possible. Yet, a true grasp of inwardness must consider the pull of transcendence.

It will be noted that in classical humanist fashion my anthropology here has been metaphysical. To think or feel that human behavior may on occasion be inhuman, that people may be 'less than human', that, unlike crocodiles, we persons may become or may fail to become our true selves, is to recognize 'man' as transcendent and not merely as an empirical concept.[26]

Human beings come to transcendence via the anthropological ideals of their culture. Each civilization offers models of true humanity which press human development in the direction of divinity.[27]

Faith is beyond apprehension because it is the human potentiality for being human: it is our strange dynamic towards becoming our true selves and becoming divine.[28]

Fearing that phrases like 'becoming one's true self' or 'becoming divine' might offend some orthodox Christians or Muslims who emphasize human depravity or stress a radical division between the human and divine, Smith recommends that these phrases be understood as pointers that indicate the direction of true humanity and leaves the various religions to fill them with their own content.

Faith is a capacity for authenticity. Persons have attained integrity by being involved in one or more of the earth's major traditions. What used to be called the religions may be thought of as historically significant attempts to be excellently human. One is not first a human being who then has Jewishness, Muslimness, Christianness, etc., accidentally added to his or her humanity. Rather, Smith argues: 'One is human by being one or another of them.'[29] Human nature is therefore not a fixed entity. Instead, what is labelled 'human nature' is a potential for cultural definition. Through culture, persons awaken to definition and to the possibility of authenticity.[30]

Faith is located in persons. In transformed individuals it reaches its highest expression. Each major religion appreciates those heroes in whom faith reached its maximum – heroes in whom the ultimates of the community were embodied. Such persons exposed the further reaches of human excellence, or in some instances of divine excellence. But Western scholarship tends not to explore the quality of persons in whom a particular form of faith is made luminous. Instead of reflecting upon exemplary persons, it has approached religious life as a system of beliefs. It has turned the focus away from faith in persons towards the objects of faith – like God, Dharma, shariah, etc., forgetting that the significance of such objects lies in the meaning they hold and the values they elicit.

Preoccupation with the objects of a culture is academically unsound and humanly alienating. Since dissimilar objects may awaken similar qualities in participants, it is erroneous to assume that when one discovers different objects one is dealing with a radically different reality. A Catholic may count his beads, while a Protestant studies scripture. Both may be engaged in the awakening of the quality of mercy. A Muslim and a Jew may engage in a similar awakening, reflecting on torah and shariah. The object which seems so dissimilar may, when explored for its human significance, reveal striking parallels. This observation has important repercussions for dialogue. It is a common observation that those who find the rituals or doctrines of an alien faith bizarre and threatening discover their anxieties allayed upon meeting a spiritually evolved representative. Expecting to find a stranger whose world picture indicated radical otherness, they may in fact find a friend. A magnetic attraction of human qualities in many instances dissolves cultural suspicions and dogmatic discord.

Conversely, similar objects of faith do not necessarily indicate similar meanings. Christian doctrines such as the divinity of Christ, the virgin birth, scriptural infallibility, etc., have meant quite different things to Christians from different periods and places. Given this instability of meaning, Smith analyses doctrinal and other aspects of a tradition in the light of their developing personal meaning.

Academic 'open' inquiry, also, even when not particularist,

has tended to be object-oriented, though in an empirical sense, rather than concerned with the relation of persons to that object. A prodigious effort over the past century, for instance, has gone into a critical study of the Bible and how it was put together; relatively little study has been made of the role of the Bible, once it had become a scripture, in the consciousness and the lives of men and women over the centuries since, to whose faith alone it owes its significance.[31]

In objectivist forms of scholarship one hears the term 'faith' used in the formula 'faith in x or y', faith in God, in the Dharma, in God and the Qur'an, in Christ or whatever. When this occurs, emphasis is placed upon the prepositional object, leaving the nature of faith (personal meaning) itself unexplored. Such an attitude presupposes that the person interested in the prepositional object understands the exact nature of faith. This is not necessarily the case.

By focusing on the object of faith, a student (or a devotee) may assume that the 'object's significance' has remained constant when in fact it has changed dramatically. One therefore ought not to ask what a concept such as 'God' means objectively (in itself) but what it has meant to particular persons in a particular age, at a particular time in their lives. Smith demands the highest degree of specificity from those who would study faith.

In an article, 'The Study of Religion and the Study of the Bible', Smith illustrates his personalist approach. Instead of studying the meaning of scripture in an absolute dogmatic sense, or according to its meaning for an original audience, Smith would have us understand how persons in different ages found significance in it. He notes that by investing the Bible with sacred status, persons have come to it with an openness to reality, with the result that it has in fact ' . . . introduced men to that which transforms, its committed readers affirm, the historical observers report, and the department of religion must note and interpret'.[32] Scripture has done this, for persons have given it the power to act upon them. It has therefore assumed various roles for the different individuals who sought instruction in its symbols, stories, ecstasies and commands: a different role in the dark ages when few could read; a different role at the height of scholasticism; and different again in the mystical theology of John of the Cross. These variations indicate the multiple ways that persons found meaning through the Bible. Faith through scripture is a way of openness to transcendence via a document.

The personalist interpretation of the task of religious studies – the apprehension of faith – has not met with a consensus in the academic community. In an article ' "Comparative Religion: Whither – and Why?" A Reply to Wilfred Cantwell Smith,' Per Kvaerne objects to Smith's insistence that the proper goal of religious studies lies in understanding the personal vision of faith participants.[33] Kvaerne rightly perceives that a personalist emphasis precludes definitive conclusions to which he assumes that 'the history of religions, like any historical discipline, must necessarily aspire'.[34] Kvaerne argues that for Smith's programme to be complete, scholars would be obliged to interview all faith participants and ascertain their unique apprehension of the meaning of the symbols, rites, doctrines, etc., of their tradition – a task Kvaerne finds to be of impossible dimensions.[35]

Smith, however, is not discouraged by the inability of historians of religion to attain definitive conclusions concerning the meaning of religious life. In fact, he argues that modest and tentative conclusions are appropriate in a field where it is impossible in practice to tabulate the full range of meaning. When dealing with the visions of others, Smith feels that it is scholastically apt and morally virtuous to recognize that 'our reports are partial and limited'.[36] They are necessarily partial because of 1. the outsider's inability fully to understand any person, much less someone from an alien culture; 2. the impossibility of querying all participants for the meaning of his/her faith; 3. the inability of the participant to express fully what he/she apprehends or religiously perceives.

These limitations caution scholarly claims to definitive

conclusions concerning the faith of others. Further, scholars, mindful of the limitations of research, should never pretend to essentialist statements such as 'Islam holds' or 'Buddhism teaches', but should instead personalize and limit such statements to read: 'Some Buddhists hold' or 'Certain Muslims teach'.[37]

Faith refers to an inner quality of religious existence. In this inward dimension faith is hidden from external observation. Yet invisible, faith can be inferred indirectly from the attributes that religious persons exhibit – qualities that members of different communities are able to admire in one another. For example, Christians have been known to admire Buddhist serenity, and Buddhists, Christian ethical fervour. Though both groups remain at doctrinal variance, the qualities they mutually admire have emerged in response to the ideals embedded in both traditions. By learning to respect the qualities of persons, one in turn comes to respect the traditions that gave them birth. Respect is therefore propaedeutic for apprehending the values at the heart of an alien vision.

Faith is also an adjective. By thinking adjectivally, instead of substantively, one places the locus of faith in nouns, objects and systems. Persons under the spell of substantives perceive themselves as members of oppositional parties, which naturally creates intellectual barriers. This is especially true in the Christian and Islamic instances. Christians have historically seen themselves through the lens of systematic doctrine and have accordingly excluded those with different doctrines. Muslims have understood themselves as a community of systematized law (shariah) and have excluded those beyond its pale. Both groups have exclusivist heritages, although Muslims, following the Qur'anic injunction about the people of the Book, have been less exclusivist than Christians.

When persons from exclusivist backgrounds conceptualize faith as a noun, they immediately reject religious insight in other traditions. This arises from the logic of nouns, though not of adjectives. If one is a Christian (noun) one is not a Muslim (noun). But if a person is Christian (adjective), meaning Christ-

like or agape-istic, one need not think of others as spiritually
déclassé. The same is true with the adjective 'Muslim'.

> A man cannot be both a Christian and a Muslim at the same
> time. The nouns keep us apart. On the other hand, it is not,
> I suggest, as ridiculous or fanciful as might be supposed, to
> ask whether in the realm of adjectives it may not be possible
> for a man to be both Christian and Muslim at the same
> time.[38]

In Islamic tradition we notice a similar substantive/adjectival
configuration. The word 'Muslim' contains both a substantive
reference, meaning formal membership in a community, and
an adjectival meaning, referring to an internal attitude of
submission to divine injunctions. The adjectival sense of
'Muslim' refers to a quality of heart, a purity of devotion in
one who submits to God. Both Christians and Muslims
therefore find themselves challenged by their adjectives.
Christians may searchingly ask how Christian they have been,
while in like manner Muslims may ask themselves how Muslim
they have been. Both will find themselves considerably short
of the qualities to which 'Christian' and 'Muslim' point.
Conversely, Christians may ask how Muslim they have been in
submission to Christ's commandment of agape, and Muslims
may ask how Christian they have been in the care of their
neighbour, which the Qur'an enjoins.

Adjectives refer us to ideals that disturb us with their call to
further growth. It is a matter of psychological fact that persons
poor in faith frequently take pride in identifying with their
particular system of faith (noun), but do not allow the ideals
of their community to call their lives into question. One takes
pride in being a Christian; one speaks of the glories of Islam;
yet one's life is neither Christian nor Muslim.

> The noun as noun is comforting, the adjective demanding.
> The noun is static, the adjective dynamic. The noun asserts,
> the adjective pleads. The noun is human, the adjective
> divine.[39]

Smith elevates faith's status above being merely *a* human quality or even *a* significant human quality. Faith may properly be called *the* essential human quality, for persons demonstrate their human uniqueness in their capacity to sustain a vision that transcends the mundane world. As *the* essential human quality, faith is necessary for psychological integration and vitality. Persons bereft of transcendent value are reduced to a state of anomie and ego-diffusion. If, indeed, faith is as essential to human integrity, as Smith suggests, one would expect it to have been highly prized throughout the major religious traditions. This is precisely what history indicates.

But if faith is an adjective, it is also a verb. One who is faithful is actively engaged, is committed, is faith-ing. Although the English language does not provide us with a verb to describe this activity (we are forced to speak of 'having faith'), the Greek of the New Testament does. The verb *pisteuo* is used there to describe Christian existence as an active state of commitment and trust. Not only Christian faith but generic faith, too, should be understood verbally, dynamically. Persons are not passive within their traditions. One engaged with faith is faith-ing, living actively in relation to transcendence.

Faith is a virtue. It refers to a human ability for transformation and may be viewed like other virtues as a form of strength. Its opposites include nihilism and disintegration – forms of human weakness. For those who participate in its virtue, faith is salvific. Though human beings are not in a position empirically to verify the activity of the divine in the lives of others, we are able to acknowledge phenomenologically that women and men appear to have entered into a relationship with the ultimate. Through faith, persons have found their lives set free (saved) from mediocrity and made capable of transformed existence. Though this type of salvation may not be viewed as 'real' by those who hold to a dogmatic interpretation, Smith holds that those who are emotionally and doctrinally free to observe the fruits of faith in persons from other traditions will necessarily notice lives of positive transformation. He comments:

> By 'saved' here, mundanely, I mean . . . saved from nihilism, alienation, anomie, despair, from the bleak despondency of meaninglessness. Saved from unfreedom; from being the victim of one's own whims within, or of pressures without; saved from being merely an organism reacting to its environment.[40]

Smith witnesses that faith produces women and men of serenity, courage and charity. He challenges exclusivisits to note that the fruits of the spirit are globally noticeable. He calls on sceptics and humanists to ponder the fact that historically the higher qualities of excellence have emerged through contact with religious traditions.

Because faith is a quality of persons, it is impossible to measure it by means of quantitative methods. Ideals, thoughts and aspirations are closed to public view. Yet we are not prevented from recognizing the activity of ideals in others. We come to know persons from their activities and creations and are thus able to infer their probable state of mind from their behaviours. As Smith would have it: 'the proper study of mankind is by inference'.[41] In the case of living persons we are able to check observations by conferring with others who can confirm or deny our interpretations. By treating observable items as clues to human aspiration, historians can approach an understanding of foreign world-views. Though this type of understanding may appear less 'scientific', according to the popular fashion of equating science with quantitative method, it is nevertheless essential in understanding human existence. Yet a danger of misunderstanding is always present, since it is impossible to infer the complete meaning of faith. Persons are never fully transparent to one another. Each consistently remains a partial mystery to the other and, given the ideal dimension they participate in, one might add, to themselves.[42]

Another reason that an observer falls short of completely understanding faith is that faith is more than an observer can observe. It does not find its full realization in behaviour or expression. Just as artists fall short of their inspirations, so too persons of faith fall short of their ideals. It is in the nature of ideals to resist formulation. One governed, for instance, by the ideal of Justice knows that there is more to comprehending Justice than present awareness indicates. He or she feels the vector of the ideal indicating that more in the understanding of Justice lies ahead.

Faith's true history has yet to be written. Though scholars have gathered factual material, they have not as yet (though here we find notable exceptions) understood what faith has meant to worshippers, nor have they apprehended faith as a quality of life.

> The history of religion has at times been mistaken for the history of its symbols; but this is superficial. . . . The true history of religion, not yet written, is the history of the depth or shallowness. . . .[43]

Though faith is essential for self and social integration, it takes perverted forms and does not necessarily result in virtue. Some have found ultimate concern in what is narrow and hateful, and faith's negative expressions have been evident in each of the world religions. Each group has produced fanatics and saints. The traditional Western apologetic tendency in both Christian and secular forms has been to compare its saints with the fanatics of others, while neglecting to mention its own fanatics. Smith prefers that we temper apologetics and match saint for saint in order to expand our repertoire of appreciation, and compare fanatic with fanatic in order to recognize that all communities have produced humanity at its most perverse. Religious persons share in the fact that they belong to communities that have produced both the highest and the most aberrant forms of human nature.

The perversion of faith is fanaticism; the opposite of faith, nihilism. As we noted, the primary disorder of today is nihilism, which results in a weakening of the capacity for profound commitment. This disorder, strong in the modern

West, likewise affects traditional societies. One should note that when Smith speaks of an atrophy of faith he is not referring to a loss of 'belief' in traditional concepts, such as miracles, a three-tiered universe or infallible revelations. Rather, he points to the breakdown of a society's ultimate concerns that give life orientation and intensity.

> In the modern world, alas, including the West, it [commitment, concern, sincerity] can no longer be taken for granted. Students who attend schools and universities but whose heart is not in their studies, who do not have faith in their own intellectual venture; teachers whose concern is with their own careers, whose heart is not in their teaching, so that, as teachers, they are then not men and women of faith; workers whose activity is aimed at their pay cheque but whose heart is not in their craft, so that the working hours of their lives are therefore lived without faith; . . . – these constitute a society in which faith is sparse.[44]

Smith is confident that sympathetic scholars will sense the authenticity of faith in the lives of those they encounter, whether that encounter is direct in the meeting of persons or indirect in the study of religious products. If, with training, we are able to sense the quality of beauty in the art of other civilizations, we are also able, if we equip ourselves with the sensitivity we offer art, to sense the integrity of a life that embodies the truth of a tradition. Educated sensitivity will convince non-members of a tradition's legitimacy more than apologetic propaganda. Yet one must add that such cultivation does not oblige a student to share the full range of a religion's world-view. One may be awed by the beauty of a Hindu guru without accepting his teaching on reincarnation. A Christian may respect the quality of a Muslim's personal islam, while regarding his or her christology as inadequate. Nonetheless, an attraction of piety remains that draws persons of faith together. The insight that God is merciful receives confirmation when one engages another established in the beauty of mercy. Two individuals from different traditions who have realized the 'truth' of mercy have a firm basis for mutual understanding. They do not share in the acceptance of a proposition; they live in the realization of human excellence – the form of a merciful person. These characteristics emerging from a life of faith draw persons of separate beliefs towards loyalty and co-operation.

Persons of like attributes recognize each other across conventional barriers. One concerned with the establishment of justice will find in individuals from other communities similar concern. They may, of course, draw on dissimilar symbols to express the demand of justice. Nonetheless, a Martin Luther King will recognize a Mahatma Gandhi as a fellow traveller. Likewise, one concerned with the mystic quest will often recognize the validity of another mystic's path. Once freed from viewing traditions as antagonistic entities, persons of like mind are freed for greater community.

Christians more than other groups have expressed their faith conceptually and doctrinally in theological systems. Many societies have not. Those of the Shinto tradition, for example, have never organized their myths, leaving them to express faith in a poetic manner. For many African tribes ritual dance rather than reasoned system can be the central expression of meaning. And in Jewish and Islamic groups the fundamental form faith has taken is law, torah and shariah.

Understanding which form is central to a religious movement radically alters the way one apprehends the ultimate values active in it. For many Christians, to speak of the 'oneness of God' is to accept the challenge of intellectually comprehending (or at least apprehending) the nature of 'oneness'. But for Muslims and Jews the oneness of God is experienced predominately as a moral command:

> . . . that one must worship only God, and serve him alone. The oneness of God is less a metaphysical description than an ethical injunction. The mood is imperative, not indicative. [45]

Within a single tradition a number of societies can exist that express their loyalty to the same object of faith through strikingly different forms. Commitment to Christ in Christian tradition reveals itself in social reformation, mystical contemplation, ritual celebration, ethical perfectionism, and intellectual reflection.

> Even within the Christian community there are certain subgroups for which the ratio of importance of ritual to doctrine is greater, for instance, for Anglicans/Episcopalians, than it is for other sub-groups, for instance Presbyterians.[46]

For persons of every religion, faith varies daily and perhaps hourly; for human qualities are not constant, nor are they equal. The ability to respond to divine reality, to be inspired by symbols, or seized by ethical injunctions fluctuates dramatically. Individuals are uneven in spiritual evolvement. A spectrum of intensity and type divides members of every tradition into a rich diversity of ways of being faith-ful.

> Faith varies. Some have faith that is large, rich, strong, serene, and that renders them generous, courageous, compassionate, patient, noble, creative. Others have a version of faith that is meager, spasmodic, or stunted, rendering them narrow-minded or distracted, unimaginative or bitter, self-righteous or hypocritical. Both extremes of faith . . . are to be found . . . in every community across the globe.[47]

For persons in the same tradition, faith varies not only in intensity but also in pattern. This is obvious when we analyse our contemporaries' religious life. Different denominations emphasize different aspects of the Christian legacy, even though they share elements of a common world view. Their unique form of faith is moulded by exposure to different aspects within the tradition. In the United States one might consider the differences between the faith of Baptists and that of Catholics, or compare the faith of rural Baptists in Kentucky with that of Baptists in Manhattan. In comparing religious life over an expanse of time, differences of interpretation indeed become extremely variegated.

. . . Tertullian's faith was different from Abelard's, Constantine's different from Zwingli's, St. Teresa's different from John Knox's, Harnack's different from William Jenning Bryan's. At a less elite level, the faith of a Roman proletarian catacombist or martyr was different from that of a hanger-on of the Crusades, and both of these from the faith of a modern Bible-belt farmer.[48]

If faith is conceived of as openness to transcendence, one immediately recognizes a plurality of ways of being open. One discerns a mystical path, an ethical path, a liturgical path, a path of social action, and so on. One might even recognize newly evolving paths such as that found in the field of pastoral counselling and name it 'a way for the healing of others' or a 'yoga of therapy'. This variety of openness helps to explain the multiplicity of doctrinal systems in Christianity that were formed to express the various communities' (denominations') relationship to transcendence.

Smith approvingly notes that Karl Rahner in *Faith Today* calls attention to the 'most diverse forms of faith' that exist among Christians.[49] Rahner serves as an example of a modern theologian who, liberated from a false preoccupation with essentialism, has recognized the authentic pluralism that flourishes within Christianity. Yet, because of the persistent dream of doctrinal unity, an honest recognition of faith's historical diversity has been difficult to achieve. Such dreams have obscured the plurality of meaning that is stored within Christian religious life.

Faith is limited. It manifests itself in cultural contexts that aid and inhibit qualities and expressions of faith. Theravada Buddhism does not encourage an openness to transcendence as personal being; nor does the Society of Friends encourage a liturgical openness to the divine; nor does Taoism create conditions helpful for a perception of reality in terms of conflictual dualism. The varieties of faith are therefore severely contained by the ambience of an age. Smith leaves us this aphorism: 'No two Hindus have the same faith, and no two Christians, and no two centuries.'[50]

Since human encounter with the divine remains limited, one may ask if Smith is able to integrate into his analysis of faith mystical testimonies in which an unmediated and limitless comprehension of the divine is said to occur. One thinks, for example, of the Hindu *jivanmukta* who in some instances is said to attain omniscience. And even where omniscience is not claimed, there exists a common belief that illumined persons have access to a knowledge of realities other than those available to logic and sensory perception.

Smith's position is Western and historical. Knowing is limited to inherited conceptualities, with space left open for creative advance. Ultimate truth is not attainable for humans. Apprehension, not comprehension, is the lot of the most evolved saint or avatar. Even the most perfect of mystics or prophets can, according to Smith, he shown to be time-bound in their imaging of the divine. He finds no evidence of a knowing that fully transcends the boundaries of the historical. However, concerning the *jivanmukta* Smith says that he himself has:

> . . . not wrestled sufficiently with the problems (surrounding the *jivanmukta's* supposed omniscience) that arise to know whether they (and the phenomena of mystic rapture elsewhere) involve realities that would in the end force a revision of the conceptual scheme with which I am operating. It is evident that I think not. . . .[51]

Smith understands the concept of the *jivanmukta* and by extension, other mystical concepts that point to a full awakening to reality as eschatological symbols, not historical facts. His reading of finitude implies that all apprehensions of reality are mediated. This position apparently stands in opposition to Hindu, Buddhist, Sufi and other illumination traditions that hold otherwise. Smith's position would therefore reject an unmediated experience of the Atman/Brahman equation. So too it would reject the Zen practitioners' interpretations of their experience as an unmediated perception of Suchness. The historian Smith finds faith's expressions too various, too finite, and too connected with specific symbol systems to indicate a radical transcendence of finitude.

He does acknowledge that *if* he were persuaded of the possibility of non-finite, non-mediated, mystical perception, he would solve the problem of whether his concept of faith applied by simply refusing to attribute 'faith' to 'those persons seen as superseding the finite'.[52] This solution parallels that of Thomas Aquinas, who found in Christ a perfect knowledge of God. Though operating with a different set of assumptions, Smith agrees with Aquinas that *if* Christ were to have a perfect knowledge of God the virtue of faith could not be attributed to him.[53]

Faith changes. Since persons are historical, new conditions require new expressions of faith – new forms of relatedness to transcendence. Populations cease responding to past sacred meanings; myths die; cosmologies change. Faith, however, re-emerges in shifting form. But Smith does not necessarily look to synagogues, sanghas, churches or mosques to find the points at which faith emerges today. New meanings, new windows on transcendence, new symbols, evolve in other sectors of society: in the new shapes and visions of art, in the new cosmologies of science, in political movements with new perceptions of justice. To illustrate, if one looks to the United States one sees an example of the birth of a new form of faith. On the Pacific coast, combinations of modern and ancient therapies unite with several varieties of mysticism to produce new configurations in the quest for personal meaning.

When traditions fail to offer their members the taste of ultimacy, historians discover values surfacing in unsuspected places. Looking for the emergence of faith, Smith does not ask for easy summaries of new beliefs. Instead he probes: Where and how are persons finding themselves at home in the universe? Where are they finding cosmic significance in themselves and others? Where and how are they finding the capacity to ground their ethical decisions beyond the conflict of relativities? Where and how are images of hope emerging? How are the qualities engendered by hope being nourished? He is, in short, asking: 'Where is faith?'[54]

On first viewing, Smith's analysis of faith may appear excessively anthropocentric. Is not faith also a gift of God? Though Smith speaks of faith as being salvific, is not the objective spiritual reality behind the awakening of faith the actual source of salvation? In this sense, is not Smith wrong in stating that we are saved by faith?[55]

Though Smith often speaks as if faith is saved by its own agency, it must be remembered that faith is not self-originating. There is no voluntaristic way of securing faith; persons may have a potential for faith, but they cannot manufacture ultimate values. Smith explicitly claims that faith is a gift:

> Some theologians, both Christian and Muslim, would say that faith is a sheer gift of God, and cannot be induced by anything that men and women do. Fair enough, I shall myself say that in a moment.[56]

Smith sees the divine saving activity as being present throughout history. God uses whatever contexts are available to bring persons to wholeness. Rather than holding Smith's analysis to be extremely anthropocentric, we would be more correct to say that his position is extremely theocentric. Faith is a universal quality precisely because God (Reality) is everywhere and at all times active in offering the gift of faith: '. . . the religious history of the world is the record of God's loving, creative, inspiring dealings with recalcitrant and sinful but not unresponsive men and women'.[57]

Understanding the faith of others is a new enterprise in the West and in the world. For the first time patient techniques have been forged to ascertain the factual content and meaning of alien traditions. Geographical isolation and ignorance of other forms of religious encounters have long obstructed cross-cultural studies of religious life. This is no longer the case. In addition, Christianity and Islam placed dogmatic obstacles in the path of serious religious studies. Persons from Asian traditions, Buddhist and Hindu, Taoist and Confucian, though demonstrating larger tolerance, remained ill-informed or indifferent to a serious intellectual interaction with other religious communities. Some Hindus further complicated the study of faith by dogmatically assuming that persons in other communities shared similar ultimate goals, and refused to notice that these others vehemently disagreed with their assessment.[58] In the light of Smith's analysis of faith, all this must alter.

Christian attitudes still occasionally oppose a sensitive study of non-Western faith. In Western seminaries alien traditions have been and are being studied as either curiosities, which one does not look to seriously for life-transforming faith, or as storehouses of factual information, helpful to facilitate the conversion effort. However, this situation has been in a state of change since Smith first voiced these criticisms. A new commitment exists in some seminaries to offer courses in non-Christian religions, given by members of these communities for the sake of furthering dialogue and understanding. One might mention, as an example, the situation at the School of Theology in Claremont, California, in which Buddhist scholars interact with Christians, to ensure that a living and faithful presentation of both Buddhist and Christian existence occurs. At other seminaries Jewish scholars offer courses in Judaism; and one looks forward to a time when the same will hold for Muslim, Hindu and Buddhist scholars.

However, the very structure of Western educational facilities fosters opposition to a serious study of global faith. Religious education in Europe and the United States is divided between seminaries and departments of religious studies. In seminaries, faith – that is, Christian faith – is studied with seriousness. Its depth and ideal dimension are assumed. In departments of religious studies the traditions of others are studied but, according to Smith, often in an external manner that misses the vision, fire and spiritual depth that participants know in their tradition. The faith of others is not seen as a serious human possibility for the student in either seminary or department of religion. That which makes a vision of the world attractive to millions of intelligent adherents is missed. Smith's criticisms, of course, do not apply to all universities. Rather, his charge is directed against a pervasive attitude of objectivism in American and European education. He appreciates the fact that some universities are already equipped with a personalist appreciation of other cultures that enables them to facilitate dialogue in earnest.[59]

As opposed to seminary and university resistance to taking other forms of faith seriously, Smith recommends a new cosmopolitanism in which the multiplicity of faith is explored and appreciated. He holds that the long era of ignorance concerning faith is drawing to a close. Although deep understanding of the faith found in non-Western traditions may take upwards of a hundred years, the era of isolation is over. The length of time needed to develop appreciation need not deter us. The recent ecumenical healing of centuries-old suspicions and misperceptions between separated Christian communities has already demonstrated the intrinsic value of understanding another's faith.

Beyond its academic value, the project of understanding faith has the vital importance of freeing individuals for community with each other. The ancient fear of strange gods begs to be overcome. A new situation exists today in which faith-ful persons of all traditions face common possibilities for planetary cooperation. They share a recently acquired knowledge of millennia of mankind's religious activities. They also share the ambivalent power of technology and the world-view of twentieth-century science. Persons of different religious communities are thrown together through instantaneous communications, and the collective fear of nuclear annihilation. And they come together in a new manner. Today, for the first time in history, persons meet with an accurate and agreed knowledge of the differences that exist between their respective traditions and outlooks. For the first time they have the possibility of authentically understanding one another.

They also come together with the knowledge that no society in history has solved the problem of inter-religious co-existence, and that this is the novel task that awaits them.[60]

Older solutions to the problem of religious plurality were found in domination, avoidance and anathema. These failed and are no longer serious possibilities. We, in effect, live with each other, do business, marry, and are concerned with one another's image of ourselves and our communities. Muslims read Christian reports concerning Islamic tradition and vision. They rightly insist on correcting misperceptions and false reports. When societies were more neatly boundaried, misperceptions were scarcely noticed. But today persons react in growing networks of cross-checking and information sharing. Christians read Jews; Muslims read Christians. Buddhists read both; and all read Marxists and secular humanists. The mixing is complex and global.

> These men are certainly aware of each other. Whether we like it or not, . . . at least at this level religious isolationism is coming to an end. To take one illustration: Presbyterians nowadays are reading Methodist books. Both are reading Buber – and Radhakrishnan. Tillich is being read in Tokyo. And I know of a Muslim critique of Karl Barth.[61]

Generic faith

Central to Smith's programme is his attempt to understand faith generically. The task consists in describing what faith has meant in the various religions, and then inductively generalizing about 'religiousness' itself in order to attain an understanding of faith as a universal phenomenon. This attempt to understand 'faith itself' should not be conceived of as an effort to discover faith's 'essence'. Smith firmly rejects the philosophy and language of 'essences', for him, 'essences' do not exist prior to phenomena. They are, rather, inductive abstractions that are more or less accurate to the data they reflect.[62]

According to Smith, three stages of research have occurred in the development of religious studies. The first two centred upon gathering and understanding the religious data of traditions.

We must learn what precisely have been and are the doctrines, institutions, and practices, the symbols and patterns, of the world's various communities. We must further endeavor to know what these things have meant to the system's adherents. It is one thing to know, for instance, that in Christian worship there is a cross; it is another to know what the cross means to the Christian who is worshipping. Something similar holds for other groups, other symbols, other ages.[63]

The third stage arises after data has been gathered and traditions understood. This is the comparative phase in which one compares the varieties of faith and seeks to unify them under a cover term, like Smith's generic 'faith'.

This may be called comparative religion proper: that is, the endeavor from a comparative study of all the diverse phenomena and their interpretation to induce some general truths. In view of man's diversity, what can one say of man's religiousness itself? . . . After the attempt to understand the fact of faith itself, in the light of its history – to understand it as well-nigh universal human phenomenon, immensely diversified in particular, remarkably persistent in general.[64]

A complete definition of generic faith, being inductive, is naturally impossible. To be thorough it would have to include what each item in every religious tradition has meant to each individual who has ever arrived at meaning. Further, this sort of tally would itself be tentative, since new forms of faith would arise in the future. Nevertheless, it is possible to discover what representative participants have declared their faith to be over the centuries. If it is not possible to have an accurate representation of everyone's faith, it is nonetheless possible to describe the faith of those who profoundly influenced the lives of millions – those whose perceptions resonated within great numbers of the faith-ful. One thinks of Ghazzali, Augustine, Ramanuja, Maimonides, etc.

Though a full portrait of generic faith is not possible, one can delineate those characteristics that an adequate description must contain.

> The new notion must be global enough to do justice to the multitude of diverse forms through which faith has kept appearing among humankind. This means, comprehensive enough to cope with communal variety from place to place, dynamic enough for the continuous changes from century to century, large enough to make room for personal diversity from saint to sinner, peasant to intellectual, aesthete to activist.[65]

A generic concept of faith requires persons of every path to expand their understanding of approaches to the transcendent. It demands that scholars bring a vitality and profundity to the study of other traditions analogous to that they perceive in their own. Only then can they hope to represent the faith of others. For secular humanists this includes the necessity of bringing depth to the study of religious traditions, and for the religious to do likewise for positive forms of secular humanism.

The formation of generic religious categories will aid participants in grasping both other traditions and their own. Those who analyse generic categories such as prayer or sacrifice are enabled to understand their own society's use of the term in light of a global understanding of the phenomena. They then become capable of perceiving the uniqueness of their own community's self-understanding in a manner not previously possible. They are freed to recognize that attitudes and ideas long held to be unique to their community are in fact shared. Further, they are now in a legitimate position to clarify which elements are indeed unique to a specific community. In addition, they participate in the insights that only a multicultural analysis of religious phenomena can offer. Smith

himself has mentioned how a study of Persian mystical literature sensitized him to the mystical insights in the Christian
tradition, for which a Presbyterian background had ill-
prepared him.[66]

Though the benefits of establishing a generic religious
vocabulary are evident, difficulties arise in attempting to
establish an acceptable definition of 'faith'. A major problem
lies in the word 'faith' itself, which is a Western term freighted
with Western Christian associations. With some qualification,
'faith' is applicable to the Semitic traditions (Islam and Judaism)
which also share a personal understanding of the divine. This
emendation, though complex, is considerably simpler than
attempting to pack Hindu, Buddhist, Marxist and Taoist
understandings of religious existence into 'faith'. But Smith
accepts the challenge of giving a collaborative and global
definition to the English 'faith'. In *Faith and Belief* he discovers
in each religion a conceptual counterpart to the term 'faith'. In
Towards a World Theology he analyses other terms that might
substitute as generic labels for mankind's 'religiousness'. These
include 'piety', 'salvation', 'liberation'; '*shalom*', 'identity'.[67]
However, he finds these terms less rich, less capable of being
extended in a generic direction than 'faith' itself.

Replies to Smith on faith

In order to create a unified vocabulary that expresses mankind's
plural religious existence, Smith must enrich 'faith' by
including within it all forms of relating to transcendence.
Scholars from every religion must be able to recognize their
own apprehension of transcendence in the term.

Smith has not been able to achieve this unanimity. Scholars
have disagreed with several elements in his programme.
However, Smith has enlivened our conversation about faith
in a way that enables us to analyse its many dimensions
and explore its personalist nature. Simplistic and objectivist
understandings have been called in question. Further, he has
launched scholars upon a world-wide effort to understand

the religious consciousness of humankind. The fruit to be harvested from this effort may indeed be greater than can at present be imagined.

Smith has not been without critics in his proposal to discard the general term 'religion', as well as its singular 'a religion'.[68] In an article 'Truth and Religions', Ninian Smart objects that: 'Because we use the word "religion" it does not follow that there is a common core. Compare "sport", "entertainment" – legitimate locutions.'[69] The argument is that Smith is not entitled to reject a term from the English language merely because he is unable to discover an essentialist core meaning. Many good words resist simple definition.

Smart is, of course, correct in attesting that many words contain a wide range of meaning, not all of which appear congruent with a central meaning. To take a word almost at random – 'canard'. 'Canard' may refer to 1. a false story or hoax; 2. a duck intended for food; or 3. an airplane whose horizontal stabilizers and and elevators are located forward on the wing. This is surely a motley group of meanings, yet despite the flagrant variety neither rumour-mongers, nor chefs, nor pilots have felt obligated to drop their shared term.

In a similar spirit, Huston Smith, critical of Smith's penchant for drastic linguistic revision, describes his solution to the problematic term 'religion' as ' . . . surgery so radical as to be raised to the art of decapitation'.[70] Both Huston Smith and Smart are correct that 'religion' can be sufficiently qualified so as not to require radical surgery. However, Huston Smith does perceive strategic wisdom in Cantwell Smith's denunciation of terms. Through excess Cantwell Smith has had an impact upon scholarly circles that moderation might well have lacked. According to Huston Smith: 'That impact could only have been achieved, it seems, by an author who championed seriously a thesis most of us consider quixotic.[71]

I readily concede that Smith's extreme solution to the ambiguities surrounding 'religion' is unnecessary. Rather than reject the term 'religion', it is possible to resolve the essentialist dilemma by appropriating Wittgenstein's concept of family resemblances. Instead of conceiving religion as a thing with an essential nature, the various aspects of what are commonly included in the term may be construed as: 'a logical relationship of partially overlapping circles where no one circle either includes or excludes all others.'[72]

Smart further argues that Smith errs in assuming that a term should be dropped from our discourse if it cannot be defined. He states: 'Even if 'religion' cannot be defined (though I believe it can), it does not matter (can we define "of", "red", etc., etc?)'[73]

If this criticism clearly set forth Smith's reason for dropping 'religion', it would be correct. Many terms are not definable in a strict essentialist sense, and the user must resort to ostensive or operational definitions. Smith is certainly aware of this. He does not reject terms merely because they are not fully definable – he finds, for example, the phenomenon of faith too rich for an adequate definition, as he does any real, as opposed to ideal entity. Yet he does not ask us to excise the term 'faith'. Smith's argument with 'religion' does not simply concern its definition, but rather the confusing nature of its several meanings. By offering 'cumulative tradition' and 'faith' as joint substitutes for 'religion', he hopes to recall as from false concern with reified 'religions' and to release us from a vain search for the essence of religion or a religion – goals that Smart also espouses in his own writings.[74]

Smith is not as inflexible in his use of language as criticism might indicate. Though he has asked us to abandon 'religion' as a scholarly term, he also speaks to those who prefer to preserve it when he writes:

> . . . one may insist that the word is used in four differing ways. And one may urge that no discussion – let alone, no definition – can be mature that is not self-conscious on this point.[75]

One further objection that might arise is that Smith has rejected one substantive, 'religions', only to replace it with

another, 'faiths'.[76] If this were the case we would be justified
in concluding that: 'This terminology implies as much reification as "religion" and "religions".'[77] This, however, is a
misreading of Smith. In his later writings Smith does not speak
of faith in the plural. He does not offer us titles like *The Faiths
of Other Men*. Nor is the plural found after *The Meaning and
End of Religion*, 1962. Faith is a capacity for ultimate valuation.
All religious visions are viewed by Smith as expressions of this
capacity in the singular. One does not speak of many faiths,
but rather forms of faith, ways of being open to transcendence.
Smith's terminology successfully resists the charge of
reification.

Some have also criticized Smith's use of the term 'faith' as
being too specifically linked to theistic experience to serve as
a generic concept for religious existence. John Cobb, for
example, acknowledges that 'faith' fits the conceptuality of
Semitic traditions, most Hindu movements and much of
Mahayana Buddhism, but he argues that it is not an appropriate
category for either Vedantic Hinduism, whose goal is the
dissolution of relationship, or Zen Buddhism, which conceives
of the purpose of religious existence as the self-awakening of
Dharma.[78] The conception of faith as a personal relation to
transcendence does not figure as the core concept or experience
in Vedantist or Zen soteriological schemes. The argument is
that Smith's description of generic faith as a response to the
impingement of transcendence falsifies the unique nature of
these traditions. This is because faith implies a relational scheme
which entails images of height, otherness and trustworthiness –
images that fit neither the Buddhist experience of emptiness
nor the Vedantist negation of subject and object.

Cobb states that behind Smith's conception of generic faith
lies the common but 'very deep assumption that when two
traditions both claim to deal with what is transcendent and
ultimate, they must be understood as relating to the same
reality'.[79] It is correct that Smith assumes that the same ultimate
reality underlies various religious expressions. For example,
he holds that Dharma and God are both inadequate (finite)

symbols for a unitary and largely unknown divine reality.[80] Further, Smith holds that each of the religious traditions is, in part, an authentic response to this reality, with no tradition capturing a complete insight into its nature.

As a process theologian, Cobb offers a different model to appreciate the plurality of religious experience. He proposes that more than one ultimate may exist; whereas Smith maintains a more traditional Semitic and Neoplatonic position.[81] Smith's model of transcendence points to the one ultimate fullness of being and value in which the transcendent ideals embedded in the earth's religions are grounded. When Smith conceives of transcendence, he cheerfully works with a model that corresponds to the parable of the elephant and the blind men, a tale which affirms a unitary reality behind disparate symbols and approaches to the Divine. A process thinker, on the other hand, espouses a model in which matter, creativity and God are each in relation to the other, co-eternal and co-ultimate, co-existing in a society of eternal ultimates. In the process model it is not necessary to postulate a single reality to acknowledge the depth dimension of each tradition. For this reason the category of faith may be thought of as appropriate only for those whose ultimate is theistically conceived. Theists ask different questions of their ultimate than non-theists. They inquire as to the why and how of things. Their answer is God. Buddhists, however, ask the question of ' . . . *what* one is and *what* all things are'.[82] Their answer is emptiness (*sunyata*), a solution that constitutes the Buddhist ultimate. Therefore, rather than finding unity behind the various traditions Cobb discovers 'complementary rather than contradictory' insights into the nature of the various ultimates.[83]

This objection to Smith's programme to formulate a generic term for mankind's religious existence ought to be given considerable weight, for it arises from years of experience with Buddhist-Christian dialogue. Cobb's conclusion concurs with that of William Johnston, the author of *Christian Zen*. Johnston likewise holds that Zen and Christian mysticism are pervasively different.[84] Emptiness is not the Christian God, and the word 'faith' is inappropriate for describing both forms of religious existence.

To answer these objections one must discuss Smith's use of the term 'transcendence'. For it is Smith's discussion of faith as a relationship to transcendence that is at issue, not his other characterizations. Zen Buddhists obviously participate in the Zen strand of the Buddhist world-view. Faith as a personal quality of religiousness or piety also applies to Zen, and anyone who has visited a zendo hall has observed such qualities in abundance. In fact, if we analyse one of Smith's late descriptions of faith in *Towards a World Theology*, we note little that does not apply to Zen understood as a way of life.

> Faith is an orientation of the personality, to oneself, to one's neighbor, to the universe; a total response; a way of seeing the world and of handling it; a capacity to live at more than mundane level; to see, to feel, to act in terms of a transcendent dimension.[85]

However, the phrase 'to act in terms of a transcendent dimension' contains the suspect word 'transcendent'. And it is important to note that Smith uses this term in several ways: 1. to refer to that which transcends us, whether objects or values; 2. to refer to values that are not empirically mundane. Smith, for example, speaks of the Marxist world-view as transcendent; for Marxist vision refers its devotees to future possibilities that transcend the present given. Further, if values have religious significance, they affect participants with a radical claim that transcends the individual. Since the Marxist illustration fits Smith's conception of transcendence, it is apparent that transcendence need not refer to 'an eternal transcendence of temporality';[86] 3. transcendence in Smith's more common usage refers to God - conceived of as the ground of being, the ultimate real, the guarantor of value.

As a historian of religion, Smith does not hold that researchers should accept the existence of a divine ground behind the various formulations of God. They must, however, have some understanding of the impact and import of perceived transcendence within a given tradition. In response to a critic, who misinterpreted him as saying that belief in a transcendent and atemporal spiritual reality is essential for scholarship in religious studies, Smith replies that Emile Durkheim correctly described the experiential fact that transcendence holds for participants, but interpreted the experience sociologically rather than ontologically.[87] Smith therefore is not asking for theological unanimity among scholars. He does, however, insist upon adequate depictions of perceived transcendence.

If we assume that the objection that relational transcendence cannot be predicated of Zen is correct, then it must be seen as valid only in relation to transcendence 3. and not 1. or 2. For transcendence 1. we simply note that there is a moreness to life that Zen practitioners are in pursuit of. For transcendence 2. we note that persons inspired by ideals transcend mere facticity. This is naturally true of any vision of life, be it Marxist or Buddhist. It would seem, therefore, that Zen has a relational orientation towards its ideal. Until the ideal is fully attained, one exists psychologically in relation to it. Emptiness, understood as the full realization of the Zen ideal, is an eschatological symbol that determines praxis and hope, and which exists for the majority of practitioners as a transcendent goal – until the attainment of emptiness. Thus the objection that the language of relation is inappropriate to Zen seems to apply to transcendence 3. and then only eschatologically.

Another objection has it that Smith maintains that faith is essentially the same wherever it is found. This statement must be clarified, for it is true only in a structural sense. Faith is the same in that it refers to the capacity to be seized by an ideal (transcendent value), which in turn leads to an organizing stance towards the world. Faith is certainly not the same in its particular forms. The forms of faith vary in each tradition, for individuals are selective and capable of novelty. Further, the intensity of faith varies constantly in each individual. Faith is

unitary as religiousness or piety in general but, once particularized, faith is manifold.

In 'On "Dialogue and Faith": A Rejoinder', Smith responds
to the misperception that he holds faith to be concretely one.
He states: 'I have tried to suggest faith as an explicitly open
category, a generic (not specific) concept, open to differing
specificities.'[88] Smith does not mean that faith is what two
religious groups have in common, or what is left over once
their multiform traditions are abstracted from. Concerning
such as interpretation Smith emphasizes: 'This is certainly *not*
what I mean.'[89] Further, he states:

> . . . My category of 'faith' should be explicitly generic – just
> as is my concept 'cumulative tradition' . . . all have a
> cumulative tradition, but it is not the same in every case (nor
> amorphous in any case); similarly all have faith, not the same
> in every case. . . . I do *not* think that faith is everywhere the
> same. Indeed, I do not even think that it is anywhere the
> same.[90]

A difficulty with using 'faith' as an open category is that if
we emend 'faith' to include a potpourri of religious orientation,
we may discover that our procedure, as John Hutchison
argues, 'stretches a good word beyond its elastic limits.'[91] This
comment is to the point, for Smith in the past has resorted to
language-building that the majority of scholars have not
accepted. For example, concerning Smith's earlier attempt to
rid scholars of the word 'religion', Hutchison says: 'For one
thing, it is late in time to seek the abolition of this word, even
if it were possible for academic scholars to command language
in this way.'[92]

In *The Meaning and End of Religion* Smith predicted that the
word 'religion' would cease to be used in academic circles
within twenty-five years.[93] Twenty-plus years later 'religion'
is strongly alive in academic English. Nevertheless, despite
Smith's prophetic error, the many qualifications he urged
concerning 'religion' have been largely adopted. Losing the
term, he has in many instances won the clarifications he sought

to gain. It may also be that 'faith' will be rejected as a generic term for religious existence, but its rejection may nevertheless richly contribute to the task of depicting humankind's multifarious religious consciousness.

Marxism and secularism are two of the most successful modern ideologies. It is important to consider whether Smith is able to incorporate them in his generic formulation of faith. Since he defines faith as a quality that arises from the impingement of transcendence, putative or real, we must ask whether this definition excludes secularism and Marxism. If the answer is affirmative, then his insistence that faith is a global and universal phenomenon stands in doubt, in that a great percentage of the modern world lives by these ideologies. One critic has raised this question and finds it related to an ambiguity in Smith's understanding of transcendence.[94] Does Smith mean: 1. 'any organizing stance towards the world', therefore a symbolic transcendence; or 2. 'faith as a relation to the transcendent', an ontological understanding of transcendence which, of course, most Marxists and many secularists would reject?

As we have noted, Smith distinguishes between two forms of secularism: positive and negative – the former inherited from the Greek humanist tradition, the latter emerging out of modern nihilism. The former is for Smith a form of faith in and through reason; the latter is a form of disintegration. Positive secularism, the search for rational structure, constitutes an ongoing stance towards the world, and is normally associated with concern for freedom from religious authorities and trust in human dignity and perfectibility. Negative secularism, on the other hand, is an attack upon all faith, including that of positive secularism, and results in anomie and ego diffusion.

Positive or humanist secularism is a legitimate form of faith, not only because it is an organizing stance, but also because it consists in surrender to the ideal of reason – an ideal whose demands lay claim upon genuine devotees. And it is Smith's analysis of the operation of ideals upon faith participants that determines whether a specific orientation towards the world constitutes a true faith expression.

His understanding of the activity of ideals in the life of faith can be surmised from a passage found in *Islam in Modern History*, in which he attempts to fathom the force inherent in the Muslim ideal of an Islamic state. He cites a Pakistani political leader saying:

> Once in Cambay I saw a boy flying a kite on a misty day, so that the kite was invisible in the fog. I asked him what fun he was having since he could not see his kite. He replied at once: 'I cannot see it; but something is tugging!'[95]

Applying this metaphor to our discussion of positive secularism, we may say that the tug of reason constitutes the faith of secularlist rationalism, just as the tug of brotherhood and justice constitutes the faith of Marxism. Understood in this sense, Marxism qualifies as a form of faith.

Smith himself was aligned with socialist and Marxist causes in his earlier years, prior to the partition of the Indian subcontinent. His work *Modern Islam in India: A Social Analysis* demonstrates throughout a socialist/Marxist orientation in which religious and ideological ideas find their primary explanation in class origin and class struggle. His commitment is transparently stated:

> Clearly these definitions [of progressive and reactionary] have been put forward by someone who believes that there is in history a basic process of ameliorative evolution . . . It is also true, and hardly less clear, that the present writer believes that socialism is the next due social form.[96]

Smith further revealed what he meant by socialism by upholding the USSR as the society most perfectly in harmony with the process of ameliorative evolution. In a glossary of terms he offered the following definition:

> **socialist**: pertaining to a society in which industry, agriculture, etc., are carried on in a planned and co-operative

manner in the interests of all those who carry them on; in which the only form of wealth is in 'consumption' goods, and in which power is democratically in the hands of the members of the society. Full socialist societies are a matter of the future, so that the definition of this word cannot be made decisively empirical. But the USSR may be given as an illustration of one society in which the basis for socialism has already been laid, and which has been moving in the direction of socialism.[97]

Yet despite his socialist orientation, Smith appears not to have accepted the full implications of Marxist determinism. For example, he speaks of 'liberalism' as having made a permanent contribution to the human community with its 'objective valuation of freedom, particularly in the individual spirit'.[98] Smith's Marxism is obviously of the humanist variety and is not to be confused with totalitarian interpretations.

His identification with Soviet socialism and his willingness to interpret the life of ideas primarily through class analysis came to an end in the 1940s with the excesses of post-war Stalinism and with his recognition that economic factors were not sufficient to explain the furious rupture of India and Pakistan during the 1947 partition. Concerning his earlier inadequate recognition of religious factors in the Muslim dream of an Islamic state, Smith later said:

> This youthful work has many defects . . . chiefly the inadequate understanding of Islam and also of the crucial role played in history by ideological and moral factors . . . The account of the sociological factors at work . . . may still be significant. But those factors, although valid, did not themselves add up to explain adequately what happened subsequently: neither the full cataclysm of 1947, nor the mood of vibrant stamina and creativity of Pakistan in the initial years of its existence, nor the subsequent disillusionment.[99]

This confession contains an altered valuation of religions

and intellectual causal forces in history. No longer understood as merely the weak reflections of 'objective' factors, religious ideas are now seen as capable of initiating historical change through their inherent attractiveness and convicting power. The dreams of faith, whether traditional or humanist, have a certain autonomy. They are causes of history and not passive victims of external reality. A free intellectual and moral creativity is understood to exist within the process of historical continuity.

Smith is not, of course, isolating either religious ideas or other intellectual creations from their formative context. He states clearly that:

> Political, economic, sociological, psychological and other factors . . . obviously affect, and in some senses of the word determine, the course of human history . . . The impetus from the past, the ongoing striving towards a dream, is influenced, molded, by them. Yet it is not obliterated.[100]

A further discussion of the semi-autonomy of religious ideas and ideals is to be found in Smith's discussion of Awrangzeb's victorious ascent to the Mughal throne rather than his elder brother's and heir-apparent, Dara Shikoh, and his (Awrangzeb's) implementation of neo-classical Islam rather than his brother's liberal, universalist and Sufistic rendering of Islam. Analysing the metaphysical disagreement between two brothers, Smith indicates how struggle in the realm of religious thought has political, economic and sociological ramifications. Concerning the origin of Awrangzeb's communalist rejection of universalism, he says:

> Marxists may probably feel that so wide-ranging and radical a change in the social climate as was taking place in India must have had economic causes at its base . . . I am left with the impression that the new movement . . . actually starts in the realm of ideas – and religious ideas at that. If so it is an example of the crucial role of intellectuals in human history. . .[101]

Despite his intellectual conversion from Marxist analysis, Smith has remained sympathetic to the moral impulse behind the Marxist critique. He in no sense questioned the need for social justice in the Third World against the forces of European imperialism. Yet in a passage of more personal tone Smith describes the disillusionment and breakdown of his earlier, simpler and more naive socialist faith.

> . . . Some of us, in addition, were socialists, in the simple days before the devastation of the Stalin terror had become revealed, before imperialist aggression in Hungary and China. Those were messianic days, with the brave new world just round the corner.[102]

Though his intellectual break with Marxism may, in part, be understood as a response to the inadequacy of his earlier social analysis of modern Islam in India, a more total rupture, this time with the metaphysics of Marxism, took place after the exposure of Stalin's internal reign of terror and the Soviet's brutal suppression of Eastern Europe. By the time of the Cold War, the same Smith who was attracted to the humane programmes of socialism rejected the nihilistic implications of Soviet Marxism, and for the same humane reasons. Writing with severity Smith argues that:

> In the rank-and-file Party members, there has been often but a shallow atheism, a dis-allegiance to the overt ideas and institutions of the historical religions, but with it a fervent piety, pursuing justice and beauty without knowing them to be divine. But the power in the massive movement has rested with men at the top who, apparently, have not been superficially but profoundly atheist, have actually repudiated truth and repudiated goodness. . . These men, standing them at the top of a hierarchy rigidly controlling a party that is the vanguard of the class that is the highest product so far of the universe's dialectical process – these men are supreme. They bow down to no higher authority.[103]

Smith rejected the Communist movement for various

reasons: its inadequate understanding of historical causality, its reliance on force to spread its gospel, its participation in a conflict dualism inherited from the Christian past, but beyond these and above all for its intellectual repudiation of ethical transcendence in the form of standards by which to judge the historical process.[104]

Two dominant orientations exist for Smith in Soviet Marxism. The first is to be found in party members' pursuit of transcendent value in the form of justice and brotherhood – values that claim ultimate allegiance. Values such as these have religious reference for Smith. For although he is a nominalist in his understanding of ordinary language, he is a Neoplatonist in his conviction that values correspond to ontological realities. As a Neoplatonist he finds no difficulty in attributing faith to rank and file party members who serve the cause of justice and have sacrificed accordingly. The Soviet leadership, however, constitutes a separate class for Smith – a class of the faith-less. Among the power élite he espies a denial of the authority of the ideal and an adoption of a nihilistic will to power. The language of faith is manipulated to control the ranks of the pious. Cynicism has replaced faith.

Smith regards a large number of Communists as faithful – as apprehending that which Christians call the will of God in the realm of justice. The question whether Smith includes secularists and Marxists within his understanding of faith receives a positive answer in most instances. Those standing under the sovereignty of the ideal can be phenomenologically described as faith-ful, regardless of secular metaphysics. Those who sense, feel, see no authority beyond themselves are bereft of faith.

Smith's later writings, from the 1960s and beyond, do not share in the militant anti-Communist rhetoric of his writings from the Cold War period.[105] Though maintaining anthropological and ontological objections to Marxism, Smith appears at present more hopeful of including a less dualistic strand of Marxist faith within the earth's newly emerging cosmopolitanism. This eirenic attitude seems to mirror the later mood of détente.[106]

2

THE VOYAGE OF BELIEF

In the first chapter, we saw that Smith's concept of 'faith' describes a personal openness to reality. Smith uses 'reality', along with other terms such as the 'true', the 'good', 'transcendence', to point to the inexhaustible mystery that Semitic traditions name 'God' and that other traditions point to with different symbols.

The dimensions of belief

Faith derives from reality or God, while belief derives from faith. The order is significant; for faith emerges from contact with that which is ontologically superior. Belief is faith's intellectual expression, whereas faith is a whole person encounter.[1] Smith states:

> Faith is not to be subordinated to belief, nor to anything else mundane. To it, all religious forms are to be seen as at best strictly secondary — as faith itself is secondary to, derivative from, answerable to, transcendent reality and final truth.[2]

Since faith finds expression in ways other than belief — in art, prayer, politics, liturgy, dance, etc., it is important not to make the modern mistake of assuming that belief is the only, or even chief, expression of faith. This assumption has been common in philosophy, religious studies and some modern theology. Smith finds this state of affairs intellectually and morally tragic. His investigations into non-Western cultures and into the West's past indicate that faith has been highly valued, whereas belief as faith's intellectual expression has been secondary. This is the case for both the intellectualist West and for other cultures, such as mythologically orientated Shinto or law-oriented Islam. Further, Smith discovers that the term 'belief' has acquired connotations that make it ambiguous and distorting for an understanding of religious life. Scholars anachronistically project twentieth-century assumptions about the priority of belief over faith, and misrepresent all known prior civilizations. This procedure is also ethically disruptive, in that it leads to misperception and mistrust between Western scholars and members of other traditions. The religious life of others is also distorted for the scholar's audience. This again raises barriers of misunderstanding, but on a larger scale.

Smith traces the history of the term 'belief' and discovers that 'belief', long a crucial religious term in the West, once referred to faith, and that linguistic changes in English over the past 400 years have led to a situation in which 'belief' has today become unserviceable as a major theological category. By unmasking what belief once was, Smith hopes to prove that in all religions, faith, not belief, is the central religious category. By returning to the central significance of faith he hopes to overcome the modern tendency of objectifying religious life, the result of which is valuelessness, scepticism and loss of faith.

The English term 'belief', like the term 'religion', has a multi-layered history. It is therefore important to clarify 'belief' by describing the various meanings that have accompanied the term in its historical journey. In the most general sense belief refers to an activity of the mind in affirming certain ideas.[3] This sort of belief is obviously not at the core of religious activity, for numerous persons believe without faith. There are persons in each religion who hold to their culture's doctrines by way of habit, without being seized by their truth, without experiencing transcendence through them. Because belief is the intellect's interpretation of an encounter with transcendence, those not party to the original faith experience may possess the intellectual skeleton of a tradition without entering into its transforming sense of truth.

Because Smith distinguishes sharply between tacit belief, which refers to an unconscious or implicit holding of ideas, and conscious or explicit belief, he recommends that the former should not be labelled 'belief'. For in contemporary usage belief refers primarily to a self-reflective acceptance of propositions, rather than participation in a world-view with tacit, unconscious or implicit assumptions. Smith restricts the use of 'belief' to mean a self-conscious holding of ideas, and uses the term 'pre-suppose' for what persons do when they implicitly, tacitly or unconsciously hold to certain ideas and values.[4]

All societies make assumptions about the way things are. These assumptions underpin the society's reflection about ontology, soteriology and anthropology, and allow participants to experience life coherently. Individuals are unable to examine their presuppositions, for they are, in fact, unable to raise them to consciousness. To call them into the foreground of reflection alters their pre-suppositional status and confers propositional status on them. This distinction is illustrated in common language. One cannot in the strict sense speak of tacit or implicit propositions in the first person. One cannot say: 'I pre-suppose', though it is quite logical to say 'I believe', once presuppositions have surfaced as conscious items of reflection.[5]

One of the major tasks for scholars of comparative religion, sociology, anthropology and history is to lay bare the presuppositional differences between cultures. This is a new venture of the twentieth century. As European forms of cultural imperialism recede, Western scholars set themselves the task of understanding multiple religious visions. As a pluralist sensitivity emerges, and as Judaeo-Christian and Graeco-Roman dominance withdraws, the West tries to apprehend and appreciate rather than ridicule or merely tolerate differing world views.

Phenomenologically orientated scholars are aware of the difficulty in applying the term 'belief', as in 'belief system', to unconscious ideational schemes. Tacitly to assume a belief system is distinct from modern believing, which is an act of judgment in favour of the truth of certain statements. This novel speech about belief-systems grows out of a history-of-religions approach that flowered first in the nineteenth century and has gathered precision in the twentieth. Prior to these developments, the concept of belief in English did not (could not) refer to the unconscious assumptions of others.[6] Smith therefore prefers not to use 'belief' to refer to the unconscious, tacit or implicit concepts of a culture.

In order to illustrate the impact of covert presuppositions, Smith tells us that no one in either the history of Islam or in the secularist or Christian West ever asked the question: 'Is the Qur'an the Word of God?' So obvious a question was never explored because each party prejudged the answer before it was asked. The Islamic side assumed a positive reply, for its truth was implicit in all Muslim activity. So apparent was the answer to the Muslim mind that those not seeing its truth were perceived as rejectors of Allah's generous offer of salvation, and therefore infidels. The West, conversely, assumed an obvious answer. The Qur'an could not be the word of God. The question was never broached as requiring serious reflection.[7]

The reason such a question was not consciously considered by Muslims is that the answer was foundational, axiomatic and self-evident. It was hardly something to be lifted up for critical self-reflection. If, however, it was an unnecessary reflection for Islamic civilization, it was an impossible one for European society. For if secularists asked this with sincerity, their naturalist assumptions would be potentially threatened. A similar threat held for Christian assumptions that entailed an exclusivist doctrine of revelation.

Smith offers a mediated position which enables persons of each traditions to appreciate the fact that whether or not the Qur'an is the word of God in an absolute sense, it has functioned as if it were for generations of Muslims. To understand Islamic life, Christians and secularists must break with their assumptions and perceive that Muslims have found transcendent meaning and experience of the divine presence because of their conviction about the Qur'an. Muslims, Christians and secularists ought to agree that in order to understand Islamic existence it is necessary to know how the Qur'an functions in Islamic life. This understanding is possible regardless of one's position concerning the status of Islam's foundational revelation.

In the modern period assumptions that are normally in the background of consciousness have surfaced because of the cross-exposure of civilizations, the science of religious studies, the social sciences, the spread of secularism and the dominance of naturalist science. Each movement has burst asunder protected assumptions of prior ages.

No longer able to exist in isolation, societies now instantly object to mis-observations and criticisms of outsiders. Brought increasingly together in the electronic age, the judgments of others become part of each tradition's self-observation. Those who have been talked about begin to perceive their own tradition in some degree from the outside, with the result that critical self-reflection and 'de-presuppositioning' occurs. Interaction with intelligent others not sharing our cultural perspectives lays bare the presuppositions of both societies. Both are revealed to be neither as universal nor as common-sensical as was imagined.

The proximity of the intelligent other is a factor in the creation of the current problem of intellectual belief. A curious process arises when persons inside a tacit world-view encounter outsiders whose presence challenges their presuppositions. The system of beliefs *through* which they viewed their world now becomes a system *at* which they look. Participants take upon themselves the observer's critical posture and in the process lose their ability to encounter the world naively. This radical process of de-presuppositioning world pictures explains in large measure the loss of faith in the modern world. Symbols and concepts that once elicited ultimate value have lost their force not only because of the erosion of ancient cosmologies by modern science but also because of the unsettling fact of pluralism. Smith writes:

Anyway, I feel that true faith has already begun to crumble

a bit, if it has not actually gone, as soon as people have reduced what used to be the data, the presuppositions, of their world-view to a set of true-or-false prepositions – I mean, when what was once the presupposed context or intellectual background for a transcending religious faith becomes rather the foreground of intellectual belief. This is one of the fundamental troubles in the modern world, and one of the fundamental problems arising from a recognition of religious diversity – that what used to be unconscious premises become, rather, scrutinized intellectualizations. At this level the believer himself begins to wonder if he really 'believes', in this new sense (and often enough finds that he actually does not).[8]

The inability of different cultures to understand the tacit assumptions of others has, of course, political consequences. The West's constant failure to understand Islamic attempts at social reform is due in part to a Western secular bias that the separation of church and state is an unquestionable good. This evaluation is congenial to Westerners because of their history, especially their reaction to the religious wars of the seventeenth century, in which Islam did not share. In addition the West is often unaware that it has inherited a double faith, the ideals of the Graeco-Roman and the ideals of the Judaeo-Christian traditions. Islam has not shared this double faith, and is consistently misunderstood by those who do, whether secularists who have rejected one-half of the ideals of the West or Christians who choose to impose their pattern of church and state outside the boundaries of their community. In *Islam in Modern History* Smith reflects on the difficulties Islam and the West have had in attaining mutual understanding:

> . . . the Western side . . . (has) yet to grasp how significant and ramified are the differences; and how they can pervade every aspect of interrelationship. On the Muslim side there has been an inability to realize and even to admit how hard it is for an outsider to understand Islamic culture and specifically the religion that underlies it.[9]

Yet, if the West has been unsuccessful in understanding the attitudes underlying the Islamic world-view, Muslims have contributed to this impasse by fundamentally misunderstanding Christian tradition. The extent of this blindness is found in a tell-tale passage:

> The present writer . . . knows no book by a Muslim showing any 'feel' for the Christian position; nor indeed any clear endeavour to deal with, let alone understand, the central doctrines. The usual Muslim attitude is not to take the central doctrines seriously at all. . . . Muslims have religious convictions for genuinely imagining that they know real Christianity better than Christians do themselves . . . (in) the faith by which Christians actually lived, they have not been intellectually interested.[10]

This passage from *Islam in Modern History* was published in 1957. It is promising to note that since this comment was made Smith has found Islamic work that reflects a profound sensitivity to the meaning that Christianity holds for its members.[11] The historical emergence of an understanding of the Christian position by Muslims signals hope for Smith that the rancorous misrepresentation of centuries has begun to wane.

Prior to the contemporary scenario of pluralism, historicism, scientific world-view and technological might, Western Christendom thought in categories that afforded its members naive religious certainty, a certainty no longer attainable by most educated Westerners. Perhaps less than a century ago the majority of Christians saw the world through the classical vision of the drama of salvation – a vision that embraced interlocking concepts of God, creation, the fall, redemption, and the cosmic significance of human life. These thoughts constituted a world. They were symbols through which generations discovered meaning and around which a culture was constituted. Such categories could not be seriously doubted while they remained presuppositional. Christians did not believe in these ideas in the modern sense of affirming their validity over against competing notions. They were not conceived of primarily as ideas of the human mind, but as cosmic realities. So long as they were experienced in this manner, ontological rather than mental, they provided the cornerstone of a civilization.

Presuppositional thought is not found only in primitive or mythological thinking. The most self-conscious of minds remain subject to presuppositions. Smith gives the example of Thomas Aquinas – one of the most sophisticated rationalists the world has met. Concerning the relationship between Aquinas's ideas and his presuppositions, Smith says:

> . . . his views on faith, like all thinkers' views on all matters, are of course implicated with his total system of ideas, are expressed in terms of what we might call his own beliefs. . . This framework we, looking back, misunderstand either if we view it simply from the outside – whereas his mind operated from within it. . . Some of what seemed to him obvious, not being so to us, we may perhaps dub his belief; but we misunderstand him if we fail to realize that for him it was not a conscious belief but an unconscious presupposition, or a platitude, or the recognition of a logically inescapable truth.[12]

Despite the growing sophistication among historians and social scientists about the presuppositional context of civilizations, persons trained in objective science remain slow to appreciate the limits of their assumptions. Smith suspects that generations hence twentieth-century scientific presuppositions will look as delightfully naive to our descendants as do those of the mediaeval Aquinas. Yet scientifically trained persons continue on the whole to view religious experience with a scepticism based on the axiom that religious positions, values and aspirations are essentially false until proven correct, a position not valid in a court of law, but assumed in the popular ethos of science.[13] Smith attributes tunnel vision of this sort to the success of science and to its legacy of exclusivism imbibed from its Christian and Greek background.

Scepticism hinders Western intellectuals from appreciating the fact that intelligent persons from other cultures do not share their naturalist rejection of other ways of encountering reality. In societies where aesthetic, mystical and ethical phenomena are more highly valued, Western concern with facts and theories seems odd, and perhaps spiritually obtuse. Smith notices that: 'Our science system is anti-mystical, and our logical systems anti-metaphor. More basic: all our systems, religious and secular, are anti-alternative systems.'[14]

He asks the Christian and scientific communities to remove their either/or straightjacket and recognize that insight is scattered throughout the earth's civilizations. One way of achieving this is to learn from Hinduism a more appreciative attitude towards pluralism. In the Hindu position, persons of quite different theological perspective are seen nevertheless to have something true to say about the nature of reality. Smith finds this multiple approach corrective to the West's anti-alternative position. Though he objects to the Vedantist attempt imperiously to absorb all religions into their system, he is on the whole impressed with India's ability to appreciate religious excellence in doctrinal positions that are quite different.[15] He remarks:

> . . . India on the whole has been critical rather than sceptical . . . there has been a general predisposition . . . that each position, especially if maintained by an intelligent person of disciplined sincerity, is to be presumed to be valid until . . . shown otherwise, rather than *vice versa*.[16]

The attitude of 'innocent until proven guilty' is academically sound. Smith observes that India's benevolent blessing of many forms of religious life has helped it develop insight into a wide range of religious phenomena. On the other hand, secular and Christian approaches have combined to produce a lack of insight into, and a disease of arrogance towards the majority of the earth's religions.

Smith is, however, aware that both universalist *and* particularist strands exist in the Hindu complex. He recognizes that

Hindus on occasion have passionately judged the positions of other Hindus to be quite wrong. Yet he remains impressed with classical Hindu thinkers like Ramanuja or Shankara who were able to see in scholar-saints of competing positions truncated versions of the truth and who did not feel compelled totally to exclude the other from the realm of salvation.

The shift of consciousness that occurs when a presupposition becomes a self-conscious proposition – or a belief – justifies Smith's position that using 'belief' to express such separate meanings is intellectually confusing and untenable. Once a statement is thought of as an item in a particular belief system rather than a self-evident truth, it becomes open to critical assessment and to doubt. It becomes, in short, an opinion. Of course, one may continue to believe ideas that were once unconsciously held; but then one believes in a radically novel manner. One can cite examples of this shift in the modern Buddhist attempt to demythologize reincarnation, and the Hindu attempt to prove it. Both movements result from clashes with sceptical Christian and scientific thought. In both attempts one observes the fading of a tacit tradition. In both instances a background assumption has moved strongly to the foreground. Rather than remaining evident, reincarnation for many contemporary Hindus and Buddhists has moved from the status of cosmic fact to the status of belief.[17] And this example is but a microcosm of the situation facing contemporary persons from all religious communities. Today moderns 'believe' many things once taken for granted.

We are today aware that our particular beliefs are neither universal nor obvious. Gone is the time when an educated Westerner believed that his or her missionaries (scientific or Christian) presented an obviously more convincing picture of reality that would convert all but the most obdurate. Instead we are left with the modern phenomenon of a plurality of beliefs. At present a cornucopia of beliefs appears before us, creating new difficulty and new freedom in choosing a religious path. It has also formed a new sophistication about the use of symbol systems.

. . . some might wish to speculate: not what we do, or shall we, believe; but rather, with what symbol system shall we operate; and now that we self-consciously know it to be that, so that we cannot naively either presuppose it or believe it, what does it mean to have faith in terms of a system of ideas and symbols that *qua* system is anthropogenetic, although the life lived in terms of it may be, as it was designed that is should be, theocentric. The ideas and the symbols, we now know, are all human; but what they symbolize, we may still find (to use, in speaking, a man-made term) divine.[18]

To illustrate the problem that the shift from presupposition to proposition entails, Smith imagines a driver searching for a parking spot and confronted with a 'no parking' sign. He can have a variety of reactions to this interdict. He may obey out of fear or out of respect, or disobey from either anger or laziness. He may trust that the authorities are vigilant or that they are lenient. Or he may decide that it is worth the risk of paying a fine. All these reactions, respectful or not, presuppose the legitimacy of the authority behind the sign. A new situation emerges when a sceptic suggests to the driver that the sign is illegitimate and put up by those having no authority. The sign now becomes not a fact but an object for discussion and decision-making. The decision-making process has profoundly altered. No longer do decisions focus around legitimacy but around the question of whether to regard the sign as authentic. The shift entails a new task of weighing evidence for authority.[19] Smith does not claim that this development is unfortunate or illegitimate, but that such questioning is a new factor for traditional societies. Prior to the emergence of the sceptic (non-participant other) questions centred upon actions taken in response to what was valid. Now the question centres upon whether something (read in Qur'anic or biblical injunctions: the doctrine of the Trinity; doctrines of reincarnation; etc.) is valid, is true.

In the experience of the modern age, few traditional signposts are accepted with the ingenuousness of our driver who lives at a time before the seed of doubt has been cast. A contemporary person is left with three basic options: to reject all signposts (all religious or metaphysical authorities) and move toward nihilism; to defend a particular signpost against those not recognizing its validity (conservative retrenchment); or to learn to conceive of signposts in new ways. Smith argues for the third solution, contending that a multiplicity of legitimate signposts exist, with each tradition having something 'true' to say about its type of encounter with transcendence. He looks forward to a time when persons will move easily from the symbolic frame of one culture to that of another, appreciating the insights that various frames offer and recognizing that all symbolic systems are finite attempts to express an ineffable reality. The ability to move among belief systems with agility is for Smith a mark of the cosmopolitanism of the future.

A linguistic history of belief

In two significant word studies, one in *Faith and Belief*, the other in *Belief and History*, Smith analyses the shifts of meaning that have occurred in the etymological history of the English word 'beliefs'.[20] He tells us that belief was once a momentous term signifying faith, trust and love, but has since become a term which refers to a detached less vital mental act. The significance of Smith's study is that he shows that belief once corresponded to the personalist core of religious life – to faith – but in the modern period has become impersonalized. It no longer carries a meaning that accurately describes the movement of faith.

The eighteenth-century assumption that believing was what religious persons were essentially engaged in was inherited by the twentieth century, and is assumed by some philosophical experts who analyse the significance of religious language. By tracing belief's meaning-shifts, Smith demonstrates that believing once described religious existence with some accuracy; today it no longer does so. He therefore asks that we drop belief as a central category in describing religious existence. He does not, of course, mean that we abandon the Western quest for accurate intellectual expressions of faith. His meaning is more modest. The term 'belief' simply no longer refers to the activity of faith. As will become apparent, it is also in the process of losing its connotations of truth, and is therefore a problematical term for expressing the intellectual dimension of faith.

In his exploration of 'belief', Smith challenges us with conclusions that seem both odd and intriguing. These include: the concept of believing does not appear in either the New Testament or the Qur'an;[21] belief is not a prerequisite of faith and no person in any religious tradition ever believed (in the modern sense);[22] or again – 'I believe' is a false translation of 'credo' in the Apostles' Creed.[23] Before exploring such irregular statements, it is important to see in detail what belief was and what it has become.

Etymologically, the Anglo-Saxon verb 'believe' originally meant to hold dear, to love, to consider valuable, to cherish – as in, to cherish a friend. In the literary archaic 'lief' a comparable meaning has survived, as in Tennyson's *Morte d'Arthur* – as 'thou art lief and dear' (that is, 'beloved or treasured').[24] In Anglo-Saxon 'lief' is written *leof*, meaning 'dear and beloved', and from it was formed the verb *geleofan*. In Middle English *geleofan* became *be-leve(n)* – meaning 'to hold dear, to consider lovely, to value, to love', which in turn transformed into the Early Modern English, 'believe', meaning – 'to belove, to regard as lief, to hold dear, to cherish'.[25]

For centuries the usual object of 'believe' was a person. Other meanings soon derived from the activity of prizing persons. One could speak of believing 'in' or 'on', or even 'to' or 'of' a person, to indicate a personal orientation towards another with an attitude of esteem, affection, trust or endearment.[26]

In these periods, if one were asked 'Do you believe in God?' the questioner would be asking whether one trusted God or held him dear. The question would be about piety, not about belief in the modern sense. Today when an individual is questioned concerning his or her belief in God, the questioner is asking about the outcome of an intellectual decision as to the existence or non-existence of deity. In earlier periods deity's existence was a given, not open to doubt. It was a truism that only a fool held in his heart that there was no God. To ask the question of belief in Old, Middle, or Early Modern English was to inquire as to the quality of one's relationship to the deity.

The noun 'belief' similarly meant holding as beloved, but included additional meanings of giving oneself to, clinging to, committing oneself to, or staking one's confidence in either persons or things.[27]

If one were to ask a mediaeval Englishman whether a particular person believed in God, in the modern sense of affirming his existence, one would find that the actuality of the divine reality was part of the accepted mediaeval world-view. For even infidels believed in God in the modern sense, as did demons; they recognized that God certainly exists.

One of the earliest recorded uses of 'belief' is from an anonymous homily of the late twelfth or early thirteenth century, in which we find '. . . Christian men' should not set their belief on worldly goods', meaning that they should not cling to or overly prize worldly goods.[28] However, by 1611, the time of the translation of the King James Version, a transition had taken place. The noun 'belief' which earlier corresponded to what today we could call faith was, in fact, replaced by the term 'faith'. The entry in the 1888 Oxford English Dictionary describes this change.

> Belief was the earlier word for what is now commonly called 'faith'. The latter originally mean in Eng[lish] . . . 'loyalty to a person' . . . as in 'to keep faith, to break faith' . . . But the word 'faith' being . . . *fei*, . . . the etymological representative of the L[atin] fides, it began in the fourteenth c[entury] to be used to translate the latter, and in course of

time almost superseded 'belief', esp(ecially) in theological language, leaving 'belief' in great measure to the merely intellectual process or state. . . . Thus 'belief in God' no longer means as much as 'faith in God'.[29]

The verb 'believe', however, was to have a different fate from its noun form. For English had no verb 'to faith' as does the Greek *pisteuo*, which indicates commitment, trust and surrender of the whole person.[30] Though the noun 'belief' had by the seventeenth century lost its religious significance and passed it on to the noun 'faith', the verb 'believe' was to lose its religious significance more slowly and retain its earlier meanings: to love, to cherish, hold dear, to entrust oneself to, to give one's heart to, to make a commitment and, with a more conceptual emphasis, to recognize.[31]

Though the verb 'believe' maintained its religious significance longer than the noun, in the twentieth century it too has lost its religious significance and has come to connote an assent to factual propositions. Once used to refer to trust, the verb in contemporary popular usage is often used in conjunction with assertions which are uncertain, so that a degree of mistrust concerning their truth value is in order. Sentences of the type 'He believes that Boise is the capital of Idaho' indicate that the believing person is actually in doubt whether Boise is, or is not, the capital.

The result of these developments is that the concept of belief has dramatically lost its erstwhile relationship to truth. The noun, for example, once referred to trust in that which is reliable and true. One could not speak of belief in that which is false. Today, however, belief is commonly distinguished from knowledge. The *Random House Dictionary* (1966) illustrates the modern situation in which belief has lost its once firm implication of truth in four telling examples. These are: 1. the belief that the earth is flat; 2. a statement unworthy of belief; 3. a child's belief in his parents; and 4. the Christian belief.[32] In these examples belief is first, false; second, unworthy; third, childish; and fourth, religious. It is doubtful that theologians would wish to see the intellectual expression of faith placed in such disreputable company.

Over the past four centuries four trends in the transformation of 'belief' have occurred. Four hundred years ago the object of believing was predominantly a person – God and Christ in the Christian case; today the object has come to be an idea, a proposition or theory. The act of believing was earlier understood chiefly as a first-person act indicating self-engagement. It has since become in academic language primarily a description of the state of belief of third persons. It now refers to the opinions that others hold and has lost the sense of self-engagement. The mood of believing once involved persons in a relationship to absolutes, to sure realities. The mood of believing today involves uncertain matters of questionable validity. And more recently believing has come to refer to what other persons do tacitly, to the presuppositions of their conceptual framework.[33]

It is apparent that religious persons have never understood themselves as believing in any of the above four senses. First, they have been aware of entrusting themselves not to ideas, but to cosmic realities which their ideas reflect. Second, they were actively involved in faith-ing, rather than merely entertaining an opinion. Third, the mood of belief was traditionally one of certainty rather than doubt; and fourth, persons of earlier times did not refer to the presuppositions of their world view – since this is possible only to outsiders, or to insiders in the process of becoming outsiders.

In view of these four shifts, one realizes why Smith contends that religious persons have never believed in the modern sense. Each meaning-shift significantly reveals how 'belief' lost its religious significance. Belief, once synonymous with faith, is today antithetical to it. It is no longer adequate to pretend to understand religious persons by referring to their beliefs. Of course, they hold (have held) ideas about reality, but they hold (have held) them in a manner incongruent with modern belief.

The first shift occurs in the grammatical object of the verb. It marks a movement away from trust in persons to belief in propositions. In the sixteenth century, the verb 'believe' customarily took a personal object, indicating the esteeming of, or the trusting in, a person.[34] By the seventeenth century in the writings of Bacon and Hobbes one discovers that the 'objects' that are believed have started to shift from persons to the *word* of persons. Hobbes, for example, uses the phrase 'believe in God' to mean that one holds God's promises and statements veracious on the credit of the speaker, or in Hobbes' words, 'to hold all for truth they hear him say'.[35] Hobbesian usage concerning trust in the *word* of a person is intermediary between trust in a *person* (sixteenth century) and the acceptance of a *statement* as true (common eighteenth century). By the time of Locke (seventeenth century), the noun 'belief' has to do with 'the admitting or receiving any proposition for true, upon arguments or proofs that are found to persuade us . . . without certain knowledge'.[36] The noun works in a straightforward propositional manner – its synonym being opinion. Nevertheless, Locke continues to personalize the verb by linking the act of belief to trust in the author of a statement. According to Smith, the verb first consistently appears in a modern propositional and depersonalized sense of believe *that*, rather than in the earlier fiduciary believe *in*, in the writings of John Stuart Mill. With Mill belief finds its definitive nineteenth-century propositional form; for Mill is of the opinion that the correct use of the verb 'believe' is encapsulated in the statement 'he believes that a is b'.[37] The object of 'believe' is here a double object. The object's relationship to truth is neutral and the quality of the person speaking is presumed to be irrelevant.

Mill's propositional understanding dominated nineteenth- and twentieth-century philosophy. Yet as Smith remarks, Mill was historically incorrect; it is not the case that throughout history, 'the objects of all belief and of all inquiry express themselves in propositions'.[38] An historian will notice that belief has most often been placed in non-propositions, in cosmic persons, revealed laws, transcendent values, ultimate states of consciousness, in reality itself.[39]

Both 'belief' and 'believe' had for centuries a strong connotation of knowledge and certainty. In the last four centuries
this connection has disintegrated, leaving the modern West
with a concept of mere belief, the force of 'mere' being that
belief is no longer firmly related to the real. One can turn again
to the writings of Bacon to illustrate this earlier linkage
between belief and reality. Bacon understands belief to indicate
loyalty to what one knows to be true – there could be no false
beliefs. Likewise, Thomas Hobbes, Bacon's contemporary,
uses 'belief' to refer solely to those beliefs which were true.
There could, of course, be false opinions, but for Bacon and
Hobbes 'belief' could not bear the meaning of opinion because
of its link with known truth.[40] It is only in the late seventeenth
century, with John Locke, that one uncovers the modern
meaning of 'belief' as opinion. A belief is now no longer a
certainty, and beliefs may be assessed as to their truth or falsity.
In Locke's works we discover 'belief' beginning to unravel its
connection with truth. The attitude of the subject towards the
truth of what is believed has shifted from one of affirmation
and trust to one of detached and neutral assessment. This
unravelling of the connection between belief and truth
continued, until today the word is often used to refer to what
is doubtful, and can connote what is transparently false.

The contemporary assumption that propositional believing
is what religious persons do finds illustration in the British
philosopher A. J. Ayer, who in his work *The Central Questions
of Philosophy* asserts that 'until we have an intelligible proposition before us, there is nothing for faith to get to work on'.[41]
The assumption here appears to be that faith, like belief, must
always have as its object a proposition. Yet as Smith indicates,
historically faith has usually been in something or someone
other than in propositions. This reduction of faith to belief is
a great distance from understanding faith as a response to
transcendence or as interaction with transcendent value. It
represents a de-existentializing of religous life and unfortunately misrepresents the bulk of religious existence throughout
history. Smith regrets that Ayer's portrayal of belief is

common in American and British philosophical circles and recommends that a true understanding of faith is necessary to correct the distortion. He returns to earlier usage to rediscover the personal dimension that belief once had, and to demonstrate the progressive impersonalization that has occurred over the past four centuries.

In the first centuries of the Christian period, to affirm 'I believe' indicated an intense commitment. Such commitment was expressed by the word '*credo*', a word now translated by most scholars as 'believe'. '*Credo*' indicated trust in God, Christ, or the community of the faithful. It referred to an act of self-engagement which by definition required an active subject in the first person. '*Credo*' retained its existential import when first translated into English as 'believe', for at that time 'believe' had that import.

However, a growing impersonalism became apparent in English usage in a shifting of subjects from the first to the third person. This development indicated a movement away from declarations of personal commitment to a description of what other persons believe. If one turns to the works of Shakespeare, one can illustrate the earlier self-engaging use of 'believe'. There one discovers that 90% of the occurrences of the verb are accompanied by either a first or second person singular subject, taking the form of either 'I believe' or '(You) believe me'.[42] Both subjects imply the activity of persons and refer to either a personal act of trust or a calling forth of trust from another. First-person usage is also standard in Bacon, Hobbes and Locke. Since the eighteenth century, however, employment indicates a movement away from self-engagement and elicitations of trust to a non-engaged depiction of the state of third person others.[43] Belief now refers to the *state* or *condition* of those who hold x or y. It has lost its emphasis upon the acts of first or second persons.

Contemporary use of 'believe', especially in academic circles, indicates that it is used today mainly to refer to what non-intimate others do.[44] These are normally persons we are not acquainted with, and therefore persons whom we would not have the opportunity to address in the second person singular. This historical change of persons has profoundly transformed the meaning of 'believe'. Since the standard subject of 'believe' is now the third person other, 'believe' is in process of severing its connection with 'truth' and 'reality'. This is because we assume that what we (first person) say is true. We may extend this trust, at least in part, to friends (second person), but quite frequently we do not extend this courtesy to those who are distant from our friendship. This development reminds one of a succinct and caustic example of how meaning shifts mirror shifts of person: 'I have changed my mind; you have gone back on your word; he, she or it has lied.' The self is trusted; the friend is considered; the other is rejected.

When a subject (first singular) states: 'I believe it is raining,' he or she is describing a state of the external world; that is, something taking place in nature. When, however, a subject declares that another subject believes that it is raining, the first subject is referring not so much to the state of nature as to the state of mind of the second subject, to his or her state of belief.[45] When first persons shift to third a loss of reference to reality occurs. This, of course, is to be expected when the third person other is not an acquaintance. We who use the verb 'believe' have shifted from being inside the action of the verb to being outside the acts of others, and still further outside when refering to the tacit beliefs of others. We have moved our attention from volitional acts (self-engagement), to the mental acts of others (presuppositional belief).

Smith finds an even further stage of impersonalist development in the habit of modern philosophers who analyse propositions in total detachment from human subjects. In this instance, beliefs are presented as if they had no reference to human beings. The locus of the proposition is in neither first nor third persons. The proposition, fully de-contextualized, exists in itself upon a blackboard, to be understood as true or false in itself rather than to be understood as a human expression. Smith states:

It has been remarked that modern philosophers are not at their ease until they have written down a proposition on their blackboard to have a look at it. Their analysis has as its locus that blackboard, where the proposition is examined minus the verb introducing it.[46]

Such procedures may, of course, be helpful in isolating the logical structure of statements as a focus for reflection. Smith's point, however, is that such gains may not necessarily facilitate understanding of the meaning of statements. This behaviour leads to a situation in which one spends a significant portion of one's time analysing statements rather than asking the author of the statement, in whom the true locus of meaning resides, what he or she meant. One must, accordingly, recognize the sociological and spiritual consequences of this procedure. When we omit the verb we omit the subject and arrive at full impersonality. Such refinement is perhaps symptomatic of a society that has become adept at analysing the objective elements of nature, and inept in recognizing the complex personal dimension of life.

Smith recognizes that earlier patterns of use continue to exist in common speech: 'Believe me', 'Englishmen believe in cold showers', 'I don't believe a word of it'.[47] These uses are, however, no longer dominant in academic writing and continue to diminish in frequency as the impersonal ideal of learning progresses. As with common speech, religious usage has moved more slowly from its personalist mooring than has philosophical speech. One thinks of the fundamentalist's plea to 'believe on the Lord Jesus Christ' or the standard theological distinction between 'believing it' (fiduciary) and 'believing that' (propositional). These illustrations are, however, minor notes in the contemporary employment of the term. In fact Smith makes the tentative observation that Protestant ecclesiastics have remained approximately a century behind secular writers in their use of 'belief', and that Catholics have remained a further century behind Protestants.[48]

As we have seen, the verb 'believe' has followed the noun,

and like it has moved from an earlier position of a sure relationship to truth, to a neutral position of weighing truth against falsity. And recently, for some contemporaries, it has taken on connotations of dubiety and falsehood. Since each of these attitudes refers to a separate relationship to truth, Smith finds it helpful to clarify their meaning in this manner: 1. he 'recognizes' that *a* is *b* (a certain relationship to truth); 2. he 'is of the opinion' that *a* is *b* (a neutral relationship to truth in which either truth or falsity are possible outcomes; 3. he 'imagines' that *a* is *b* (a complete separation of belief from truth, with the verb referring to either error or delusion).[49]

It is apparent that religious persons have not committed themselves to that which they held to be false. Nor have they normally committed themselves to an ultimate value or vision of the world after a detached and neutral weighing of its truth or falsity. Few persons approach religion from the viewpoint of Pascal's wager. Religious persons normally commit themselves to either that which is assumed to be true or to a perceived truth which has seized them with the force of insight.

In the twentieth century, 'knowing' implies certitude and correctness; one cannot know what is false. Believing once had similar implications, but today implies lack of certitude or falsity. Though modern 'believing' does not describe the religious existence of past cultures, it does reflect the situation of being cast out from the certainties of traditional belief. Modern 'belief' describes today's individuals who exhibit uncertainty and indecisiveness in their beliefs.

Belief and the world religions

Having indicated what 'belief' has come to mean, it is not difficult to offer evidence that persons from the world religions have never, in this sense, believed. Muslims have not traditionally believed in the modern sense of assessing a proposition. Nevertheless, modern Muslims have borrowed the language of belief from the West and are themselves subject to the pressure of modernism and pluralism. They have followed the

West in entering into a process of objectifying their past religious assumptions. For those who still live in a traditional atmosphere, in the naive aura of a corporate vision, the problem of belief had not yet arisen. The number of such persons is rapidly diminishing. Yet the bulk of Muslims in the past have not believed; they have held their truths with certainty, or as tacitly obvious, rather than sceptically, or on the basis of considered evidence. Outsiders may disagree with the way Muslims experienced their truth, but if they wish to understand Muslim religious life they must understand it was not constituted by 'believing'. On the contrary, Muslims understood themselves as responding to a divine address, not approving a proposition.[50] They did not view themselves as proposing statements for scientific scrutiny. Instead, they held that human beliefs (opinions) are the creations of men and therefore cannot offer certitude. The Qur'an, on the other hand, speaks in the Words of God and calls the reasonings and imaginings of men into question.[51] Even today a Muslim does not say that he or she *believes* that there is no God but God and *believes* that Muhammad is his prophet. Rather, a Muslim *bears witness* and *proclaims* these as cosmic.[52] Further, Islam does not confuse faith with its belief system. Islamic theologians have long recognized that persons may belong to the Islamic cultural world and yet not have faith. Faith is not automatic. Not all have truly surrendered, or appropriated the gift of revelation; not all are truly Muslim.

Turning to Smith's analysis of Buddhist tradition we note that Buddhists likewise do not believe in the Dharma, the cosmic moral law which enables those in harmony with it to attain salvific peace. Naturally, Buddhists assume the existence of the Dharma; but the Dharma is not presented as a belief or an opinion, but as a cosmic fact whose efficaciousness has been proved true in millions of personal experiments. Those living by the Dharma, by the ethical teachings, experienced salvation. Belief in the Dharma did not entail a philosophical analysis of whether the Dharma existed. Its presence was not seriously doubted, since for Buddhists, the Dharma is reality, is truth.

To live by it is to participate in it. And participation naturally does not lead to a detached or neutral attitude. A relationship to the Dharma is not comparable to a relationship to an opinion. Life according to it demands commitment. One does not believe it; one lives it. The modern concept of belief is clearly not applicable, and a modern Western philosopher or historian who relates that the Buddhist believes in the Dharma misconstrues the Buddhist manner of encountering the world. An outsider sees beliefs, concepts and assumptions; the insider sees *through* concepts and assumptions. Even abstract discussions on the nature of the Dharma when offered by Buddhists have a radically distinct flavour from the discussions of outsiders. The insider who has lived according to precepts of the Dharma has penetrated into the reality that lies behind the precepts. This reality is thought to have been previously encountered by thousands of *arhants*. The insiders' concept points to a growing experience more profound than formulations. For the outsider it remains a concept.

In the Hindu tradition Smith finds two terms which correspond to the English 'faith'. These are '*astika*' and '*sraddha*'. Yet, he finds nothing in Hinduism which corresponds to the Western notion that belief constitutes the centre of religious life. The emphasis appears rather to be on *jnana*, on the realization of cosmic truth, on the awakening of supreme knowledge rather than on belief. *Jnana* does not refer to the knowledge of a proposition but to an immediate knowing that involves a rich participation between knower and known.[53] Though outsiders observe Hindus believing this or that, the insider will not find belief an appropriate category for describing his/her activity.

Smith is not claiming that Hindus hold to the same doctrines or that doctrinal dispute is insignificant in Indian history. His claim is more subtle. In the Hindu tradition one does not find preoccupation with belief.

The Sanskrit '*astika*' refers to a positive attitude (an ortho-attitude) towards the Hindu spiritual tradition and is unlike both the ortho(praxis) of Jews and Muslims and the ortho-

(doxy) of Christians. Though *astika* excludes non-believers like Muslims, it does not necessarily exclude atheists or non-theists, since these persons are also recognized as religious participants in Hindu tradition. *Astika* refers to a 'yes-saying' to the Hindu complex *and* a 'yes-saying' to the transcendence which the complex points to. It may, therefore, also be described as 'an awareness of transcendence' that lies behind the Hindu tradition.[54]

Another central category in Indian religious thought is the term '*sraddha*'. Like *astika* it, too, refers to a human quality. Each of the major sects, Vaishnava, Shaiva and Shakta, postulates *sraddha* as a prerequisite for success in the way of salvation.[55] Composed of two words *srad* (heart) and *dha* (put), it literally means 'to put one's heart upon', to commit oneself to, or become involved with.[56] *Sraddha* is predominantly conceived of as a quality of persons. Further, it is an open term that does not specify the object upon which one puts one's heart. Instead, it refers to a capacity for intense personal involvement. Without the object specified it remains similar to Tillich's 'ultimate concern', when this is understood subjectively rather than objectively. *Sraddha's* opposite is not disbelief but ego-diffusion and indifference. Further, *sraddha* has connotations of truth. Whatever one is committed to should be true.[57] Smith's analysis of *astika* and *sraddha* leads him to conclude that the Hindu religion is more concerned with the quality of religious life and with a relationship to Reality than with belief.

In *The Meaning and End of Religion*, Smith noticed that in the Christian tradition faith has been predominantly expressed in prose, doctrine and systematic theology – more so than in other traditions.[58] The standard of being a Christian has been expressed in 'orthodoxy' rather than ortho-attitudinalism or orthopraxy. At the time of publication (1962) Smith held that Christian focus on the rational explication of doctrine was due to the inheritance of Greek philosophy, which was itself an expression of the Greek faith in reason.[59] Further research (*Belief and History*, 1977), however, led him to the observation that Christians, like persons of other traditions, have not believed in the modern sense of the term, even though they characteristically expressed their faith in doctrine.[60]

Smith is sympathetic to making ortho-attitudinalism the criterion for determining whether a person ought to be counted as standing within a given religion.[61] Using this standard Muslims, Jews, Christians, etc., are persons who have found relevance within their tradition and who approve of what the tradition has been attempting to get at. If one defines a Christian or a Muslim as one who believes x or does y, then one must exclude Christians and Muslims of excellent quality who have lived in the past and have not held x or practised y, or who live in the present and do not believe x or do y. Smith therefore finds ortho-attitudinalism rather than ortho-doxy or ortho-praxy the more appropriate criterion for deciding membership.

'Belief' as the intellectual expression of faith remains significant in Smith's thought. But the word's associations with neutrality, tacit world-views and dubiety prevent him from using it. Instead, he asks that we retranslate those texts in which religious activities that differ from modern belief have been translated as 'belief'. He also suggests that 'belief' is no longer the most adequate term for expressing the intellectual expression of faith, and reformulates the traditional question of the relationship of faith to belief as 'the relation of faith to intellectually apprehensible truth' – an awkward phrase, perhaps, but one that circumvents belief's contemporary associations.[62] The phrase 'intellectually apprehensible truth' serves to correct the misguided attempt of religious enthusiasts to demand rational assent to that which has not been personally encountered.

Belief in the New Testament

When Smith turns to the New Testament, he again discovers that the concept of belief does not appear within its pages. Naturally, early Christians held to many presuppositions of their milieu. But if modern believing means: 1. the holding of ideas rather than the perception of cosmic realities; 2. an uncommitted assessment of facts or values rather than acts of love and loyalty; or 3. a belief system, then one must quickly state that early Christians did not believe.

Smith does not claim that earlier translators of the New Testament erred in translating faith as belief. As long as belief maintained its dynamic personal reference, it well described early Christian existence. However, contemporary translators are advised to cease using the term. A call to drop 'belief' and 'believe' altogether in the New Testament may perhaps sound radical. Yet it is not. If one turns to the King James Version of 1611, one finds that 'faith' occurs 233 times, whereas 'belief' occurs but once, and that occurrence is in II Thessalonians 2.13, where it does not actually indicate belief in the modern sense.[63] In contrast, the verb 'believe' occurs 285 times.[64] As we have seen, the English language did not possess a verb 'to faith', and translators, rendering *pisteuo* as 'believe', pressed its earlier meanings into service.[65]

New Testament 'faith' (pistis (n.) *pisteuo* (v.)) in its nominal, verbal and adjectival forms is found 603 times.[66] In the overwhelming majority of cases, it is used either absolutely with no object, or with a person or thing as its object. In only 4% of its 603 appearances is faith followed by a propositional or *hoti* (that) clause.[67] This statistic indicates that a propositional understanding of belief was at best minimal in the New Testament. An analysis of the *hoti* clauses which do occur indicates that a propositional understanding was not intended. Though Smith does not deal with all *hoti* clauses, he selects three as representative. These are: James 2.19: 'Thou believest *that* there is one God; thou doest well: the devils also believe and tremble'; John 13.19: . . . that you may believe *that* I am He'; Hebrews 11.6: 'without faith it is impossible to please him: for he that commeth to God must believe *that* he is and *that* he is a rewarder of those that seek him'.[68] Since in modern English 'believe' can mean to hold an opinion that is either correct or false (a usage common in the nineteenth century and the early part of the twentieth) or to hold an opinion which is dubious or false (usage common in the second half of the twentieth century), it is apparent that 'believe' is an inappropriate translation of *pisteuo* in the given instances. In each of the above *hoti* clauses, the verb orientates itself on that which is most certainly assumed to be true, not on opinion or falsity. Smith therefore translates *pisteuo* as 'recognize' in order to maintain a link with the truth of what is being presented, which the original clearly intends. If we take James 2.19 as an example, we see that *pisteuo* requires a sense of 'to recognize'. The devils which the author has in mind have a firm certainty that God exists, not merely as an idea in their minds, but as a cosmic reality. If we think of our devils as being merely of the opinion that God exists and entertaining the possibility that they might be in error, we would surely misrepresent the author's appraisal of their situation. A similar analysis can be offered for other passages having *hoti* clauses. Smith therefore maintains that despite the existence of several *hoti* clauses modern propositional belief is not found there.

New Testament faith when presented as a noun is most frequently found without an object. *Pistis* occurs 246 times.[69] In 217 instances it is used absolutely without a genitive object or following preposition.[70] The bulk of instances of absolute usage indicates that *pistis* is primarily understood as a human quality. It should be understood as a virtue, like courage, loyalty or hope.

Re-understanding faith as a personal quality is essential for moderns (including biblical scholars) who have been linguistically conditioned to see faith in terms of its object. But emphasis on the object of faith misses Christ's understanding of faith as a capacity for trust, receptivity and openness. Though often faith undoubtedly had a tacit object, it appears to have been used absolutely in a large number of instances. Smith reminds us:

Certainly for Christ, faith was something by which a person is characterized less or more: 'I have not found so great faith, no, not in Israel', 'faith as a grain of mustard seed', and so on. This appears to have been the case also with those who heard him. 'Lord, I have faith: help my lack of faith' (9.24). It seems evident that for Jesus, faith was a quality of the person, rather than any externalized viewing.[71]

Rather than assume that we understand the nature of faith, and are free to concentrate on faith's object, Smith recalls us to meditate on the nature of New Testament faith. He does not wish to minimize the importance that the New Testament object of faith, either tacit or stated, was Jesus Christ. Instead he asks us to explore the nature of the subjective capacity to be faithful in order to realize how faith, as apparent from the words of Christ, is a virtue.

> I am asking, however: what is this 'faith' that enables, compels, one who has it towards Christ to be loyal to Him even before the lions? Or is 'faith' another name of that very loyalty?[72]

The verb '*pisteuo*' is standardly found with either a direct or indirect personal object or with the prepositional object.[73] *Pisteuo's* primary object is persons: human beings, God and Christ. The verb is fiduciary and refers to obedience and fidelity, activities apparently other than dogmatic assent.

A less common usage than either faith in a person, or faith as a quality of persons, is found in passages where 'faith' is followed by a single non-person object. Such usage is more common than use of the double object found in *hoti* clauses.[74] The single object may be a person's word, or it may occur in constructions such as 'to have faith in the Lie', or 'in Truth', or 'in Love'. Examples of the latter may be found in II Thessalonians 2.10–13 and I John 4.14.[75] In these selections *pisteuo* takes a single object and refers to persons offering their allegiance to evil or good. In exegesis of II Thessalonians 2.10–31 we find:

> . . . it is quite evident that the point at issue is where one puts one's allegiance, where one gives one's heart, to which

of these two contrasting forces one consecrates one's life
. . . (*pisteuin toi pseudei*) means to align oneself with the Lie,
to enlist in its (his) service, to devote one's living to it. The
parallel is, 'had pleasure in unrighteousness'. There is no
question here of mere intellectual error. (For most modern
readers, a rendering 'believe what is false' is simply wrong,
if I may say so with due respect to the modern translators.)
It is a matter, rather, of delighting in a Lie, or taking pleasure
in what one knows to be false.[76]

The significance of Smith's analysis is clear. Though
'believe' is found in New Testament translations, it is apt to
be misunderstood. Unless translators have fully intended
earlier fiduciary connotations, they have distorted the nature
of New Testament belief.

Christian tradition and the evolution of belief

Smith challenges not only New Testament translations but
also the translations of the creeds. He finds contemporary
rendering of the early Latin '*credo*' inadequate and misleading.
In conjunction with a growing consensus of church historians
Smith holds that the ritual of baptism in the first three centuries
AD consisted not in the acceptance of a propositonal creed, but
in the dedication, or personal engagement, or, more literally,
in a *credo*, a setting of one's heart upon, or a giving of one's
heart to Christ and his Father.[77] The words of the baptized
meant that the person uttering the *credo* experienced him or
herself engaged in a decisive step of self-commitment, in the
taking of a loyalty oath to the divine. The act called '*credo*'
inaugurated committed existence.[78]

Smith is not suggesting that early Christians had no beliefs;
rather, he insists that their beliefs were tacit.[79] Some were
shared with the surrounding society; others were shared within
the commuity and assumed to be true. He suggests that the
word '*credo*' had no propositional meaning except and perhaps
in a rare occasional circumstance.[80]

Naturally there were instances when Christians were aware of possessing a vision not shared by their environment. These tensions called forth a self-reflective expression of difference. When early Christians articulated their distinct view of the world they did not choose *credo* or *pisteuo* to indicate their uniqueness. Instead they chose terms that are translated 'to see', 'to know', or 'to announce'.[81] Each of these terms insures a strong relation to truth, and immediately suggests that when early Christians were conscious of holding truths that set them apart, they spoke in terms of discovery, recognition and involvement.

After the first three centuries AD the church, when using *credo*, slowly began to place greater emphasis upon the predicate or object of the verb, rather than upon the act of the subject. With baptism now standard practice in the late empire, the victorious Christian community turned to the intellectual task of formulating the object of commitment. Although concern with doctrinal clarity emerged as a strong issue, even at this late date persons did not primarily concern themselves chiefly with doctrinal issues. Through most of its history the church remained concerned with faith as a quality of life.

Even in formulations of the Apostles' and Nicene creeds, the principal verbs are performatives – indicating commitment and allegiance rather than abstract understanding.[82] Though the objects of faith within the creeds are qualified and explored, they are not expressed as propositions. The dominant emphasis remains upon surrender, trust and self-engagement.

The earliest official church statement that contains a propositional form does not appear until the fifth century in the Athanasian Creed, and even at this date only a few propositions are found.[83] The early existential focus on self-commitment is maintained despite a growing concern with intellectual articulation. If moderns read the creeds as propositional matters, they are, Smith argues, reading back their own preoccupation with 'belief' rather than understanding them as previously understood, as expressions of the recognized truths of the community. Given modern belief, translations of both *credo* and *pisteuo* as 'believe' are misleading and falsify a true understanding of the Christian self-image in the period of the Empire.

Smith turns to Thomas Aquinas, the master rationalist, to test his thesis that Christians have historically been concerned with faith rather than with belief. Aquinas is selected as a representative of that portion of Christendom in which one would expect to find a propositional emphasis. Yet despite Aquinas's massive commitment to intellectually expressing faith, he does not equate faith with belief. Aquinas is concerned with the act called *credo*; but he holds that *credo* as the act of faith is more than *opinio* or propositional believing.[84] For Aquinas and for the mediaeval schoolmen in general *credo* stands for an act of loyalty to the truth. It represents both a recognizing and an accepting of truth – truth being ultimately another term for God.[85] Both faith (*fides*) and (*credo*) signify an act of loyalty. As with the *pisteuo* of New Testament and the *credo* of the creeds, Aquinas's use of '*credo*' is incorrectly rendered 'believe'.

A person who knew truth but was not loyal to it, or one loyal only to such truth as he or she had already apprehended but with no openness or commitment beyond it, no reaching out in pursuit of yet fuller truth, would in Thomas's eyes not have faith, in his language would not be said to have *fides*; the act called *credere* would not be ascribed to him.[86]

In Aquinas's understanding, *fides* is close to knowing. Yet it refers to a knowing that is not yet a total understanding. Smith calls it 'an apprehending that is not a comprehending' and 'not *savoir* but *connaître*'.[87] Apprending is not believing; it is a recognition of what is true. Aquinas believed many things moderns do not. He saw these beliefs as universal truths and descriptions of the way things are in the universe. He named these assured truths faith's 'preambles', his name for the accepted conceptual background.[88]

Aquinas held that faith-ful persons are able to recognize that which is true and therefore able to state true propositions about truth itself (God). However, he emphasized that these propositions never contain the whole truth but instead point mystery-ward. Propositions are human constructs that express apprehension, but precisely as human constructs they can never express comprehension. For Aquinas, faith is not in a proposition but in that which insures the truth of propositions, that is reality, or God.[89] In faith we intellectually apprehend God, yet partially. The temporal mind is unable to grasp the simplicity of reality.[90] Though faith has an intellectual component that is expressed propositionally, it includes an orientation towards reality that remains mysterious to the earthly intellect.

Opposed to modern 'belief', 'faith' (*fides* and *credere*) implies a personal commitment to truth. Contrary to 'belief', 'faith' does not indicate the acceptance of opinion but the acceptance of truth. Faith is the acceptance of that which is 'clearly known to be right'.[91] As used by Aquinas *credo* maintains a clear connection to truth. It is not, as 'belief' would indicate, opinion, or possible truth. Aquinas goes so far as to say that persons may hold wrong beliefs, yet still have a correct orientation towards truth, and that this constitutes true faith.[92] Aquinas certainly did not 'believe', though he indeed possessed (or was possessed by) faith.

Later developments in the Roman Catholic tradition continued to maintain this distinction between faith and belief. Smith illustrates this continuity by analysing Vatican I's pronouncement on faith, '*De Fide*', the article '*Foi*' in the *Dictionnaire de théologie catholique* (1899–1950) and the volume '*What is Faith?*' in the *Twentieth Century Encyclopedia of Catholicism*.[93] Each of these works makes the point that faith is more than belief. In this sense their authors are consistent with the statements of most modern Protestant theologians. Yet Smith's position is that faith is other than belief and that tacit belief provides the framework in which faith arises. Smith predicts that once theologians understand how belief has been altered into its twentieth-century form, and how it significantly differs from earlier meanings, they will cease using the term as a religious category. He states: 'No future age . . . will ever again translate *credo* as "I believe".'[94]

Smith gives further examples of the linguistic change his analysis demands. He predicts that no one in the future will translate Anselm's aphorism *credo ut intelligam* – 'I believe in order that I may understand.' Against this Smith offers: 'I became involved, in order that I may understand; I dedicate myself, I give my heart, in order that my mind may truly penetrate'.[95] He also anticipates alteration in the translation of Augustine's '*intellege ut credas, credo ut intelligam*' (understand in order that you may believe; believe in order that you may understand).[96] Smith offers instead: 'Understand in order that you may become committed, become committed in order that you may understand.[97]

By returning to a traditional understanding of *pisteuo* and *credo* Smith hopes to enable contemporary Christians and contemporaries in other religions to understand the life that lies buried beneath a propositional understanding of Christianity. It is important both to free ourselves from holding that belief is at the heart of Christian spirituality and to return to a serious contemplation of faith as openness to transcendence.

Though Smith insists that to understand religious man we must grasp the priority of faith, the intellectual expression of faith is not ignored. The intellect has legitimate demands. Smith rejects anti-intellectualist tendencies in modern theology that reduce faith to either an act of will or to a state of feeling. Faith as the expression of the entire person is inclusive of intellect.

Reflection on belief must be adequate to the intellectual situation. Smith, therefore, recommends that belief statements should have the following characteristics: 1. be genuine expressions of faith; 2. reflect the recent awareness that genuine faith occurs universally within a plurality of limited symbol systems; 3. express the consciousness of a new pluralistic situation in which traditional beliefs have become self-conscious; and 4. be sensitive to the historical relativity of the intellectual formulations of faith.[98] A consideration of these items makes formulations of modern 'belief' tenuous and difficult at best.

Persons attempting to formulate modern belief are under moral and intellectual constraints. Moral constraint urges them to reject items of belief that can no longer be held with intellectual integrity.[99] Smith insists that the intellect must never bow to irrational belief for such is the way of dishonesty, a vice opposed to the character of faith. He likewise insists that we must not reverse priorities. Beliefs must be subordinate to faith, and faith again subordinate to truth.[100] Intellectually, beliefs are under constraint to be true. But this entails understanding what Smith intends by 'truth' and is the topic for discussion in Chapter 3.

3

AN UNDERSTANDING OF TRUTH

A realist epistemology

Before analysing Wilfred Cantwell Smith's use of the term 'truth' it may be helpful to locate his epistemological position. He is a realist for whom objects transcend our necessarily incomplete apprehensions of them. Categories of perception are historically conditioned. Perception occurs through conceptual filters which to a large extent determine the limits of the known world. But persons are not thereby totally locked into a sociological pattern of perception. Individuality and creativity offer some freedom from the patterning of a cultural epoch.

Values, like objects, transcend persons. They have their own form of existence and are significant determinants of human action. Further, they are central ingredients in world-views that determine behaviour. Given the transcendence of objects and values, Smith's realistic approach entails the acknowledgment that the richness of being exceeds schematic representations. Concerning the use of 'transcendence', he states:

> I use that term more or less literally, to refer to that which transcends – transcends us, our grasp, our definitions, among other things. Now my suggestion is that maybe it is relevant to our concerns that the modern intellect has tended to deny transcendence and therefore to stultify itself.[1]

Among that which transcends is ultimate transcendence –

God or divine reality. Though things and values are real, they, together with the divine, are not known in themselves, but only in the manner in which they appear to finite percipients.

With the existentialists Smith teaches that human beings can enter into a plurality of relationship with reality. Like Kierkegaard and Buber, he is concerned with elucidating the various stances that an individual may take towards objects and values. The primary stance chosen by a majority of Western intellectuals is, of course, an objectivist position in which objects and their scientific descriptions constitute the only, most important or primary form of knowledge. But, as Smith points out, this stance is but one among many. Other civilizations have preferred non-objectivist positions that emphasize aesthetic, mystical, symbolic, personal, intuitive, participative and ethical orientations. These ways of relating to reality reveal something true and valuable about the world that mere objectivity is unable to offer. All orientations, however, fail to exhaust transcendence, and in Kantian style Smith suggests that things in themselves remain for ever elusive, for ever transcendent.[2]

Transcendence, however, refers to more than the *Ding an sich*. There are elements of transcendence that are beyond our present grasp, but not unconquerably so. 'Transcendence' is here used to refer to the sense of moreness, richness and complexity that persons are aware of in their interaction with life, but have as yet failed to explore or explicate. It is this which convinces us that there is more to ourselves and the world than we currently know. This is a fact that historians are able to demonstrate; for the future persistently proves that those who claim to have attained final understanding in a sphere of human thought are invariably incorrect. New discoveries, values and methods continuously arise.

Despite his reflections on the mystery of the not yet known and the thing in itself, Smith is not an epistemological sceptic. Persons do know, and increasingly know, a good deal about reality in the natural, social and historical sciences. The species has gathered a vast harvest of information about the various 'levels of being'. Smith uses the language of 'levels' to indicate that values, along with ultimate reality, transcend persons by laying claim to them. In this sense values and divinity may be imaged as 'higher than persons'.[3]

At the level of things, scientific understanding obviously advances. In the social sciences, knowledge about human behaviour has demonstrably increased. Nonetheless, Smith argues that social scientists with a behaviourist bias have consistently failed to understand or recognize the significance of other cultures. Some advance has been made by historians of religion, who are beginning to see within the religious visions of other peoples. Since religious vision refers to a culture's way of organizing reality, Smith is stating that our understanding of world-views is only beginning to approach adequacy. Yet he confidently views the present advance in scholarship as a watershed period that holds promise for a mutual co-understanding between cultures.

Smith is also a realist in his approach to history, treating it as a study of the development of past *events*, rather than a mere study of past *accounts* of events offered by historians. This latter form of history has its reality in the minds of historians rather than in events occurring outside them. It is the event which is primary; for the event gives rise to historical reflection.[4]

This concern for the primacy of actuality over interpretation does not indicate that Smith is indifferent to theoretical issues. His writings are proof of this. He is, though, alert to avoid the intellectual disease of preoccupation with theoretical conception at the expense of attentiveness to the actual. He wishes to avoid this modern 'narcissistic, and self-destructive' attitude that pays 'attention not to the world around us, but to our ideas about that world'.[5]

He finds contemporary academics in the United States infatuated with ideas about subject-matter rather than with subject-matter itself. This orientation presages the arrival of a new scholasticism, fascinated with ideas at the expense of reality. Smith's wariness about the new scholasticism helps to explain his strictures against methodology at the expense of content. His criticisms, though directed chiefly at practitioners in religious studies, are intended to apply more widely to the academic community of the liberal arts and social sciences. The contemporary love affair with methodological and epistemological issues has resulted in a loss of sensitivity to the real, a loss of sensing both that which is mundane and transcends current explication, and that which is mysterious and transcends definition and grasp. This lack has led to a lapse in creativity; for when scholarship moves away from direct contact with its subject matter it degenerates into stereotypical thought. It becomes obsessed with the known and is unable to venture into fresh perspectives:

> If we are not more concerned with our subject-matter, which we do not know, than with our methods, which we do know, we have ceased to be true inquirers. (When I say that we do not know our subject matter, I mean of course that we do not know it except partially, inadequately.)[6]

An object such as stone may transcend human knowledge, but its existence is axiologically subordinate to that of persons. On the other hand, transcendent values and the divine are axiologically and ontologically 'higher' than human beings. This fact gives the humanities and the social sciences a special task, in that they study human creations which to some extent embody transcendent value. These areas of thought study expressions of value which persons must open to, surrender to, and in some degree stand in awe of, if they are to learn from or understand them. Smith's meaning can be illustrated by turning to literature and, more specifically, to the dramas of Shakespeare. Modern persons approaching the plays with well-honed methodological tools will certainly discover what these tools were designed to search out. They will uncover information such as the economic background or sexual customs of Elizabethan England. Though this discovery is, of course, legitimate, it may happen that persons busy in this sort of research will fail to engage the work, fail to sense the world it reveals, fail to be illuminated by the insights into human nature it offers, and fail to perceive the force of the work in its presentational immediacy. For Smith one necessarily risks and ought to risk much when genuinely encountering a literary work; for in this process a person exposes his or her actual self to his or her potential self. The same may be said for encountering the subject-matter of each of the humanities and social sciences. And it is only after an effective and repeated encounter with the subject-matter that one should take up more abstract methodological concerns. For only then is the experienced reality of the subject-matter assured. Only after a thorough acquaintance with the material at hand should methodological concerns arise, and then in a creative sense, as method responding to material, rather than method imposed upon material. It is indeed Smith's concen for the presence of reality, that leads him to say: '. . . I claim that the methodological emphasis threatens to disrupt knowledge, to distort it, and to obstruct understanding.'[7]

Rather than use the common image of mastering a field of material as proof of one's expertise, Smith recommends that instead we first be mastered by that which we study, in order that the significance, presence and value-dimension of it be actuated in us. His attitude to the proper study of method is similar to that of Gerhardus van der Leeuw, who refused to countenance the study of methodology in comparative religion until the student was generously exposed to the original texts.[8]

In a footnote to *Faith and Belief* Smith maintains that unless persons accept the dominance of the real over the conceptual, they will fail to apprehend the insights of other civilizations.[9] This represents a tragic loss; for something of the nature of reality is present in the works of other civilizations. When scholars forget that reality transcends their concepts and is more complex than their culture's orientation they fail to understand.

> . . . two modern social scientists have popularized the unfortunate phrase 'the social construction of reality'. . . This is a thesis fundamental to my own argument . . .

Nonetheless, by speaking of the social construction of 'reality', when they mean that of the perception of reality, they fall victim to and enhance the modern incapacity to recognize (*sic*) that reality precedes and transcends our apprehension of it . . . If interpretations of reality differ among groups not because each is but an approximation to or an abstraction from reality itself, where are we? Can we never improve our apprehension; or never be insane? And if reality does not transcend our perception of it, what is our awareness of transcendence an awareness of?[10]

As the above quotation indicates, Smith is in harmony with Michael Polanyi's attempt to reintroduce the concept of reality as a necessary guiding thought for understanding nature. Without the concept of reality one is unable to explain the fact that humankind seems to be attaining an ever-increasing advance in knowledge, in a growing adequation of concept and thing.

Knowledge is always knowledge by someone and does not exist in itself apart from persons in a timeless realm. For this reason Smith prefers to use active nouns like 'conception' rather than abstract nouns like 'concept'. Likewise, he prefers to speak of knowing rather than knowledge, in order to remind us that knowing is a human act. In these linguistic choices he is concerned with reversing approaches that view personal knowing as a liability rather than an asset. In taking a personalist position, he is deciding against Karl Popper's position that knowledge exists apart from knowers. Smith states:

Popper holds that knowledge exists in, for instance, the British Museum, rather than in people's heads. It would be possible to contend that in this matter he is wrong. For if biological warfare obliterated human life on earth . . . but left the British Museum . . . there would be no knowledge on our planet (even if the means of re-attaining knowledge remained for some future race of intelligents).[11]

In *The Faith of Other Men* we find concrete examples of

Smith's realist convictions. Two are sufficient to indicate his position that the study of value reveals important non-subjective aspects of reality that are not available to the natural sciences. Concerning the validity of aesthetic perception:

> Surely we must train our children not to *believe* that x is beautiful, but to see that it is, to appreciate it, deeply and inwardly and truly and personally. . . I aspire not only to see things as beautiful myself, but also to see as beautiful what is beautiful, really, and only that . . . My goal is to recognize as lovely what is in fact lovely, without deceiving myself and without being deceived – once again to combine integrity and validity, subjective judgment with objective truth.[12]

A similar emphasis on the reality of non-objective perception may be found in this account of the moral sphere:

> I am not moral if my act merely conforms to external standards that I myself have not accepted, if I act without inner conviction. Yet neither am I moral if I am merely paving the road to Hell with well-meaning stupidity. . . . You must do what *you see* to be good; and you must see to be good what actually is good.[13]

These examples indicate that insight into the realm of the beautiful or the good constitutes a form of knowledge (insight into the realm of the true). Transitions among these realms are easy in Smith's ontology, for all three are aspects of reality, and reality is for Smith synonymous with truth. It is perhaps unusual to find such an active neo-Platonic imagination in the twentieth century;[14] but the neo-Platonic model legitimizes those insights into reality that a sceptical and reductionist philosophy fails to perceive.

Smith's eirenic concerns are jeopardized by reductionist models, for if one is not able to authenticate the central perceptions of other civilizations, the possibility of dialogue is undermined. Reductionist methodologies encourage Western scholars to insult rather than appreciate. This approach alienates and prohibits mutual understanding. It also cuts off the possibilities of new forms of personal individuation that draw on the insights of a multi-cultural mix. Smith's realism therefore not only reflects a theoretical preference, but also has pragmatic consequences for person-making.

For Smith 'truth' is a term containing ideal, ontological and scientific connotations. As an ideal, truth is a value that constitutes (or ought to constitute) the ultimate concern of intellectuals. Less idealistically, it refers to the structure of things, to the facts and processes of both the natural and historical universe.[15] As an ultimate, 'truth' refers to reality and therefore to the divine.

When Smith speaks of truth he is not referring principally to propositional truth but to the reality which grounds such truth, the reality which includes all forms of being, ideal or actual. In understanding 'truth' in this manner Smith represents himself as standing in the tradition of Aquinas, for whom also truth did not refer to propositions but to the reality behind propositions.[16]

Placing a high regard on being an intellectual, Smith defines the intellectual as one who has surrendered to the ideal of truth and is thereby empowered by it. Truth so conceived leads by way of habit to the creation of persons whose characteristic virtue is that of truthfulness. In this position, intellectuals through the exercise of this virtue enlarge their humanity and become more authentic or more real. A genuine intellectual is one whose motive remains the search for truth itself and who follows its demands regardless of personal inclination.

It is apparent, therefore, that Smith does not use the term 'intellectual' to refer to those skilled in technological praxis. For the pursuit of truth is not primarily an exercise of the practical intellect. It refers to the operation of the autonomous speculative intellect that remains free of external authorities.[17] Such an intellect for Smith must be separate from self-interested ideologies, including theological authoritarianism, technological will to power, Marxism, and forms of nationalism and parochial patriotism. Those who live by truth as an ideal, live by a form of faith, namely that the world, and to a lesser extent ultimate reality, can be intellectually apprehended, and that such an apprehension constitutes a good in itself. In taking this position Smith aligns himself with a Socratic understanding of knowledge as a love of truth that leads to virtue, rather than with a Baconian understanding of knowledge as the pursuit of power.[18]

All perceptions of truth are personal. Despite the social nature of intellectual enterprises, truth remains a personal apprehension of the way things are. The primary locus of truth is in persons. For all knowledge, insight and perception is enacted by persons. It is important to recognize that Smith does not intend to subjectivize the concept of truth; nor is he propounding an epistemological idealism. Reality transcends persons, as both common sense and common language attest.

Though the term 'knowledge', is commonly used in the twentieth century to indicate the intellectual dimension of truth, Smith accepts many forms of truth other than intellectual. Perceived truth includes recognizing the validity of a theorem, the legitimacy of aesthetic insight, the authority of a moral ought, the reality in mystical vision, together with the validity of inferences and deductions in the natural and social sciences. True (synonymous here with real) knowing is seen as requiring more than an abstract belief that x is true, good or moral. What is true must be personally recognized as such, for personal truth requires acquaintance.

> There is a difference between knowing that something is true and knowing its truth, recognizing it. (As a minimal example, one may take the case of propositions . . . 'It is warm today': in this there is a range of potential knowing, from sheer information to varying degrees of realistic appreciation and sensitive awareness. . . . More abstractly, $e=mc^2$. All informed people know that this last is true, and some even understand it; but few recognize the truth that it expresses.) There is a difference between knowing that a joke is funny . . . and personally 'seeing' the joke. . . . Two

school-children may successfully learn and repeat on an examination a proof in geometry, but one of them may see the point of the argument and the other not.[19]

Truth is bi-polar, melding together that which is true and that which is real. It is a synonym for what is 'really so', and refers to both the 'really real' and to actual aspects of reality. Smith finds this bi-polar perception of truth in at least three evolved civilizations. In the West, it is found in the Latin 'verus', which also signifies reality and truth. In Islamic and Hindu civilizations 'haqq' and 'satyam' likewise contain a double significance.

When I first learned Arabic, I was taught that *haqq* sometimes means 'true', sometimes means 'real'. Now this same remark, actually, had been made also about the Latin term *verus*, which can mean real, genuine, authentic, and also true, valid. When I came to learn Sanskrit, I met the same point again with regard to that language (and civilization's) term *satyam*: it too denotes both reality, and truth. Eventually I came to realize . . . that all these people were [not] somehow odd folk who had confused . . . two concepts, . . . but rather that it is perhaps we who are odd, or off the track, we who have . . . allowed our conception of truth to diverge from our conception of reality.[20]

He notes sadly that Westerners have largely lost the sense for this dual concept. And this absence is especially present in linguistic philosophy which insists that propositions alone are true or false, and that it is illegitimate to speak of the truth or falsity of things or persons. Yet it is precisely this sort of truth that other peoples (including those of an earlier Western civilization) referred to when they used the term 'truth'. This early misunderstanding still echoes remotely in certain English phrases:

Even in the West today we harbour remnants of this usage. For our own civilization . . . was built upon concepts of this type. We still at times can speak of a true courage, or false modesty; of true marriage or a true university; even of a true note in music. I mentioned this once, however, to a philosopher only to have him dismiss it as metaphorical, and not really legitimate or even significant.[21]

Smith suggests we again learn to listen to this earlier (what he calls Platonic) tradition in order to reawaken a sense for the truth of things and persons.[22]

Historically, the error of limiting the attribution of truth to impersonal propositions may be traced to John Stuart Mill. Contemporary language philosophers are the direct heirs of this mistake, namely that 'All truth and all error lie in propositions'.[23] Smith, instead, locates truth in persons and in what they encounter in the outer and inner world. Truth is therefore said to have a double locus, in persons who 'see' the truth, and in the world they see, but not in propositions which are merely expressions that represent personal encounters with the world.

Earlier, in Chapter 2, we noticed that Smith credited Mill with having definitively moved 'belief' in an impersonalist direction, away from its earlier engaged sense as 'trust' in a person, or in a statement held true or false on the worth of a person. It was Mill who gave 'belief' its contemporary philosophical form: x believes that a is b. This nineteenth-century interpretation subsequently became dominant in the English-speaking world, and according to Smith, has led many contemporary philosophers to misconceive the nature of religious existence by encouraging them to project an impersonalist understanding of belief into the religious writings of earlier ages.

Reading back this later notion into the literature of earlier times led philosophers to conclude that religious people had always 'believed' in the modern sense. Since Smith is concerned with correct historical knowledge of the religious past, he insists that what we find in early literature is an exercise of faith rather than an exercise in belief. He therefore focuses his criticisms upon the linguistic tradition's reduction of faith expressions to propositional statements. For it is this distortion that most thoroughly prevents a correct understanding of religious life.

Objectivism and the linguistic tradition

Some of Smith's most severe criticism is directed towards linguistic analysts. Yet it is somewhat ironic that Smith singles out this group for special censure, since it can be argued that his own writing demonstrates a concern shared by his opponents, that is, an intense preoccupation with linguistic and grammatical precision. One writer, more sympathetic to the linguistic school, proposes that Smith's clarification should be thought of as a contribution to the analytical tradition:

> All one has to do to see that philosophical analysis is not, per se, a barrier to theological understanding, is to read on. For Smith demonstrates this for us himself, many times over, in the latter two chapters, where he proceeds to do, far far better, the very thing he appears to be rejecting in the first . . . The theses of these two chapters are argued with . . . an attention to the logic of human thought and conversation that would do credit to the most Austinian philosopher. . .[24]

In fact Smith acknowledges a resemblance between his manner of scholarship and that of the analytic tradition. Speaking of the type of work he has put together in *Faith and Belief*, he explains:

> Our study is historical. Furthermore, it is comparative. It is also in a preliminary way theological, and in various senses philosophic. These four approaches are seldom combined. I call it 'in some senses' philosophic, since much in present-day philosophy (in the English-speaking world) is scarcely historical and not at all comparative, so that a study that is primarily these may hardly be admitted − not one that is concerned with ultimate as well as with 'technical' questions.

Yet this work is directly concerned with the clarification of concepts and the careful analysis of the usage of words, in the modern fashion.[25]

Yet despite parallels of concern, major differences remain; and Smith approaches his opponents with the caution of one wandering into the philosopher's den. He relates that he is not 'expert' in modern philosophical technique, but is instead an historian with critical observations to offer concerning the assumptions and procedures of modern philosophy. This caution and modesty, however, is not the full truth. For Smith is also a formidable linguist and grammarian, at home with the delicate weighing of words in several languages and time periods. His challenge to the analytic tradition is therefore worth serious hearing. Though he claims innocence of the techniques of modern philosophy, one discovers that this innocence is a choice, due in part to an original, fundamental disagreement.

My own capacity to effect a synthesis of my historian's view with the current philosophic, stems at least in part from lack of serious acquaintance with the positions from which mine differs . . . Yet that failure of familiarity stems . . . from the radical divergence between us. The fact is that on and off for a couple of decades now I have . . . looked into the growing literature . . . It has tended to strike me . . . from the point of view of my concerns rather superficial and irrelevant . . . I find that the observations of such critical linguistic philosophers of religion as I come across . . . from Ayer to Neilson – do not seem much to impinge on anything that I am doing. They are not merely not helpful; they seem not even pertinent.[26]

Smith first criticizes the analytical tradition for its seeming ignorance of, and insensitivity to, the nature of religious experience as illustrated in its focus on belief rather than faith. Although this approach can be explained in part by tracing it to Mill, it may also be understood as a development arising from contemporary pluralism. Today, even religious persons have shifted from presuppositional to intentional belief. Even the faithful have been forced to become believers, for the presuppositions of earlier ages have been called to question by their encounter with other systems, both scientific and cultural. Further, the success of the scientific tradition, which aims at universal impersonal statements, has created an atmosphere of impersonal thought, so that even 'believers' themselves often assume that the language of belief lies at the heart of religious existence. It is therefore readily understandable that analysts, reflecting the scientific bias of objectivity, misunderstand the nature of faith.

However, more importantly, analysts lack any serious acquaintance with the philosophical and religious literature of other traditions. Smith finds this state peculiarly parochial, especially for persons using the designation philosopher, since philosophers have customarily addressed the question of truth from as universal a perspective as was available. Smith is not unique, however, in his dismay of the lack of knowledge of non-Western traditions that characterizes the linguistic movement. A similar appraisal has been made by Ninian Smart, himself an historian of religion and a philosopher in the analytical tradition. Thus Smart speaks of his surprise at discovering that philosophers of religion at Oxford knew little about the Christian tradition and next to nothing about alien religions. He tellingly describes this inadequacy.

However, it remained very obvious that the Achilles heel of so-called linguistic analysis of religious language lay in its lack of concern with the context and plurality. By context I refer to the actual milieu, including ritual in which religious language is actually used. The trend was to take religious utterances simply as metaphysical claims (note here objectivist orientation). This was bad analysis . . . By plurality I refer to the variegated types of religious claims and languages – even within the ambit of the Christian tradition little attempt was made in the philosophy of religion to identify the nature and particular commitments and sentiments of the 'believer'. . . Even more seriously, there was little concern for religions outside the Christian tradition, or . . . systems of belief such as Marxism which might betray . . . characteristics of religious faith. . . To repeat the main point in a nutshell: how can we philosophize about something without knowing what it is really like?[27]

Terence Penelhum, also an analyst, confirms Smart's observation: 'It is also especially galling . . . to find philosophical sceptics claiming, as they are very prone to do in this century, that their incomprehension is not a calamity but an intellectual advance.'[28]

According to Smith, analytical philosophers are more than heirs to the objectivist tradition and the fact of pluralism. Though these influences have hindered attempts to understand less self-conscious religious activity in earlier ages, they do not explain the astonishing inexpertise in the knowledge of alien religious traditions. Nor do they explain the fact that:

Much recent anti-religious philosophy of religion seems to display an animus, and to be motivated by a deliberate seeking to depreciate. Although this seems evident on reading, one would be hesitant to make such a charge against presumably serious scholars. Yet Nielsen virtually admits it explicitly (though presumably inadvertently). He says in so many words that the critical analysts were engaged in an 'attempt (sic) to find a general meaning criterion in virtue of which the putative truth-claims of religion can be shown to be unintelligible or incoherent'; and when this failed they have worked 'instead . . . in an attempt (sic) to establish (sic) the actual incoherence or at least the baselessness' of such 'claims'.[29]

Carrying forward the legacy of intellectual imperialism, these philosophers have failed to enter the conceptual world of other cultures. This would constitute no fault in itself, except that the analytical tradition has felt entitled to adjudicate on the truth or falsity of concepts derived from both the Judaeo-Christian tradition, with which they were somewhat acquainted, *and* on the truth or falsity of concepts evolved from other traditions, with which they were not familiar. According to Smith, these latter concepts were simply not understood. But understanding is necessarily prior to adjudication. The prerequisite is a large acquaintance with the primary documents of a tradition and its religious life, plus mastery of its language and a sympathetic feel for its worldview. Even beyond such scholastic requirements Smith suggests that successful knowledge requires acquaintance, even friendship, with participants. This is necessary so that scholars may be enabled to verify whether they have understood what participants intend by their concepts, symbols and rituals, etc. Since such representatives of the linguistic tradition as Nielson (quoted above) approach the religions with an effort to depreciate rather than to understand, it is not difficult to recognize why Smith considers such philosophy both irrelevant for an understanding of religious traditions and destructive for his own programme of global inter-religious understanding.

Smith notices a lack of foreign-language qualifications among members of the analytical tradition, a lack that makes serious understanding of other philosophical positions impossible. This Smith finds puzzling, since analysts have correctly seen the necessity of a contextual approach for revealing the intricacies of the English language. Failing to recognize that the same sophistication is required for treating the concepts and values of other people, Smith concludes that linguistic philosophy is unhelpful and even non-pertinent for historians or philosophers of religious existence.

Something calling itself a philosophy of science that proved irrelevant or boring to historians of science . . . would seem odd. This might not matter decisively provided that the theories proffered were serviceable to the practising scientist in his laboratory. If, however, an interpretation of science had bearing neither for the careful observer nor for the practitioner, one would feel it strange. Critical linguistic philosophy of religion seems to fall into some such case; it does not illuminate empirical studies, either of religious belief; and religious persons themselves keep protesting that they have been misunderstood.[30]

One of the primary functions of religious language is to proclaim and invoke encounter with transcendent value and/ or reality. Philosophers who place an *a priori* naturalist ceiling on religious experience, and who reject religious language as nonsensical or meaningless, are not in a position to help us understand faith and enter into dialogue. This perspective requires that religious experience be rejected as merely emotive or illusory. But it is the task of religious thought, and to a certain extent of metaphysical thought, to reflect on the reality of precisely those non-naturalist experiences of transcendent value, the numinous and the mystical.

Some representatives of the linguistic movement (Professor Ayer being the best known) popularized the notion that statements ought to be classified as either meaning*ful* or meaning*less*: meaningful if they refer to that which can be objectively and publicly observed. Religious statements naturally fall outside the criterion of objective verification and are accordingly deemed meaningless or subjective. But Smith argues that non-verification is due to the fact that religious concepts are meaningful within a group context and are not objectively (i.e. universally) available for a detached observer. He objects to the meaningful/meaningless scheme because it arbitrarily limits the concept of meaning to the lowest common denominator of agreed-upon perception – the obvious facts of the sensory world.

It should, however, be pointed out that Smith's accusation that analytical philosophers have so restricted the meaning of meaning that religious discourse seems non-sensical, useless or absurd should perhaps be limited to the logical positivists of the 1920s-40s. More recent philosophers have on the contrary rejected the simplistic verification theories that Smith refers to.[31]

Smith is likewise incorrect when he implies in *Belief and History* that analytical philosophers think that religious communities in the past have 'operated for millennia in a meaning vacuum'.[32] As one critic has aptly put it, Smith overlooks the fact that:

> . . . meaninglessness is a technical term for logical positivists. Smith treats their assertions about it as if they were talking about meaninglessness in general. And to say that those who hold theism to be meaningless are 'altogether right' in so far as they speak 'as modern philosophers' . . . is to overlook the fact that two of the most respected philosophers in America today (William Alston and Alvin Plantinga) are founders of the Society of Christian philosophers. . .[33]

Since much more openness to religious and metaphysical ideas exists in the analytical movement today, it would seem that Smith is concerned with opponents of an earlier time. This perhaps reflects, as he admits, that he is not expert in the field. Though wrong on specifics he is nonetheless correct in his depiction of the anti-religious mood that has accompanied the linguistic movement. As much as A. J. Ayer, Kai Nielsen or Anthony Flew may allow religious language a modicum of meaning, be it emotive, pictorial or poetic, they nevertheless are agreed in finding religious language bereft of cognitive status. As Huston Smith remarks: 'Analytic philosophy is not the monolithic enemy he makes it out to be, but Smith is not paranoid in seeing it as such; for this is the face which, until recently, it has shown the world.'[34]

Smith chooses to restore to the term 'meaning' its original broad extension, arguing that all statements have meaning to those who make them, and that they tell us a great deal about human reality; for at a minimum they tell us about those making them. Also, if a statement is about reality external to the speaker, then the statement is about both the person and his/her experience of reality.

Statements concerning religious existence are meaningful for a particular group while meaningless for those outside the community of experience. For example, neither positivists nor Muslims comprehend the ongoing witness of the Christian church that Jesus is Lord. Nor do Marxists or Naturalists comprehend the Hindu maxim that 'Atman is Brahman'. In each instance the outgroup lacks an experiential context for appreciation and/or verification. This misunderstanding of the communal nature of religious language leads Smith to affirm that the linguistic tradition is unqualified to evaluate the truth or falsity of religious statements made within other traditions. In limiting themselves to the study of ordinary twentieth-century language, these thinkers bind themselves to the thought-forms of a single time period in a particular civilization. They thereby encapsulate themselves within the insights and limitations of modern European and American civilization and forfeit the insights of earlier epochs, both within and outside their own civilization.

Smith also rejects the assumption, common since the Enlightenment, and shared by the linguistic tradition, that religious statements refer directly to a transcendent reality. According to Smith, who reflects the position of Schleiermacher, religious statements refer to the divine indirectly through the inner lives of finite subjects. Statements ought not to be conceived as a straightforward and immediate depiction of metaphysical realms. Rather, they are derived from faith, and should be treated primarily as clues to faith. As clues to the nature of reality itself, they are indirect. Yet, it is important to reiterate that Smith does not reduce religious statements to the status of subjective utterance. He does not claim that personal encounters with transcendence tell us nothing true about the nature of that which is encountered. Rather, he believes that religious experience does not and cannot reveal a complete conspectus of transcendence. The divine, like all that is actual, is known only as experienced; human beings have no access to that which is independent of the human observer.

Smith invites scholars to move beyond appraising religious language as emotive, illusory or pre-scientific, and enter into a search for what is humanly significant and personally true in religious expression, even when they occur in pre-scientific, pre-modern, non-Western cultures. To offer an example, in classical Chinese metaphysics one finds the pre-scientific concept of spontaneous generation. One also finds mythological elements masquerading as fact. The rationalist temptation is to reject all statements within Chinese cosmology as false. However, if one does so, one fails to perceive the religious significance of Chinese cosmology which is based on the yin/yang patterning of nature. It tells us: 1. about the human need to order reality and to perceive harmonies in nature; 2. about the human need to attain a sense of union with these harmonies; 3. also something about nature itself; for it is true, despite some arbitrary instantiations, that harmones can be discovered within nature. Reflecting on Chinese cosmology, we learn about human values that nourished the lives of billions. We also perceive something about the structure of nature. To reject such a world picture as pre-scientific and therefore false is to say that a knowledge of human need, a history of how much of the human race has encountered nature, and ways of living in harmony with the world, are insignificant.

To find what is valuable and true in alien traditions and in one's historical past requires a reversal of egocentrism. This includes a commitment to discover personal truth and value in statements that are scientifically 'false'. One may, for example, reject the mediaeval assumption that the earth is the centre of physical reality, yet hold to the value implied by such a concept: namely, that human beings are terribly important and even loved by their creator. Human beings, though not at the physical centre, may indeed remain at the value centre. It is possible that de-centred earth beings may still be valued by their creator, even in an Einsteinian universe.

To reverse egocentrism it is necessary to suppose that

religious statements made by millions of persons for centuries approximate to reality and are, at least in part, true. In *The Faith of Other Men* Smith uses the Buddhist *Shin Byu* ceremony to demonstrate his approach to the 'truth' in other traditions.[35] The ceremony is based on the 'going out' legend of Siddhartha Gautama. Historians refer to the 'going out' as legendary because they are unable to confirm it in the Buddha's life. Smith shows, however, that without being Buddhists we are able to appreciate on various levels the truth of the tale and the ceremony it gave rise to. The ceremony is an adolescent initiation rite, containing the psychological truism that parents cannot indefinitely shield their children from the reality of old age, poverty, sickness and death. Further, the 'going out' is a symbol of renunciation. These two truths remain, whether the 'going out' is mythological or not. One who limited the label 'truth' to 'objective' facts might readily fail to discern any insight in this sacred tale.

In holding that statements held by millions are probably partially true, Smith reveals himself to have an approximation theory of truth. Since truth has degrees, Western bi-polar categories of truth and falsity are inadequate. Tracing the West's fondness for dichotomous thought to Palestinian and Greek roots, Smith uncovers simplistic culture–bound elements in both traditions, rendering them unserviceable for dealing with pluralist truth.

> The simplistic true/false dichotomy was encouraged in the West not only by recent scientific rationalism, however, but also, although in less restricted fashion, by the earlier dominant ideology of the Church ('the saved and the damned); and even to some degree by classical Greek thought. In each case the view was held for reasons internal to the positions espoused; it was not induced by a consideration of the world scene now available to us. Once this scene is seriously confronted, the ineptitude of the position emerges.[36]

An either/or attitude leads to an unfortunate psychological

dilemma in which persons, convinced they have perceived something of the truth, feel compelled to reject other positions lest their own position be called into doubt. This anxious attitude can be found in the West both in religious groups and in modern secularism. In a mitigated form it is also present in Islam.

Smith once again lifts up the Hindu attitude as a corrective. He finds in Indian thought a consideration of truth in terms of degrees, rather than in absolutist fashion.

> In India, for example, a contrasting alternative perceptual disposition has been widespread: that if two statements contradict each other, probably both of them are at least partially false – although also, if each is held by intelligent and sincere persons, especially by large and lasting groups, then probably also both are at least partially true. (More accurately, in India the standard opposite of truth has been not falsity but ignorance. Of ignorance there are, of course, degrees.)[37]

India's degree theory of truth is similar to Smith's approximate truth. His position can be illustrated in the case of Copernicus. Copernicus' insight that the sun is at the centre of the universe (actually, according to Copernican calculation, slightly off-centre) is neither meaningless nor true in an absolute sense. Nor was Copernicus' statement absolutely true or false when first presented. The insight that he expressed was a closer approximation to the true nature of siderial truth (reality). It was an insight which, although true, was yet limited. Though Copernicus understood that the earth was not at the centre of the universe, and that it circled the sun, his central premise that the sun was at the centre of the universe was indeed false. For Smith, therefore, it is legitimate to say that modern science which built upon the Copernican heritage is 'based on an insight that was true expressed in statements that were false'.[38] Truth always reflects the limited frame of the individual. Naturally, Copernician insight falls short of today's astronomical knowing. Yet each successive knowing is an advance in depicting reality.

> Indeed . . . even the proposition that the earth is flat is itself not flatly false. It is (has been) an approximation to the truth. The surface's curvature approximates to a straight line more closely than most approximations to the truth with which we live our lives or think our thoughts, and the flatness idea serves well for a great multitude still of practical and contemplative purposes . . . Copernicus's idea is a closer approximation. That the sun hastens around the galaxy while the latter retreats swiftly from its neighbors, is still closer. That all scientific, and religious statements have been and are, expressions of historical approximations to truth . . . many of them valid, none of them absolute or final, is an interpretation consonant with theses developed later in our present argument.[39]

The scientific world-view excels previous cultures' attempts to control the natural world. Nevertheless, it has failed to make sense of the aesthetic, moral, interpersonal, mystic and numinous experience of mankind that has loomed so important for most of human history. To understand these dimensions Smith recommends that we turn to cultures that have evinced greater interest in such phenomena. He sees a more adequate perception of the nature of transcendent value in neo-Platonism and a larger grasp of religious pluralism in Indian metaphysics than he does in positivism. Further examples are at hand. Westerners often find more insight into the realm of the beautiful in Chinese aesthetics, or in the Japanese tea ceremony, than in Western art and culture. Others have discovered a more profound understanding of the religious significance of the body in yoga traditions than in the ascetical traditions of Christianity, etc. Each cultural system opens participants to aspects of the real not available to other systems. Persons from each tradition need one another to introduce them to partial but important glimpses of being that are wanting in their own culture.

Smith argues that some philosophers have not yet grasped the fact that the manner in which truth is understood is itself historical. If they considered the historical dimension of their own apprehension of truth and compared it to other cultures, they would come to perceive truth in new ways. They would notice that truth is not only conceived variously, but that the opposite of truth is also conceived differently. For the Indian, the opposite of truth is not falsity, but ignorance; for the Muslim, the opposite of truth is neither falsity, nor ignorance, but the lie.[40] Both ignorance and the lie are personal concepts. And in viewing their opposites, one immediately sees that truth is likewise a function of persons. Like ignorance and the act of deceit, truth accordingly lies not in propositions but in acts of persons. Propositions are therefore not true or false in themselves, but in the meanings their authors intend. Propositions are vehicles of meaning, not containers of truth or falsity; for words do not mean they are given meaning. They are vehicles for acts of thought.

If Western philosophers are to participate in global philosophy, they must understand the nature, function and purpose of philosophy as conceived by other cultures. At present, attempts to philosophize (or theologize) in a single culture-specific ideational system have become naive – a sign of pre-cosmopolitanism. Smith asks those who wish to theorize about truth generically to remove themselves from insularity and move towards a comparative perspective. The entrance requirement consists in having philosophers from different cultures demonstrate to one another that they have grasped the other's concept of truth and notion of the philosophical enterprise.

Smith does not, of course, deny the linguistic tradition its own mode of truth. It has rightly explored the importance of precise, objective, impersonal statements which are personal statements containing the lowest common denominator of personal experience. The analysts represent the attitude of natural science in which statements are valued independently of the one making them. This approach has had success in exploring nature, less success with cultural existence, and perhaps least success with religious life, where self-engagement is uppermost.

> . . . there is perhaps a range of types of proposition, with the personalist element being lowest (or merely: most universal?) when the proposition refers to natural-science matters, higher when it refers to social-science matters, very high in various special cases, and highest in the religious realm.[41]

Smith not only disagrees with the analytical tradition about the locus of truth (in persons, not propositions) but he also finds fault with the common distinction between statements and propositions. Statements are here understood as declarative sentences whose meaning can be demonstrated to be historical and culture-specific, while propositions are sentences which reputedly express universal and therefore timeless meaning. If we turn to a standard text in modern logic we find: 'The difference between sentences and propositions is . . . that a sentence is always a part of a language, the language in which it is enunciated, whereas propositions are not peculiar to any of the languages in which they may be expressed.'[42] Smith, on the contrary, argues against the existence of universal statements that are not peculiar to a given language or, at least, a language group. Propositions cannot be deemed timeless or universal when they are not, in fact, universally understood. Where they appear to be cross-culturally apprehended, agreement is due to the sharing of a common world-view. A proposition that appears to a Westerner to contain universal meaning actually consits of what two statements have in common for those participating in a similar meaning-world.

> It is not the case that all languages, or all eras, are such that a proposition can be expressed equally in any of them. Statements are constructs in words expressing concepts; every proposition exists . . . in one or another conceptual system. Its validity, and indeed its meaning . . . have their locus within that system . . . more accurately: they have their locus in the historical persons and groups of persons

. . . [who] have participated in, who have understood, that particular system. . . . It is the task of modern thinkers who know and understand the history of thought, to construct new concepts able to express in propositions of wider generality the previously incommensurate statements and propositions of until now disparate systems.[43]

If one takes the paradigmatic syllogism 'All men are mortal; Socrates is a man; Socrates is mortal', one sees Smith's point. The categories of both mortality and manhood are culture-specific (Greek), and take their meaning from a larger system not shared by other traditions such as the Hindu or Buddhist. Mortality in these last traditions is applicable only to the current incarnated self, not to the entire individual, which includes the causal remains of prior individuals. The lesson to be drawn from this example is that Western philosophers are not entitled to make judgments on the truth or falsity of statements without understanding their context. Propositions do not refer in fact to a common reality; for the terms of a proposition, if not purely formal, are culture-specific and to a degree individual-specific. An artist does not perceive the same chair that a businessman does. There may, of course, be agreement as to a state of affairs, such as that a particular chair is brown (or that snow is white), but the meaning of the chair differs for both individuals (as does the colour brown). Given a radical contextualism one sees why:

It is no longer permissible to ask what does it mean inherently, statically, absolutely; but rather, what has it meant? What has been its meaning in this or that century; in this or that part of the world; to this or that community?[44]

Smith interprets the difficulty of analytical philosophers with religious language as sociological rather than logical. When an earlier generation fails to communicate its vision of reality to a later one, its language appears meaningless. Smith is not surprised that later generations fail to understand earlier ones, or that persons of disparate cultures talk past, rather than to, each other.

The business of understanding is arduous. It consists in setting aside one's own criteria for meaning and learning from others. Most communities have been unwilling to take up this task. It is more common for one community to stand against others and demand that outsiders subject their perception of truth to the dictates of the more aggressive tradition. In this way Smith understands the posture of the linguistic tradition towards users of religious language.

> The historian of religion or of culture is quite accustomed to finding the propositions of one group, or century, not understood by members of another. A slightly curious note is added when, in addition, those who do not understand become rather zealous missionaries endeavoring to persuade others not to understand, either. Of curiosities, however, the history of religion is full. . . What actually is happening here is that the missionary zeal is directed, via the attempted undermining or destruction of an alternative world-view, to proselytzing on behalf of one's own. This is historically standard. . . Modern anti-religious linguistic analysts are not only fundamentalists but iconoclasts; and missionary.[45]

One reviewer has applauded Smith's presentation of the missionary nature of secularism's critique of religion. Like the dogmatic theologian, the secularist thinker is more than ignorant of other traditions. He or she uses the technique of:

> . . . interpreting the faiths of other cultures in terms of its own, according to the principles and criteria of their own context . . . distorting what *they* say in order to show the sole truth of what *we* affirm. . . Thus . . . the religious is interpreted as 'belief', that is, as a set of subjective, dubious, projected notions and therefore easily replaceable by the 'reality' known in our own modern scientific and technical culture. . . Missionaries called other faiths 'idolatries'; secularists call them 'projections' or 'fantasies'. Each thus drains out of the other culture's views all of their meaning and validity – and thus does it hope to conquer.[46]

The fact that religious communities do not ask the same questions about truth is difficult for outsiders to comprehend. Western philosophers may find Hindu statements about ultimate consciousness to be unscientific, unverifiable, non-sensical and even uninteresting, since the facts that many Westerners deem important are verifiable and common, not requiring radical internal transformation. The Hindu on the other hand may readily reject the Western philosopher's preoccupation with ordinary objective fact. He may also experience concern with ordinary language and ordinary experience as a form of bondage to the trivial, a state of untruth, that leaves one unillumined.

These two understandings of truth remain fundamentally separate, as do the world-views they presuppose. They point past one another, rather than interact. Given this lack of contact, Smith rejects not only the ability of Western philosophers to assess the truth claims of non-Western systems, but also the very language of 'truth-claims', insisting that the word itself is part of the arsenal of a Western philosophical attack on religious language in general.

> . . . I am ill at ease . . . with the notion of 'truth claims'. . . It distorts . . . When a religious man makes a statement, especially of the 'I believe' sort, and is then asked (more or less peremptorily), 'Do you claim that this is true?' he probably answers 'Yes' – poor chap: what else can he do? (The question is of the 'Have you stopped beating your wife?' sort, although not obviously.) Yet the original statement was not put forth as a 'claim', and to dub it so is insensitive at best. Especially insofar as religious affirmations are . . . either the asseverations of saints or the interpretations of these by theologians, they are not primarily claims, since sensitive religious persons do not go around making claims.[47]

The Western analytical assault is not unlike earlier theological attacks upon the 'truth-claims' of Muslims and other 'heretics' and 'pagans'. The language of 'truth-claims' prema-

turely assumes the existence of conflict in advance of the
necessary knowledge that would warrant the fact of conflict,
and before any mutual understanding of positions has been
secured. Smith does not minimize the real differences that exist
between cultures; but to see difference immediately as conflict
is a decision typical of the Western attitude towards truth and
falsity. It is Smith's hope that the West will end its epoch
of dichotomous thought, and enter into an era of nuanced
appreciation for degrees of truth.

> Hence my unresponsiveness to the offer of allowing that the
> conflict may be only apparent. One does not in fact know
> that in the end conflict may not be real; but in the meantime
> what appears is not conflict but difference. It may be
> interpreted, if we choose, not as the threat of diminution
> but as the promise of enlargement. . . . To choose polemics
> rather than irenics at the present stage of our new encounter
> with each other – even in surreptitious theory – is
> unnecessary and, surely, unwise.[48]

To choose a word like 'conflict' to open a discussion of
religious difference sets the scene for conflict. One must
consider alternative terms that elicit more propitious connotations. One thinks of 'bearing witness' as a phrase with
positive associations, one which Muslims use to speak of that
which they have encountered. Christians, on the other hand,
speak of good news, and Hindus of the reports of the ancients.
Scholars desiring to facilitate mutual learning might use terms
that positively represent the others' self-understanding. Smith
speaks of a diversity of good news, or a plurality of truth
reports; or varieties of witness-bearing, rather than of truth-
claims.[49]

In the West 'belief' once described a vital relationship with
reality; it has now ceased to do so. Though a term of considerable historical significance, it now fails to signify ultimacy to
contemporaries. Given the historical nature of terms, even the
most adequate formulation of community insight remains
meaningful but a short while. Even ultimate values change

with the tides of history, though some motifs such as compassion or mercy may remain relatively constant. Even so, the manner in which these are understood shifts dramatically. When values alter it is a sign that peoples are concerned with other aspects of reality. It makes, for example, a real difference whether a community understands the essence of Christian love to consist in mystical transformation or in ethical activism. Values and words once pregnant with insight take on new associations or even lose their capacity to express faith. Given this metamorphosis of changing value and changing meaning Smith states:

> . . . humankind's awareness of the Truth, in the past and still to-day . . . may outrun its capacity to form propositions that embody that truth in any but transient and culturally specific and always vulnerable ways.[50]

By shifting the locus of truth from propositions to persons, Smith hopes to repersonalize the West's attitude to knowing, especially religious knowing. In order to accentuate this focus, he uses words that maintain a strong personalist connotation of truth, such as 'seeing the point', 'insight', 'awareness', 'recognition', and 'understanding'.[51] His concern to formulate a language of insight as it is revealed in personal situations parallels Ian Ramsey's attempt to speak about 'disclosure situations' in which terms like 'insight', 'discernment', and 'vision' are similarly used to refer to personal perceptions or religious truth.[52]

Sensitivity to multi-cultural forms of truth will inevitably effect an alteration in the self-understanding of Western philosophers. They will come to view themselves as contributors to the global discussion of truth rather than as imperial adjudicators. Such a shift in self-image could readily lead to a philosophical renaissance that initiates the formation of a truly world philosophy.

Smith's pluralism does not presuppose that every perception of truth is equally valid. That which is more true is to be separated from the less. However, the sorting process is not to be the work of one culture. The work of discrimination requires a team of international philosophers to confirm the attainment of mutual understanding. Understanding here does not mean agreement in doctrine, but rather agreement that participants have been understood. At present we cannot offer adequate judgment on the validity of the various communities' approaches to truth. Decisions on the adequacy of conceptions of truth await the formation of an international scholarship.

Personalism and truth

Since Smith argues for an appreciation of personalist truth, it is necessary to grasp what he intends by 'personalism'. This is somewhat complex, for he does not align himself with a specific personalist thinker, even though he mentions several 'personalists' who apparently share aspects of his outlook. In *Faith and Belief* he mentions H. H. Farmer.[53] Although Farmer's personalist orientation is not discussed in detail, Smith's writings agree with Farmer's perspective that the study of religion should focus on an individual's dynamic relation to the divine, rather than on doctrine, and that doctrine should not be conceived of as objectively true apart from the particular divine-human encounter that helped to give it birth. Smith's concern with faith as the core of religious existence also matches Farmer's conviction that scholars should deal with:

> . . . *living* religion . . . religion as it continually and spontaneously springs up in the soul of man in the midst of human life and of history as a creative and originating energy; . . . that in religion is the source of its validity, when it has vitality, and of its power to persist as a distinctive and irreplaceable factor in human affairs.[54]

In Farmer's theology God is the supreme personal reality whose dealings with men take place in the personal realm. The great central concepts – revelation, faith, grace, sin, reconciliation – are expressive of personal relationship and are perverted when construed in non-personal ways. However, though emphasis on personal encounter is also apparent in Smith's picture of faith, he does not remain solely within Farmer's framework of theistic language. Smith often uses a more abstract philosophical terminology, speaking of reality or transcendence in order to accommodate non-theistic encounters with the divine. Unlike Farmer, he does not argue for the superiority of conceiving the divine as a person, even though he personally appears to continue to think in theistic terms.

Smith highly esteems the work of Martin Buber and cites his I-Thou/I-It distinction as a valid description of the difference between personal and propositional faith.[55] He also approves of the experiential outlook of Roman Catholic thinkers like Maurice Blondel, Karl Rahner and Jean Mouroux, who in their interpretations of faith have moved Catholic thought away from the old, scholastic, objectivist orientation.[56] Yet despite these parallels a reading of Smith's work indicates he is not a follower of any thinker. He does not argue for the superiority of the Christian faith as the one, final, unlimited faith, as does H. H. Farmer.[57] He refines Buber's helpful but inadequate distinction between Christianity as a propositional form of faith and Judaism as an interpersonal form. He rejects the common Catholic view of faith as more than belief, and suggests that faith is other than belief. He also uses the term 'personalist' more broadly than technical theological usage and locates personalists in the far past, in figures as varied as Nanak, Muhammad, Jesus and the Hebrew prophets.[58] In this sweeping sense 'personalist' applies to anyone who encounters the divine in an engaged way, in distinction from those attempting to know the nature of reality by propositional reflection. Here personalism means the opposite of formalism and scholasticism, whose orientation is 'merely' conceptual.

Since Smith finds personalists among prophetic heroes and modern scholars, it is necessary to clarify the use of the term in his writings rather than define it through hypothetical influences.[59] 'Personalism' and its opposite 'impersonalism' are orientations towards persons, values and things. Impersonalism describes the orientation of the natural sciences, whose goals include impersonal description, prediction and, when applied, control of objects. A personalist orientation on the other hand does not primarily concern itself with objects but with individuals and values. When a personalist concerns him- or herself with objects, the focus is not so much on the object as upon the valuation of the object made by the subject. Smith, like the existentialists, is troubled by a society whose social sciences value the manipulation of human beings. Personalism includes a decision to say no on both empirical and moral grounds to an objectifying of humanity.

Smith encourages a moral approach to the study of man. This entails regarding human beings as centres of freedom and self-reflection. In contrast, some social scientists consider such an assumption soft thinking that is sentimental and subjective. Smith's answer to this objection is *ad hominem*. He argues that persons who so argue are themselves the product of impersonalist alienation; for they theoretically deny what should be apparent in their own lives. The majority of individuals experience themselves as free, open to transcendent value, creative, etc. For Smith, the value that 'hard' thinking objectivists deny have been amply demonstrated. These are facts that can be personally experienced, and readily inferred from statements of most of the race.

> Human qualities such as self-transcendence, a sense of justice, a creative and destructive imagination, a capacity to respond to and create beauty, a capacity for wickedness and also for dignity, freedom, compassion, rationality . . . these are manifest facts; and, frankly, it strikes me as rather stupid . . . to put up with theories that . . . fail to do justice to such facts. The advocates of such theories, when challenged, usually fall back for defense on the plea that their theories, however seemingly absurd or inhumane, are 'scientific'; which succeeds only in giving science a bad name.[60]

Those who deny these qualities are engaged in an enterprise that robs human beings of their sense of self-transcendence and produces in turn the contemporary moral nightmare in which persons view themselves through the categories of robotics. Such persons are ill-equipped to shed light on the spiritual creations of others, and Smith takes an aggressive posture towards debunkers of nobler qualities. His argument constitutes an appeal to self-evident experience and to the *consensus gentium*. He insists that those who reject the wisdom of the majority of the race must consent to the burden of proof. He sees this burden as great – especially in that it contradicts common sense and self-observation.

In an article entitled 'Thinking About Persons' (1979), Smith considers the significance the adjective 'real' has in popular language, as in the phrase 'becoming a real person'.[61] Such speech implies that men and women experience themselves as being under a moral obligation that has ontological implications. Persons are aware of an internal demand to become 'more'. More authentic, more loving, more learned, etc., therefore more 'real'.

Persons remain inaccessible in their inwardness. Their inner world is approachable only by inference from their expressions. Therefore students of human existence retreat into objectivity because of the difficulty involved in understanding the inner life. But a retreat into objectivity is an admission that one has nothing significant to say about the values that humankind has prized above all else. To have nothing to say about creativity, the love of freedom, the urge to justice, the capacity for hope, etc., or the ways these experiences have been celebrated in art, or sought after in the rush of history, is indeed to have little to say about the uniqueness of the human.

Persons are transcendent to their present; they experience varying degrees of control over future possibilities. Smith does not, however, envisage a theory of absolute freedom. Rather, freedom is rooted in actual possibilities that are projected into the future and empowered by the lure of ideals via the imagination. We are not indentured to the present.

Persons are constituted by self-reflection, meaning selection, and meaning shaping. Anthropologically, human beings can be described as those who are for that which is not yet. Yet, academicians often ignore this transcendent-ideal dimension and thereby misrepresent concrete life. In doing so, one fails to see the way most people perceive themselves. Since the goal of understanding others includes recognizing their self-understanding (which includes their self-reflections, ideal projections and future hopes), the denial of transcendence leads to shrunken perception of the human world.

Many of Smith's observations on self-transcendence may impress the reader as common sense eloquently rendered. Yet it is precisely a failure of common sense that Smith espies in the social sciences, whose task is to enrich our understanding of human existence. His argument is not against those who for methodological purposes deliberately bracket aspects of personal existence in order to pursue theoretical models – as in the case of a behaviourist who acknowledges the legitimacy of other approaches to human experience but chooses to neglect the symbolic and self-reflective aspects of consciousness. Smith targets instead those who deny reality to obvious aspects of the human world which most civilizations consider significant.

Smith's understanding of the nature of historical research stands in the tradition of Wilhelm Dilthey, who likewise argued that effective historians must use their full humanity in studying other peoples, and that sympathy and passion are necessary tools for apprehending the meaning of persons in both past and present.[62] Applying Dilthey's recommendations to social scientists and practitioners of the liberal arts, Smith finds the current split between humanities and social sciences artificial and unfortunate – for both areas are engaged in studying the meaning- and value-laden productions of humanity.

A personalist analysis of religious life begins after the task of gathering objective material is well advanced. There are four historical (also logical) stages in the West's intellectual encounter with alien religious traditions. The first is that of ignorance. The second consists in subjective and impressionist awareness of the elements of a culture that strike the outsider as curious or interesting – the Marco Polo stage of study; the third stage refers to an objective, systematic knowledge of facts; while the fourth, and most significant stage, is the personalist, which has only recently begun.[63] At this point the meaning that the facts of a culture have for participants is ascertained. This requires researchers to use the full range of their humanity in order to create (and thus re-present) a foreign world-view. For just as a work of art is not present for study until it has been re-created in the act of appreciation, so too a world-view is not present for understanding until it stands before the appreciator in its re-created intensity.

Since the concept of 'understanding' has received much attention from scholars in the history of religions, pre-eminently in the writings of Joachim Wach, it may be helpful to present Smith's position, even though he unfortunately does not give us a systematic discussion.[64] Smith's essential concern is with contemporary faith rather than with faith of the past. He therefore relies on participant others for verification in order to confirm whether understanding has or has not occurred. His focus on contemporary religious life does not indicate that he is not concerned with the problem of 'understanding' historical texts. A survey of his corpus corrects any such idea. Smith, though, has been criticized for a lack of theoretical discussion of the understanding of understanding.[65] This appears as a weakness to those committed to the Western epistemological tradition. What is not apparent to critics of this persuasion is that other cultures do not share a concern for this hermeneutical enterprise. It is specifically Western and *therefore* a stumbling block to those committed to forming intellectually shareable statements about religious life between members of different religious traditions. Interpersonal reasons explain Smith's apparent aloofness from the 'meta-questions' of religious studies. As one author puts it:

> There is danger in a concentration upon such issues, for they are meaningful only among one's colleagues and within the context of the Western philosophical tradition. Thus they

are not and cannot be broached for the purpose of more constructive relationships with non-Western peoples about whom they are made, nor with the intent of seeking out their criticism. The result is a strengthening, not a weakening, of the barriers between peoples, and no aid at all in understanding the faith of other men. The prominence of meta-questions is a sign of intellectual incest.[66]

Smith's personal encounter with representatives of other religions (primarily Islam) has led him to suggest that understanding another culture's religious life is improbable, if not impossible, unless verified by participants. This suggestion may appear obvious; but it has not been obvious to scholars in the past who, for missionary reasons, have not been concerned with sensing the meaning that a religion has held for its members. Western missionaries of either stamp (Christian/ secularist) are (have been) concerned with conversion at the expense of conversation, and therefore at the expense of understanding. Smith, on the other hand, describes how knowledge arises within the context of dialogue. He speaks of a meeting in which Westerners grappled at length with Islamic concepts in the presence of Muslims, till at long last a Muslim exclaimed: 'Yes, (at last) you have understood us!'[67] It is this type of confirmation that generations of scholars so often lacked. Though they were experts on the data of Islam, and spent considerable energy 'explaining' Islam or other religions, yet, for lack of the confirmation of dialogue the faith of others eluded them.

In an introduction to *Religious Diversity* Willard Oxtoby observes that when Smith uses 'understand' he not only means comprehension (Oxtoby's word), but also 'shades of sympathy if not outright agreement'.[68] Oxtoby is correct that Smith's conception of understanding includes sympathy, for friendship may be a vital ingredient in realizing the depth and complexity of another's faith. Agreement may, however, be too strong a word. Smith uses 'understanding' to include seeing the point of another in the other's context, and apprehending the position of another as partially valid. This is easier for Smith than for those who do not share his approximation theory of truth.

A personalist view of religious existence holds that the meaning of faith lies in persons rather than in systems, creeds or institutions. A study of religion must deal primarily with meaning rather than with objects which are the expressions of faith. Further, a personalist study refuses to assume that transcendence is not real. However, it is also not the purpose of such study to confirm the ontological status of the divine. It is enough for the researcher to recognize that the impact of transcendent values and mystical phenonmena on religious existence is an historical fact of vast consequence. Even though these 'facts' remain invisible to the observer (except in their manifestations), it is absurd to agree with 'objectively' orientated social scientists that behaviour is not influenced by unobservable factors. The reality of such factors may or may not be as their participants claim; they may be illusory, or even genuine in ways not understood by participants. In any case their impact on society is massive, and a personalist study of religious existence gives considerable weight to the 'invisible' dimension of vision, ideals, ideologies, hopes, ecstasies, etc.

As we have seen in Chapter 1, a personalist outlook rejects an essentialist understanding of religious life and understands terms like 'Buddhism' or 'Christianity' to refer to complex traditions rather than ideal or static entities. This is due to the fact that what traditions have meant to persons has been various. The personalist approach likewise rejects dogmatic religious method as inappropriate for a scientific understanding of religion. It rejects theological prejudgments concerning the truth or falsity of alien traditions as harmful to the task of knowing.

A metaphysical anthropology underlies Smith's term 'personalism', for the Western concept of person stems from a unique blend of Christian and Greek thought. Smith argues that the term's limited historical provenance should not deter us from using it as a generic category.[69] Accordingly, he uses 'person' to refer to the depth dimension of human existence. For him the term preserves the unique dignity of humankind over against things and beasts. It reflects the fact that human beings are able to interiorize and incarnate ideals. Understood in this way, 'person' is a term of resistance to every form of reductionism. But personalism has more than an anthropological dimension; it entails a way of ordering reality that has obtained in most civilizations. It holds to a pattern of reality similar to the now unfashionable 'chain of being' model, which for centuries in the West joined nature, persons and the divine in a natural hierarchy of values.[70] Smith regrets that the contemporary West is the first civilization to reverse this order by deriving man from nature, valuing it as primary and thereby reducing the transcendent to the status of human projection. He hopes to contribute to a re-ordering of nature, person and divinity that will re-establish for the present the classical order of being in a way which is responsible to the facts of science, the findings of history and the earth's drama of religious life.

Truth and reality

Having discussed personalism and truth, we are now in a position to analyse personalist truth. Smith locates the basic cause of the West's struggle with meaninglessness in the conceptual (and resultant existential) failure to create a convincing paradigm for the modern mind that offers a non-subjective understanding of the relationship between truth and reality, truth and morality, and morality and reality.

A divorce between truth and reality is clearly exhibited in the modern philosophical insistence that truth cannot be predicated of things or persons, but is limited to propositions. Smith argues that not only is it meaningful to speak of true persons and true things, but that it is historically curious not to find truth paired with persons, with virtue and with things. Our period has seemingly lost the ability to recognize what was apparent to other ages. For centuries Westerners found it appropriate to speak of true courage, true marriage, a true university or a true note in music, in which 'true' obviously referred to the reality or presence of the thing in question.[71]

Another divorce that Smith finds symptomatic of our malaise is the cleavage between truth and morality. This separation is apparent in the prevalence of subjectivist theories of morality that undermine the moral dimension of existence. Smith reminds us that common language still echoes a linkage between truth and morality, and that such a bond was common in earlier periods. The fading of this style of speech reflects the successful march of objectivism and impersonalism in the intellectual community. Yet despite the success of objectivism, one finds persons for whom it is still meaningful to join truth to ethical behaviour and speak in terms of being true to one's conscience, vocation, destiny, spouse, office, etc. Conversely, one can speak of a false conscience, vocation or spouse. Linguistic reflection reveals the fact that 'truth' was originally cognate with both 'trust' and 'troth'; and one can readily be false in both trust and troth.[72]

A third divorce, that between reality and morality, also marks our time. Here, too, a bond is glimpsed in ordinary speech. When x is described as a 'real' person, indicating moral genuineness and large heartedness, this is synonymous with describing x as a 'true' human being. Here truth, morality and reality are conjoined.

Western philosophers argue that the divorce between these factors constitutes a gain in clarity. Without denying that this has on occasion resulted, Smith asks whether the clarity produced is not in fact spurious. Has it not created a loss in the perception of reality by oversimplifying the relationships between persons, truth, morality and being? Smith prefers to remain loyal to the insights of ordinary language; he contends that when a society's idea of truth breaks true courage down to subjectivity, or morality to emotive utterance, social disintegration is inevitable. He finds the massive student unrest in the 1960s and 70s an instinctive reaction against the inadequacy of objectivist notions of truth.

> In particular, an unreality and an impersonalism are sensed, in much of what passes for truth in what the university is engaged in pursuing; a lack of correlation either with absolute significance . . . or on the other hand with the inner integrity and wholeness of those persons who are invited to pursue it.[73]

Under the dominion of objectivity, sensitive and committed reflection upon the nature of reality and morality is banished from the 'truth concerns' of the university. Science is left to pursue its interests 'objectively' while 'subjective' morality is weakned by being denied status as a form of truth and assumed to have no connection with reality. Surface analysis and amoralism result when the truth of persons, qualities and things are excluded from serious discussion. The presence of reality is violated.

In order to offer a model of personalist truth, Smith turns to a language analysis of the Arabic concept of truth in which truth is most clearly a function of persons. Three different relations to truth exist in Arabic in the terms *haqqa, sadaqa* and *sahha*. The first term describes the truth of things; the second the truth of persons; the third the truth of statements. Number three, which describes the dominant sense of truth in the West, is the least significant in Islam. The first two terms contain the dominant Arab perception of truth, which is conceived of as inseparable from both persons and reality. If for the West propositions are truth's primary expression, this is not the case for an Arabic-speaking world.

Haqqa means both true and real. It refers to the single complex truth/reality. It is also a denotation for God, the ultimate real, but refers likewise to what is genuine and authentic, and contrasts with that which is vacuous, unreal, phony.[74] That which is genuine is understood as being true. The English language preserves a sense for this distinction in speaking of true courage, of false modesty, a real performance, a true pitch, etc. Truth here is the truth of being.

In the Arabic *sadaqa* one finds a specific reference to the truth of persons. The term resonates to the Western concept of integrity. It includes being true to self, to others and to one's situation. It includes propositional truth, but this is subordinated to the personalist concept of *telling the truth*.[75] Truth is not understood as limited to being 'in' propositions, but includes instead both the truthfulness of the person and the correctness of his communication. The opposite of *sadaqa* is *kadhiba*, which translates – to be a liar.[76] Here the concept of mendacity does not refer to unintentional inaccuracies in reporting, but to the intention to deceive. English, of course, has an equivalent term to indicate a person who wills to deceive (liar), but has no equivalent to *sadaqa* (truth-teller).

Nor has English developed a term that covers the meaning found in *sidq* – the generic or abstract noun of *sadaqa*.[77] *Sidq* is used to refer to speech which is both true and conforms to the intention to speak the truth. Questions are not *sidq* (truthful) in Arabic if they are of the 'Have you stopped beating your wife?' variety.[78] Commands such as, 'Return my pen', are *sidq* or *kadhib*, truthful or lying depending on: (*a*) whether the addressor truly wants the pen back; and (*b*) whether the addressee genuinely has the pen.[79] Other examples of speech that is *sidq* reveal a personal/objective inter-relationship in the understanding of truth. The paradigm for a true statement for Muslims is 'Muhammad is the Apostle of God.'[80] Yet, though this statement is perceived by Islamic society as cosmically true, it is only half *sidq* when spoken by the insincere. *Sidq*, therefore, refers not only to true statements but to an appropriate personal relationship to the truth of what one speaks. In this sense, it can be applied to human acts other than speech, such as 'he fought with *sidq*', meaning he fought with zeal, was truly aligned with his cause, and was truly effective in the struggle for his cause.[81] Smith summarizes:

Throughout, *sidq* is that quality by which a man speaks or

acts with a combination of inner integrity and objective overt appropriateness. It involves saying or doing the objectively right thing out of a personal recognition of its rightness, an inner alignment with it.[82]

Speech is a bridge between inner life and outer reality. It expresses both poles. Therefore in order for speech to be truthful (*sidq*), both poles must be in an appropriate relationship. To be truthful, speech must reflect the integrity of the subject and the (objective) correctness of his or her action and/or perception.

The inseparability of truth and persons expressed in *sidq* becomes intensified when one considers *tasdiq*, the verbal noun of the causative (*tafil*) form of *sadaqa*. The intensified form carries the meaning – to regard a sentence or a person as true, that is, to regard an individual as a speaker of truth and (more propositionally) to regard a sentence as truly referring to that which is the case.[83] In both instances, truth is based on the trustworthiness of the speaker. In English a possible rendering of *tasdiq* would be to 'believe', as in to believe a person or statement; but since the modern verb 'believe' has lost its earlier sense of considering something as true, based on personal trustworthiness (common seventeenth century), it fails to catch the flavour of *tasdiq*. Further, since the modern 'believe' can take an object that is either true or false, it cannot properly translate *tasdiq*, which maintains a strong sense of the validity of that which is held.

When one recognizes a speaker to be *tasdiq*, this refers to recognizing his or her sincerity and correctness. If a subject gives *tasdiq* to someone, he or she not only recognizes the truth spoken as objectively correct, but sees it as correct for others and therefore, in the act of giving *tasdiq*, the subject recognizes its truth for him- or herself.[84] In recognizing what is true one is obliged personally both to affirm and interiorize its truth. *Tasdiq* refers to the art of making what one knows to be true existentially true.

Tasdiq may also refer to a past act wherein one did not

previously hold a person to be a speaker of truth, but has subsequently discovered him or her to be so.[85] It also refers to the active searching out the truth of another. One may actively verify or confirm for oneself another's truth. In this sense *tasdiq* has become the term for scientific verification, of proving something true, and in so doing vindicating the truth of the experimenter. Smith offers the phrase '*saddaqa al-khabara al-khubru*' to mean 'the experiment verified the report and the reporter'.[86] One further meaning may be noted: *tasdiq* can mean to take steps to make a promise, one's own or another's, come true by fulfilling the promise.[87] Summarizing:

> *Tasdiq* is to recognize a truth, to appropriate it, to affirm it, to confirm it, to actualize it. And the truth in each case is personalist and sincere.[88]

The objectivist ideal of a statement being true or false in itself is apparently impossible in this mode of thought. It resists depersonalization.

Since propositional objectivism leads to value-scepticism, Smith rejects what he calls a 'bilateral theory of truth', namely that the truth of a statement is 'a function of the relation between it and the overt facts', and recommends instead a trilateral theory in which statements purporting to be true involve: 1. the person making the statement; 2. the statement; and 3. the facts it describes.[89] In some areas, especially in the social sciences, where the meaning of human behaviour is uppermost, he recognizes the need for a quadrilateral theory of truth, which includes the above plus a verification of reports about outgroups by cross-checking with those under study to see if one's observations tally with the self-perceptions of those observed.

Applying the trilateral conception of truth, which he derives from the Islamic *tasdiq*, to academic research Smith asks what we should mean when we declare a journal article to be 'true'. The question here refers primarily to articles in the humanities and social sciences, where human values are more to the fore. Yet, the natural sciences may be included to a degree. He answers that, first, the content of the article must correspond to the facts in a verifiable way.[90] Second, the writer must have the proper intentionality, in this case to communicate something that is recognized as true. If an article is instead published primarily to attain a reputation or a promotion, it lacks *tasdiq* and is false or at best half-true.[91]

Third, a person writing about an aspect of the cultural world who does not sense its significance or depth, or who fails to communicate the values that are embodied – be they in plays, political movements or religious rites – has failed to attain a trilateral realization of truth.[92] Similarly, one who ferrets out facts but stops short of their meaning has failed to represent that which is truly significant to his or her audience. This person has failed to make real to one's self and to one's audience that which is real.

Fourth, statements or theories which are not appreciated by their authors, which make no difference in living, ought to be rejected as false. For example, theoretical determinists who do not live their lives according to the principles of determinism are not *tasdiq*; they fail the trilateral requirements.[93]

Also false are the articles of scholars who write in impenetrable jargon for the exclusive benefit of members of their profession. Though heavily technical language is to a large degree necessary in the natural sciences, it is not so in the social sciences, where cliquishness gives birth to distortions of language. These distortions prevent a sharing of findings and concepts with those outside the 'profession' and shield them from the criticisms and/or appreciations of intelligent readers. The result is a breakdown of the ideal of a unified approach to the truth, an approach that is essential when what is studied is complex and requires reflection from several disciplines.

The reader may view Smith's version of what ought to constitute academic truth as fanciful. Yet what he has done is to show us a way to repersonalize our conception of truth. He would have us recognize that various cultures perceive truth in disparate ways and that our current choice to limit truth to objectivist statements contains the potential for disastrous social consequences. He invites us to consider that the dominant understanding of truth in the West is, in fact, but one among several legitimate ways to reflect on the nature of truth.

4

A NEW METHOD: CRITICAL CORPORATE SELF-CONSCIOUSNESS

Comparative religion

Smith describes himself as a practitioner of 'comparative religion', a phrase he prefers to the more accepted 'history of religions'.[1] His objection to the label 'history of religions' is that both secularists and Christians use it as a blanket term to refer to religious communities outside the West. Smith is fearful that this terminology will intensify the us/them orientation that is already strongly represented in the Western outlook. He is apprehensive that acceptance of 'history of religions' will institutionalize the dichotomy between one's own faith (studied in seminaries) and that of others (studied at universities).

A further difficulty centres upon the term 'history' and the assumptions that attend the world-view of large numbers of historians. History is frequently conceived of as a closed system of natural events, not open to the pressure of transcendence.[2] 'History' in 'history of religions' suggests for Smith connotations of an unproven naturalism which reinforces the prejudice of social scientists, and even religious intellectuals, who presume an absence of transcendence in the religions of others.

Accordingly, Smith prefers 'comparative religion' to describe the study of all religious systems, including Western ones. He feels that the phrase does not bias the reader against the possibility that genuine divine/human encounters may occur, and more specifically that they may occur outside the Christian community. 'Comparative religion' for Smith has had 'an honourable history in Britain as in Canada'.[3] But his preference for this traditional wording is more than a clinging to the established usage of his native Canada. One may find concern over labels mere quibbling, but the implications are serious. Since comparative religion is the study of the human species in its religious diversity, it is important to know what we assume when we refer to it as a branch of knowledge.

In the twentieth century, humankind's diversity of faith is becoming self-conscious; humankind is awakening to the full spectrum of an aeons-long divine/human interaction. The role of comparative religion is to make universally known the insights and the follies of religious life on planet earth. Therefore 'comparative religion' must be an inclusive phrase, like its analogs 'comparative literature' or 'comparative anatomy' – phrases that embrace all members of the same class. Smith says: 'Part of what one wishes to convey is the sense of including oneself, at the same time as embracing pluralism, at the same time as using a singular.'[4]

No religious tradition is excluded from comparative religion, neither Christianity, nor Marxism, nor secular humanism. Since one's own faith tradition is included as a legitimate area of study, comparative religion suggests that those who study the faith of others should do so as they would have others study their own.

Though comparative religion has a noble academic role in making the faith of others intellectually available, its practice should not be thought to be a replacement for, or an improvement upon, concrete religions. Nor should its task be construed as a search for a perennial philosophy underlying the numerical vastness of historical symbols. Instead, it studies and generalizes about existing religions and does not engage in building new ones. For Smith is of the opinion that academic attempts to construct new religions have 'fatuously failed'.[5]

Nevertheless, comparative religion has a significant role in affecting the evolution of religious history. Though it cannot create, it can guide. Religious research can shape historical consciousness by dividing myth from history and by interpreting the meaning of one religious vision to those submerged in another. In this regard, comparative religionists have an essential function to perform as mediators between representatives of the various faith positions and as custodians of honesty concerning the historicity of religious events.

Smith sees the role of comparative religion as consisting in inter-cultural bridge-making by constructing statements about the religious life of one community that are intelligible to members of at least two traditions. As an example, Christian scholars narrating the faith of Muslims should be intelligible to both Christians and Muslims. Further, since scholars are academics they are also responsible for making their material lucid to those in a third tradition, that of secular scholarship.

The comparative religionist who is expert in world-view analysis is able to offer a unifying model to those in the social sciences and liberal arts who study more restricted aspects of human behaviour such as economic, literary, or political activity. These studies are more limited in that they do not have the world-view of an entire people as an object of investigation. Yet it is only within such a whole that the significance of aspectual studies is revealed. For each aspect of human behaviour finds its integration within a world-view. For this reason, Smith indicates that comparative religion does not have a unique method and is not to be defined by a technique, but rather by its special object – the world view.[6] Comparative religion is therefore a unificatory science which is polymethodic and which draws upon the results of the social sciences and liberal arts as food for reflection.

Most importantly, Smith sees comparative religion as standing at the foreground of an emergent phase in the history-of-religious consciousness. The scholar of comparative religion is a participant in the creation and heralding of a global religiousness. It is novel in the history of the earth to find men and women who can accurately represent, appreciate and cross-culturally validate the meaning that religious life has held for humankind. Through a collaborative study of the world's religions, a new form of reflection that embraces the entirety of the earth's religious patrimony is emerging. This event presages the birth of an attitude that excludes all parochialisms. The consequences are large. No longer do all Westerners say 'Greece and Palestine, and no more, for these are the streams that have formed me'. A sense of the legitimacy of multiple sources of religious wisdom has developed. A new atmosphere is forming in which people experience the length and breadth of religious history as a universal acquisition and a portion of their own past. To the vastness of the religions past, there is a sense that this is our own.

Though Smith has accurately described the distortions that the phrase 'history of religions' can hold for some, his own preference for 'comparative religion' is open to similar charges. Both ways of speaking contain the ambiguous term 'religion', and in order to be more consistent with his earlier criticisms of 'religion' a more neutral term may be preferable. Some scholars may find negative connotations in the older phrase 'comparative religion', which was frequently used in contexts where non-Christian religions were unfavourably compared to Christianity as proof of their inferiority.[7] For pragmatic purposes either phrase is viable so long as proper qualifications are delineated. One might also suggest that other terms such as 'path', 'world-view' or 'way' be used in place of the problematic 'religion'.[8]

Humane knowing

'Humane knowing' is Smith's phrase for intersubjective knowledge. It refers to the meaning dimension peculiar to human existence. The term 'meaning' is here used to refer to what persons are getting at when they speak of life as being meaningful or meaningless. This entails giving a pattern to one's living that determines one's actions in a way that discussions of a theoretical nature do not. Unlike 'objective', study which concentrates upon external processes (objects), humane knowing reflects upon the meaning of human creations.

Humane knowing also raises the issue of how one understands the relationship of an observer to the observed when both are subjects. A subject/subject relation, unlike a subject/object relation, acknowledges the often overlooked fact that individuals who are objects of study are themselves, like the observers, capable of free acts and distorted when analysed as objects. Objectivism implies impersonality, behaviourism; it denies significance to the operation of values. It concerns itself with the externals of religion such as beliefs, rituals and institutions, rather than what these mean in the life of those using them. From a moral point of view, the objective outlook is a powerful force in disrupting human community. It alienates people. Intellectually, it fails to acknowledge the real power of the symbolic dimension of mind. And by 'symbolic' one means that certain objects, words or events have, and have had, the power to express and elicit ultimate value.[9]

Smith is especially critical of the inexpertise of behaviourist social scientists when they apply their tools to non-Western peoples. The objective orientation not merely alienates humanists in the West, but has evoked fierce resentment from Third-World persons who find themselves the object of an aggressive scholarship.[10] Carelessness towards non-Westerners has, according to Smith, become standard fare for large numbers of social scientists who, having appropriated the methods of physical science, proceed to apply them ineptly to the human realm. In making this criticism, Smith refuses to be disturbed by the charge of being 'non-scientific'. He is concerned with valid knowledge and appropriate methodology, not with an imitation of methods suited to the natural world. Validity is constituted by one's effectiveness in illuminating religious existence. One's responsibility as an intellectual is rationally to reveal the unique facets of religious life, not to force all forms of life into a Procrustean 'scientific' mould. Reason must prove that it is responsive to subject-matter.

As an illustration how an objectivist approach hinders

insight and dissolves community, Smith tells how a Western anthropologist he chanced upon in Lebanon readily admitted to having no interest whatsoever in Lebanese villagers as persons.[11] He had come to Lebanon to test some general theories that his discipline had formulated. His interest in observing these 'others' was to advance the theoretical state of anthropology and promote his academic career. The primary task was not an understanding of concrete persons but the development of abstract theory. One might, of course, defend a social scientist's right to develop a theory of human behaviour and test it. But Smith is concerned that an observation of human beings that does not seek an in-depth (personalist) understanding of them is superficial and leads to surface and incorrect generalizations.

Smith is sceptical of statements that are not based on the unique particulars of each culture. As an illustration consider the fact that rituals designed to constrain aggressive behaviour are found universally. Yet to know this gives one only the most abstract information about a particular family or tribe. There are many reasons for particular aggressive behaviour that abstract theory does not address. The way aggression fits village ideology, the manner in which individuals purge themselves of hate, their attitude towards revenge, etc., are all necessary items of investigation for a fully concrete portrait of living people. Yet it is impossible to gain this information unless one has entered the meaning pattern of a particular culture. Generalizations about behaviour that do not consider such issues in depth offer little to the understanding.

Smith is certainly not against the use of objective and technical procedures, but he objects to focusing upon fact-gathering at the expense of world-view analysis that gives facts their meaning. He states:

Humane knowing – the knowledge of man by man – is an exercise in the meeting between persons, be it across the centuries or across the world. It is, therefore, not technical, not subordinate to methodological rules. In personal relations, whether face-to-face or mediated by man's symbolic forms of expression, the use of technical procedures, unless rigorously subordinated to primarily personalist considerations, is not merely inappropriate but potentially disruptive. Man cannot know man except in mutuality: in respect, trust, and quality, if not ultimately love.[12]

Though externalists promote the measurement of behaviour apart from subjective meaning, Smith observes that in many instances their programme is not actually carried through. A person wishing objectively to describe a cultural activity such as temple worship has already included certain preconceptions in his or her study. In knowing that a particular building is in fact a temple the researcher demonstrates some notion about the nature of worship. The concepts of temple or worship are human constructs that do not exist in a state of nature. To understand these concepts, no matter how inadequately, is already to practise a form of humane knowing in which questions of intentionality and symbolic meaning are inescapable.

Even the impressionist accounts of 'strange' cultures related by Renaissance merchants displayed a modicum of humane knowing. Smith expects students of comparative religion to demonstrate superior skill to their mercantile forebears. He acknowledges that studies done by so-called objective researchers are occasionally full of insight, but he also notes that these achievements are usually gained within the researcher's own society. The behaviourist approach, applied to foreign cultures, has remained woefully unskilled.

Ineptitude is inevitable when investigators fail to penetrate the meaning of behaviours. Without adequate world-view analysis researchers are more likely to project their subjective interpretations upon behaviour. Those striving to be the most objective, by avoiding the complex issues involved in the way ideological factors influence the perception of reality, may actually find themselves in a situation of not knowing what to

look for, what to measure, or how to proceed. Familiarity
with the values of a culture gives the social scientist clues to
theories that may be later confirmed or validated. A person
who is not familiar, for example, with the complicated web
of values surrounding racism or sexism in the United States is
not in a position to measure their importance in national life,
or even to know where to look. The same holds true for those
measuring behaviour in other societies.

Theoretical inadequacies have practical import. Experts in
the West have amply demonstrated their persistent misunderstanding of foreign peoples. The Islamic revolt in Iran came
unexpectedly for Americans who profoundly underestimated
the force of Islamic values. This is not surprising when one
realizes that American political scientists normally assume a
state/church separation, an idea foreign to Islam. Likewise, the
Vietnamese value system continued to baffle American experts
armed with objective studies and confused by alien values.

Objectivity is naturally a value Smith wishes to preserve.
He is not recommending a scholarship of whim or subjective
impression. As its original goal, objectivity sought to super-
sede subjectivism and to obtain knowledge valid for all investigators. This orientation, effective in the natural sciences, can
also work in the social sciences when the investigator has a
pre-understanding of the political, religious, sexual, economic, etc., values of the group. A sociologist who has spent
his childhood amidst the lower class of Chicago has had a rich
education in the signs of class hostility, religious authoritarianism and certain forms of political conservatism. In this
instance the researcher is a participant in that which he studies.
His efforts may be thought of as a portion of society analysing
another portion that is known through shared acculturation.
A sympathetic understanding pre-exists.[13] A feeling is present
in this instance that 'we Americans' are studying ourselves. In
such study the researcher knows where to find collective ideals
that are inconsistent or moribund, recognizes how religious
considerations permeate economic motives and how these
vary among diverse ethnic groups. The researcher also has a

'feel' for how his studies will affect those reading them. He understands why some of his peers will value his labour, given their scientific commitments and their participation in a certain reading of the American way of life – American faith.

Intelligent members of the researcher's society, be it his professional group or a larger informed community, will recognize in his study something of importance concerning the actual social forces present in the United States. This recognition is precisely what Smith and members of other societies find absent in Western studies of foreign cultures. It is often the case that in so-called objective studies, the objects of the study do not recognize themselves or the actual forces of their society. Nor do they understand why or how they are being observed, for the goals of the researcher's actions are not explained to them. This misunderstanding is inevitable when the researcher is not interested in the self-perception of the native, but only with his behaviour.

Persons under study are likely to resent being discussed without being conferred with. Within many societies there are no critically-minded persons to question the methods and assumptions of the investigator, since he writes for a learned group on another continent. Smith calls this type of study 'idiosyncratic'.[14] Previously, Christian missionaries demonstrated this form of idiosyncrasy when they wrote for Christian groups at home to describe how the natives fell short of European and Christian ways. The missionary was the West's forerunner in failing to recognize the importance of the native's self-understanding. So too, modern social scientists follow in missionary footprints, studying only those things relevant to the 'folks back home', their particular sectarian group who 'share certain presuppositions (and whose ritual is certain methodologies)'.[15] This type of sectarianism is additionally reinforced when researchers read only within their own discipline and accept only the criticism of their peers (sect). Smith describes this state of affairs:

. . . subjectivity with a vengeance! Group subjectivity, no

doubt, but subjectivity for all that. Objective knowledge of man leads to subjective knowledge by man. The importance of this has been little understood, but is major. Its contribution to fragmentation (of knowledge) is serious.[16]

Sectarian practice is doubly insulated from criticism – criticism from those who are studied and from the larger group of university scholars who might question the value or adequacy of his or her procedures.

In order to secure a first-hand knowledge of other peoples, field-work is of course essential. For in the immediacy of another culture preconceptions are challenged. But American social scientists in the past have arrived in the field with predetermined methods, knowing before they have contacted the unfamiliar that they are looking for.[17] A preconceived methodology has already measured the possibilities of experience. With tight blinders on, there is no way to experience what is lacking in one's own understanding. It is as if a botanist arrived at a new continent intent on studying only the flora familiar to him from his own land. He would perhaps find oaks and elms that varied slightly from his native soil, but would miss birds-of-paradise, exotic ferns and unheard of medicinal herbs. Knowing ahead of time what one wants to know ensures that one will come to know only that. This approach, being unresponsive to the novel, might be called ineducable.

Smith is not suggesting that a researcher can come to the study of another culture without preconceptions. It is apparent that implicit and explicit theories are operative in all students. However, he rejects an emphasis on method that prevents the power of the real from suggesting new approaches.

Smith holds that foreign societies have valuable lessons to teach researchers. He assumes that change, growth and insight on the part of the researcher are an integral part of humane knowing. Objective methodologists, on the other hand, seem to Smith to be unconcerned with the personal qualifications of the researchers, and seem to prize fact at the expense of human growth. This policy too frequently ensures that the researcher is not sufficiently sensitized to apprehend the inward life of other peoples. Detachment prevents one from thinking, feeling or loving like a participant in a foreign tradition.

If a certain orientation is valued in the social sciences, it will naturally become institutionalized. Funding will then be dispersed to secure reduplication of a certain type of professional. And Smith is not pleased with the sort of student he finds rewarded in academic circles. Speaking of his service on fellowship committees in foreign areas studies, Smith regrets that the person invariably rewarded was one destined to be closed to the unobvious.

> I was struck by the fact that the predisposition was to award fellowships by preference to applicants who had formulated with some exactitude the research project that they were going to India or to the Near East to execute. A well thought out, tightly knit, neatly packaged proposal was expected, and was rewarded. I was much disquieted at this. It was my experience that those persons learn most from especially their first visit to India or the Near East who recognize ahead of time that they do not yet know the best questions to ask: that more than half the point of their trip is to ascertain what is worth investigating, how to formulate one's queries, how to modify one's preconceptions, and the like. Sensitivity, openness, creative response to new awareness, are inimical . . . to the pre-articulated methodological neatness . . . that wins the heart of the methodological school.[18]

Though all knowing is human, only the knowledge of persons by persons qualifies as humane knowing. Thus Smith speaks of 'humane sciences' to distinguish the knowledge of objects from the knowledge of persons, and to unify two areas of intellectual activity, the humanities and the social sciences that he finds artificially divided in the modern university. This separation is especially acute in the English speaking world, less so on the Continent.[19]

The term 'science' in the phrase 'humane science' is justified by Smith in his resolve that the study of human meaning be rigorous, critical and rational – therefore scientific in a broad extension of 'science'. But 'humane' is perhaps the more essential word, since all knowledge of persons by persons requires an act of self-awareness. The world of another is available only by means of a sympathetic use of the researcher's self-consciousness. One, for example, who understands the intentionality of prayer in a foreign culture does so mainly because of the ability to extend one's own perception of the life of prayer and qualify it in light of new information. Even within secular societies religious motifs are apprehended in a similar manner. The hush that transpires before Lenin's tomb is understood by those who have known reverent awe before the icons of their own ultimates. This same extension occurs wherever self-awareness is used to understand the human forces of history. The historian understands dictatorship because he or she recognizes the pervasive temptation to lay down the burden of freedom in one's own society and in one's self. More specifically, in understanding religious history the researcher has a modicum of familiarity with the Buddhist thirst for Nirvana if he or she has also taken an honest inventory of life's traumas and has noted that suffering pervades human existence. He or she understands a longing for a further shore of freedom. Such examples are innumerable and serve to indicate that humane knowledge is truly a form of self-consciousness. It is appropriate to think of cultural creations as variations on one's own humanity. Whether researchers explore religiously motivated violence in Sri Lanka, the art of Persian miniatures, or the diagrams of Taoist geomancers, they are probing human meanings as possibilities for themselves. Though they may not be serious life possibilities for oneself, they must nevertheless be seen and felt as genuine ways of being human.

Western traditionalists may object to this emphasis on self-consciousness as the royal road to unearthing non-Western meaning, arguing that Westerners have been so thoroughly formed by the Graeco-Roman/Judaeo-Christian culture that they cannot (should not) experience other world-views as genuine personal possibilities. Yet the evidence is against this. The difficulty for a Westerner in apprehending the faith of others lies not in the capacity but in the will. To see alien perspectives as potential stores of insight presupposes a commitment to extend our identity by risking a portion of ourselves.

The West has already been enriched by its incorporation of the values of two disparate civilizations. Having learned from Hellenic and Jewish modes of thought, we have insisted on the irreplaceable value of both. Yet convincing evidence does not exist that Hindu, Buddhist or Chinese cultures are less valuable than the Greek and Semitic complexes. Nor are they necessarily more difficult to absorb into Western thinking than was the Semitic view of life that was incorporated into the Graeco-Roman world via Christianity. Smith holds that the various ways of being human are in some degree integrable. He sees humankind as potentially, though not actually, one. The anatomical oneness of the species does not constitute a true human oneness; this requires a knowledge of, and a sharing in, the consciousness of others.

Two options lay before us in our intellectual encounter with diverse world-views. We may choose to appreciate alien views of reality and enter into partial community with those that hold them; for community is created by shared values and symbols. We may thereby receive the inheritance of others, at least in part, as our own. Or we may choose to spurn the opportunity of establishing a larger community of value and retreat to a safe objectivity by refusing the benefits of riskful growth. In choosing the latter path we create a comfortable distance from the challenge of another's truth. This posture ensures that we shall not entertain the consciousness of others as aspects of our potential self-consciousness. Instead, we shall continue to view the religious and cultural existence of others like:

> . . . flies crawling on the outside of a goldfish bowl making accurate and complete observations on the fish inside, meas-

uring their scales meticulously, and indeed contributing much to our knowledge of the subject; but never asking . . . never finding out, how it feels to be a goldfish.[20]

One might extend the fishbowl metaphor adding that the observer never inquires of the goldfish what it knows, sees, or feels about the observer's activities, which must appear queer or rude to the goldfish.

For Smith, humankind is at a point where we can in an evolutionary manner move beyond the earlier plateau of objectivity. Though evolutionary language sounds peculiar in today's climate, in which a nuclear winter seems apocalyptic-ally feasible, Smith maintains an optimism similar to evol-utionists such as Julian Huxley and Teilhard de Chardin. Like them, he has not been captivated by pessimism and continues to be fascinated by the potential of the planetary situation. He shares in the evolutionists' imagery that speaks of advance arising from greater complexification. He sees the twentieth century as unique in that a part of the web of humanity, the West, has for the first time dominated the entirety of humanity, though for a short period, and in so doing has created an interacting network with all civilizations. They in turn have reacted to the penetration of Western imperialism and are in the process of redefining themselves in the light of Western political ideology and technological ability. All cultures are thus at present reflecting on the significance of their newly experienced interaction with all other cultures.

Smith's delineation of human ascent points to three crucial moments. The first occurred in the awakening of reflexive consciousness. The second happened in the birth of critical consciousness, that is, science.[21] The scientific state marked the advent of objectivity which impelled humanity to establish criteria to which all rational beings might uniformly consent for the measurement of natural processes. Beyond this stage Smith sees the further emergence of critical self-consciousness. This is a contemporary development which consists in a humane understanding of the persons of one culture by those of another. Such an undertaking is critical and self-conscious. It is also corporate, requiring the involvement of the person under study.

As a safeguard against misperceptions the new method requires that the person to be studied be consulted as an active agent in verifying whether his/her world-view has been correctly recognized. A researcher has not demonstrated a true apprehension of doctrines or symbols if he or she represents them in vitiated prose. To say, for example, that Christians believe that Christ rose from the dead offers little that explains the joy present in the faces of Geek Orthodox Christians when icons are uncovered with the proclamation that Jesus Christ is risen today. A student wishing to penetrate the faith of this congregation needs the worshippers to be informed, perhaps corrected, and to a degree challenged by the faith he studies.

Corporate critical self-consciousness

Corporate critical self-consciousness is a method designed to transcend the subject/object dichotomy by recognizing the unique status of a subject/subject relationship.[22] This, coupled with an awareness that the participant is now a partner in study, helps to allay the natural resentment that persons display when excluded from conversation about themselves. Resentment is particularly abated when the nature and purpose of the study is explained to participants. Corporate critical self-consciousness has the effect of muting suspicion on the part of the researched by fostering in both parties the sense of a shared task. Smith hopes to advance the concept of corporate critical self-consciousness in that it both creates an adequate approach to learning the faith of others and strengthens the moral quality of fostering community. He summarizes:

> By corporate critical self-consciousness I mean that critical, rational, inductive self-consciousness by which a community of persons, constituted at a minimum of two persons, the one being studied and the one studying, but

ideally by the whole human race, is aware of any given particular human condition or action as a condition or action of itself; as a community, yet of one part but not of the whole of itself; and is aware of it as it is experienced and understood simultaneously both subjectively (personally, existentially) and objectively (externally, critically, analytically; as one used to say scientifically).[23]

Corporate critical self-consciousness is an attempt to preserve what is true in objectivism and subjectivism. If one takes the example of deciphering the meaning of a Hindu temple, one realizes that it is necessary to be familiar with the temple's factual components – age, composition, artistic style, etc. In fact, as objective students of Indian architecture we may be more correctly informed in matters of history than those who worship within the temple. We will also have impressions as to the meaning of the rituals performed in the temple and hope to confirm our perceptions, which at this point are subjective. There is only one way to do this once we have declared our interest in the meaning of the ritual. We must inquire of the devotees as to the intention of their behaviour. Of course, one might instead approach the ritual with a so-called universal interpretative key. There are many such keys – Freudian, Jungian, Marxist, etc. – though none of them stands up fully to empirical testing. This is not to say that these perspectives offer nothing of value; however, Smith is distrustful of interpretative schemes which minimize the conscious self-understanding of the primary actors.

Since a temple ritual may signify various things to different persons, conversation with many devotees is in order. However, when we involve a participant in understanding our project, we may need to search out an Indian intellectual, one able to appreciate our findings on the objective data of the temple. It is difficult to say how much mutuality of learning is possible with uneducated villagers. One wonders how possible it is to share one's factual findings when mythic exaggeration and indifference to history may distort an historical understanding of the origin and purpose of the ritual.

Ideally, one might find an educated Hindu who understood the researcher's objective concerns. This, however, is not sufficient for a reconstruction of the past faith of earlier devotees. To explore how a temple has functioned in the life of the community over centuries, one would have to do without the advantage of living witnesses. Reconstruction would need to be established from texts, religious auto-biography, travel accounts, historical records, etc. Without a living informant, hermeneutical issues would become more pressing and more difficult. But once the researcher returned to the temple's function in contemporary life he or she would again be on solid ground. Inquiry might begin with the way architecture signifies the cosmos, or with the worshippers' implicit or explicit anthropology, or with how the efficacy of prayer is thought to vary in temple environs, and so forth. Gradually, the temple as a powerful symbol in village life would be transparent and the inquirer would be able to validate or invalidate his or her initial intuitions about the meaning of Hindu existence as embodied in stone.

At this point I would observe that Smith disagrees with Eliade's and Jung's interpretation of symbolism, finding in their positions a form of objectivism that seems to hold that symbols contain their meanings in themselves.[24] He accuses those practising 'phenomenology of religion' (he has Eliade in view) of 'positing a Platonic idealism of symbolic forms'.[25] Smith objects that no object is a symbol in itself and that 'the historical evidence suggests . . . that the empirical symbol does not itself participate in that transcendence'.[26] He does not dispute the fact that when a symbol becomes luminous with significance it appears to the experiencer to participate in transcendence. But he adds that since most individuals do not experience the symbol as revelatory it is best not to argue this way. He also disagrees with Jung and Eliade in their belief that a symbol has a universal meaning, stating that as an historian: 'I am inescapably aware of diversity and change . . . the meaning of things lies in their relation to persons . . . and not in themselves as objects.'[27] There is some difficulty with Smith's voluntaristic way of speaking. It sounds as if persons bestow meaning on symbols. Yet experientially this is clearly not the case, for one must be grasped by meaning to have a genuine religious symbol. If symbols are the creation of persons, they are most certainly not conscious creations. Yet Smith is aware of this and on occasion he does speak of the effect of the subconscious on symbol formation. A person is not limited to his or her conscious mind. One must ask Smith, however, whether meaning is always humanly created. Are symbols human constructs or are they vehicles of divine meaning? One suspects that Smith would say both. But how? How much is donation and how much creation in the formation of symbols? Smith is not clear on this point, and one hopes that he will present his understanding of the workings of the deep mind in relation to the emergence of religious symbols and their effect on the conscious mind. Perhaps this unclarity reflects Smith's apparent lack of strength in psychological studies, for his volumes attest to few references.

For Smith, the participant other adds to the adventure of knowing another's faith 'a decisive new principle of verification'.[28] Verification here differs from that found in objective knowledge in which the discovery of one observer is capable of being publically retested and reconfirmed. In critical corporate self-consciousness one's findings are not so much objectively tested as inter-subjectively proven by both researcher and participant. Presumably if other observers were present they also would be able to understand the explanations offered by participants. Critical corporate self-consciousness is therefore capable of offering agreed upon descriptions of faith, and in this sense is both public and objective. Smith gives this maxim to describe the type of validity that critical corporate self-consciousness calls for:

No statement involving persons is valid, I propose, unless

its validity can be verified both by the persons involved and by critical observers not involved.[29]

This statement summarizes the corporate dimension found in critical corporate self-consciousness. As a method, it ensures that one culture will not be able to impose its interpretation upon another since a cross-cultural community of verification will readily block and correct such attempts. This type of reaction increasingly occurs today in academic publications where representatives of the major religious groups respond to interpretations of their communities' religious (or political, economic, etc.) life.

A peculiar, though common, passage of mind takes place when an exotic vision is transformed into a familiar one, when one becomes acquainted with another manner of seeing reality. Once a student passes over into the vision of another, that other becomes less strange and a portion of an alien way of seeing becomes a portion of oneself. That which is curious is recognized as a genuine possibility rather than a mere form of behaviour or belief. Though such a process sounds unusual, it is actually repeated daily by students who study human meaning in a number of fields. One might take the example of one studying Chinese painting who comes to accept a form of beauty that was initially experienced as odd. By extending his or her aesthetic sensibilities the student has ranged beyond typical modes of Western perception. It is in fact not unusual for students of Chinese painting to prefer Chinese forms of beauty to those offered in Western culture.

Mutual transformation is a challenging possibility for scholars exercised in the practice of critical corporate self-consciousness. When the participant is a partner in value exploration the values of both parties will be called into question and, hopefully, expanded. The process of interrogating a member of another culture at a profound level necessarily raises questions centring upon ultimate valuation. The participant may inquire, for example, why the researcher appears interested in historical detail rather than in timelessness, or why the researcher finds theoretical or doctrinal formulations of the divine more significant than meditative experience. Since a researcher's task is to think into another way of life, rather than apologize for his or her own, he/she begins to realize how curious his or her own way of perceiving appears to the participant. His or her values will at this point appear curious when seen through another's eyes.

One wonders if Smith is not excessively sanguine in his trust in an inter-personal, inter-subjective method of verification. Does not a Freudian or Marxist legitimately uncover negative elements in a religious tradition, such as that of escapism and sanctioned class oppression, that piety precludes from serious entertainment by devotees? Smith, I believe, would answer 'no'. He accepts the possibility that new experience will challenge and alter traditional frames of thought as people interact. Critical corporate self-consciousness has a revolutionary aspect precisely because it exposes the assumptions of the researcher and participant to each other. An orthodox Freudian interacting with gurus in the Indian sub-continent may arrive at a less regressive interpretation of samadhi, while an orthodox Hindu may recognize that psychoanalysis has something to say about unconscious conflict, even in the lives of saints.

Occasionally, Smith speaks as if religious knowledge is capable of being shared in such a fashion that not only understanding but even agreement about issues of religious truth is possible between researcher and participant.

I personally tend to feel that there is probably no statement about my faith that I would wish to make that I could not on principle hope to explain to an intelligent, modern, devout, informed, Muslim or Hindu friend – and explain so that he would understand, and yes, in the end, would accept. Especially, I suppose, if he were something of a mystic, as well as a rationalist. Nor should I expect him in turn to 'believe' anything, if he were intelligent, that I should not find both intelligible and intelligent. (What reason would he have for believing anything that I would not?)[30]

The reader may react to the quotation above with sceptical amusement concerning Smith's optimism about cross-cultural acceptance of religious insight. He does, however, add a proviso to guard his position. For he appears to be operating with an extremely select group. He defines his intellectual partners as rationalists and mystics. It may not be difficult after all to find a high level of philosophical concord among a select company; for Smith has excluded fideists, non-mystics, supernaturalists, secularists, dogmatists and a multitude of others who do not fit his limited sampling. In the company of a more differentiated gathering it is doubtful that he could remain so hopeful of agreement. Optimism is problematical here. Since what appears reasonable depends a great deal upon one's unique experience, it is not at all certain that such persons would reach agreement. Critical corporate self-consciousness would be better advertised if one did not postulate a hypothetical friend whose basic orientation turned out to be identical with one's own.

Yet Smith is to be congratulated for his bold trust in the human ability to enter into imaginatively novel contexts and sense therein what is excellent, sacred and true. His position appears more justified than either a pessimistic or relativistic attitude which assumes that cultural differences makes value sharing virtually impossible. The large number of Americans and Europeans who have recently incorporated elements of Eastern metaphysics into their world picture and who have taken up spiritual disciplines developed in Asia tend to support Smith's more cheerful hypothesis. Further, he is surely correct that faith should be made intelligible and that communities of faith are called to give explanations for the faith that is within them, trusting that this can in some measure be successfully communicated to intelligent outsiders.

Though Smith is chiefly interested in creating understanding between scholastic representatives of religious communities, his method can be applied to other situations. It contains unifying potentials for countering the fragmentation of thought found in separated university disciplines. By promoting critical corporate self-consciousness in the academic situation, scholars could experience a broader intellectual community and develop a more adequate response to the work of their peers in neighbouring fields of study.

The political and social implications of critical corporate self-consciousness are likewise significant. An enlarged and confirmed understanding between divided groups such as blacks/whites, males/females, hetero-/homo-sexuals is necessary for reconciliation. Such conflicts are costly to national health and are replete with cultural misperceptions. Critical corporate self-consciousness is therefore not to be thought of as a valuable tool merely for unlocking distant and exotic religions. It can readily serve in the home arena.

Reflecting on the political dimension of social research, one sees that misperception of studied groups has frequently occurred. These distortions have long been apparent to outsiders who are not white, male or middle-class. Minorities have persistently shown scepticism concerning the findings of researchers whose task is to observe and evaluate their 'problems'. In many instances minorities have been forced to mimic the behaviours and values of the majority, sometimes unconsciously, but often with self-conscious cynicism, in order to gain majority acceptance. In these situations the otherness of the other is negated by absorption into the dominant culture. Those studying the problems of minorities are frequently members of the oppressing class – men studying women, whites studying blacks, straights studying gays. The exercise of critical corporate self-consciousness would diminish this sort of implicit domination; for in it the one to be studied is acknowledged as a serious partner in the process of understanding. At the same time, critical co-operation of this type may easily constitute a threat to the self-perception of investigators who are comfortable in their role as external observers and adjudicators. Smith writes:

. . . at issue is the point that the intimate dynamic interaction
. . . between the subject group and the object group in each
case is in part constitutive of the situation of the object group
– to its discomfort; that the subject group . . . has had a
hand in perversely making the subject group what it is. This
fact inevitably introduces a distortion into such research . . .
partly on the grounds that true knowledge in each case is
resisted because it would involve the knower in a new
awareness of his or her own self.[31]

A solution to these social difficulties, both methodological
and personal, lies for Smith in the formation of intellectual
communities containing equal numbers of the polarized
factions. Research in race relations should, for example, be the
joint product of white and black scholars who, without
rejecting their separate identities, are able to agree upon
what constitutes legitimate data and interpretation. Failing to
achieve this, one hopes to attain at least a clear appreciation of
the other point of view, since committees established along
the lines of critical corporate self-consciousness would raise
group presuppositions into consciousness.

There is an important psychological truth in Smith's depiction of critical corporate self-consciousness and its relation to
the development of community that is consistent with insights
drawn from the popular Rogerian method of counselling.
'Method' is not perhaps the correct word here, with its
connotation of technique and manipulation, though it is used
here simply to describe a manner of interacting between
persons that intends to be authentic. In Rogerian theory, bonds
of trust are established between client and therapist when the
therapist demonstrates to the client that he also (the therapist)
has non-judgmentally heard and understood what the client
intended. In some instances the therapist hears the deeper
intention of the client revealed in the mode of expression rather
than in overt speech. In this relationship the therapist may
possess objective information concerning the client which the
client is unaware of himself or herself. This is because the latter

does not commonly possess a knowledge of psychological dynamics. In the therapeutic process the therapist discloses whether he or she has genuinely perceived the client's situation by reflecting back the client's point of view, attitudes and emotions. When the therapist's depiction of the client's inner state rings true, the client develops a bond of trust and positive regard for the therapist. Barriers of loneliness are lowered and the sense of isolation is overcome. A developing spiral of confidence takes place which allows for a deepened sharing until the most profound and intimate values are disclosed. Often the bond of trust even allows the client to discover his or her own hidden concerns; for once the security of being accepted and understood is established, the client is set free to explore the unconscious assumptions of life. Being accepted, the client develops positive regard towards the self, which in turn enables him or her to find the ego strength necessary to acknowledge weaknesses, strengths, fears and hopes that under normal circumstances of insecurity and guilt could not be made explicit.

On the therapist's side, the practice of empathy had led to an enlarged capacity for self-insight. The therapist has been enabled to acknowledge to him- or herself the full play of human disorder, though in attenuated form, that is present in the client.[32]

The Rogerian model emphasizes: 1. the need to indicate to the other that he or she is understood; 2. the importance of empathy; 3. the importance of a non-defensive, non-adjudicatory orientation; 4. the necessity of creating conditions of trust so that profound values can be inter-subjectively shared. This last condition is necessary for allowing a self-criticism of one's own tradition to be shared with outsiders.

Of these four points, Smith has insisted upon the necessity of 1. and 2. and like the therapist he relies upon the subject's testimony to confirm whether the historian has successfully heard the subject's world-view. 2. is also seen as a necessary pre-condition for the development of empathy, while 4. is a prerequisite for the establishment of mutual learning.

Critical corporate self-consciousness does not presuppose a client/therapist modality. A therapist is after all turned to as one who knows more about the psyche than does the client. However, in critical corporate self-consciousness the investigator is in need of instruction and cannot be thought of as superior in her understanding of the faith of those studied, even though she may possess a more complete knowledge of the content of the tradition. One reason Smith has created this model is to dismantle the sense of superiority that he finds in Western investigators. Parallels exist to the Rogerian model, but in critical corporate self-consciousness therapy is applied to the fragmented psyche of the human race rather than to individuals. It is a tool for gathering into a whole the divided forms of insight that create conflict between civilizations. Perhaps it is also a therapeutic life-style for becoming truly cosmopolitan.

Those who have attained an in-depth conversation in which the we/they fallacy is overcome are able to read the world through foreign symbols. A number of things may then occur. They may discover that a particular insight is truly unique to the tradition they are studying. Or they may discover that the wisdom they assumed to be possessed by their own tradition is also available elsewhere. In either instance they have been altered. An external tradition has become internalized. This process occurs in greater or lesser degree depending on one's sensitivity and on the nature of what is studied. As critical corporate self-consciousness becomes a primary organ for interaction between peoples the process will intensify.

It is important to recognize that the internalization of cross-cultural values erodes the concept of a 'religion' as a bounded community of salvation. Critical corporate self-consciousness is a contemporary Western expression of the Indian and Chinese practice of savouring truth from many sources. It facilitates the collapse of cultural and religious exclusivism. The approach holds promise for the healing of the nations, for it facilitates the termination of a monolithic understanding of truth which has figured so largely in disfiguring one's image of one's neighbour's faith.

However incipiently, the boundaries segregating off religious communities radically and finally from each other are beginning, just a little, to weaken or to dissolve, so that being a Hindu and being a Buddhist, or being a Christian and not being a Christian, are not so starkly alternatives as once they seemed.[33]

In the US State Department a fear is often found that diplomats who live abroad may 'go native'. A diplomat, in sensing the reasonableness of the attitudes of the host country, may come to prefer the betterment of the host nation to that of the United States. In a fashion Smith is arguing that in the cultural and religious sphere it is best for the sake of humanity that all of us 'go a bit native'. For it is only when catholic-minded individuals place themselves under the rule of excellence, whatever its geography, that the limited vision of each culture can be surpassed. When this occurs, insights and symbols that were initially strange come home in ourselves. We find ourselves part of an experienced community of 'we-all'.[34]

A key to the psychological profile of any human being is contained in his or her use of the pronoun 'we'. The barometer of one's sympathies is revealed in a careful analysis of the use of the language of identification.[35] But more important academically is the intellectual gain in learning to utter 'we' in authentic fashion.[36] The ability to assimilate disparate world-views convincingly requires a movement away from an us/them to a we-all orientation.

If such thoughts sound utopian, it must be made clear that Smith's programme does not exhibit the normal patterns of idealism. His programme is not abstract, nor does it consist of an imposition of theoretical unity from above. Rather, it is a hopeful challenge to wrestle with concrete persons and their otherness until both they and their perspectives are known as sharing in one's own humanity. Though critical corporate self-consciousness is an intellectual method, it does contain an ideological element; for it is a programme that is hoped to result in both knowledge and peace.

A more sombre tone infects Smith's recent writing. There appears a heightened sense that we may fail to create a more harmonious interaction between civilizations. Humankind may indeed fail to survive. A less sanguine Smith now confronts the possibility of global catastrophe rather than evolutionary advance.[37] Though he is not resigned to this point of view, he calls on religious people to heed the advice of the Bhagavad Gita and strive for world peace and love in full awareness that success is not assured, yet confident that such work is the will of God.[38]

This realistic exhortation may be a sign that Smith is becoming more sensitive to the recalcitrance of evil. Even though he mentions, on a number of occasions, humankind's capacity for fanaticism and destruction, one is nevertheless more impressed by his contagious optimism. Those who live in darker spaces of the soul and find Pascal, Luther or Kierkegaard their travelling companions, may find in Smith's writings a limited but lovely exuberance characteristic of the first-born. I believe they would not be totally off-target. I was surprised to hear Smith refer to Calvin's concept of radical evil and Gautama's summation that life is suffering as ways of suggesting that this is what life would be without faith.[39] This analysis is clearly incomplete. Both Calvin and Gautama reflect a profound sense of personal unease with unredeemed existence. Both concepts have the firm ring of the autobiographical. Because Smith's writings do not show this sense of estrangement, one critic has wondered if Smith is not in danger of replicating the unguarded hope of turn-of-the-century liberalism.

> . . . advanced liberal theology (ca. 1880–1936 in the Anglo-Saxon world) emphasized the univeral presence and so the universal revelation of God and, as a consequence, the salvific efficacy of 'religion' (here termed 'faith'). Character-

istically such theology had difficulty with both the ambiguity of history and of culture, on the one hand, and the demonic possibilities of religious faith itself, on the other.[40]

This appears to be a danger in Smith's analysis of faith. For, although he speaks inspiringly about the force of ideals in religious life, one hears little of the need to be saved from the ways in which ideals are twisted by the depths of sin. True, Smith names the problem of evil, but he offers little in the way of a subtle analysis of depravity.

Though Smith is not utopian, his failure to portray sin in stark terms may give this impression. Yet if there is to be a future for our planet, Smith's hopeful programme for increasing respect, learning and mutual insight between cultures is essential. If we cannot trust that our effort towards bringing the human family into greater harmony reflects a divine purpose, we are left with an enervating pessimism towards history.

5

THE SEARCH FOR A GLOBAL THEOLOGY

In the West theological reflection has customarily taken place in isolation from the religious thought of other cultures. This situation was understandable for geographical reasons which no longer apply. Isolation, however, has also been the result of an exclusive mindset that portrayed non-Western faiths as pagan or heretical. Consequently the West assumed that its religious counterparts had nothing of import to say about the life of faith or the nature of reality. Given this history, Smith finds theological activity in the West both dangerously inbred and arrogant in its ignorance of world religious life.

Once the faith of other cultures is seen as valid, Western theologians are challenged to integrate into their thinking whatever insight they uncover outside Western traditions. This task is not merely an intellectual obligation but has become a pastoral necessity! For the spectrum of faith has fanned out wide. Westerners who one or two generations ago were confined to a choice between Christian and secularist faith now experiment with Hindu, Islamic and Buddhist modes of thought and practice.

Western theology and comparative religion

If one feels that Smith underestimates the performance of Christian theologians in understanding other traditions, the story of Paul Tillich may serve as an illustration. A student letter to the editor of the *Harvard Crimson* revealed that Tillich's presentation of Asian religious traditions was superficial and in fact incorrect.[1] An undergraduate was able to fault one of the notables of twentieth-century theology. Though Tillich had combined elements of German Idealism, Christianity, Marxism and the social sciences into a formidable synthesis, he nonetheless remained the product of a generation that, to a large degree, was uninformed about non-Western religions. When information was present, it was of the objective sort, a type of knowing that in itself helped to produce incomprehension of non-Christian communities.

In his last years Tillich widened his acquaintance with Eastern literature, pursued an intellectual friendship with historian of religions Mircea Eliade, and enlarged his religious education first-hand in Japan. In 1963, with the publication of *Christianity and the Encounter of the World Religions*, Tillich demonstrated that he had transcended his earlier pre-cosmopolitanism. Prior to this, Smith in 'The Christian in a Religiously Plural World' had charged that: 'Tillich belongs to the last generation of theologians who can formulate their conceptual system as religiously isolationist.'[2] It is perhaps the measure of Tillich's stature that this criticism, originally presented in 1961, was to be later emended in *The Faith of Other Men* (1963).[3] Future historians will perhaps recognize Tillich as a watershed figure who aided the Christian theological escape from the corporate subjectivism of the West.

Though disclaiming theological expertise, Smith challenges theologians to consider the serious consequences that comparative religion holds for the enterprise of theology.[4] Yet before analysing these we must first note what Smith means by theology. For in a strict sense 'theology' is a misnomer when applied to non-Christian religions. Other traditions do not have a theology that corresponds exactly to the Western discipline with its concern for rational and systematic dogma and unique history of theological problems. Islam and Judaism, the orthopractic traditions, have not placed their emphasis upon the development of dogma. They have been more concerned to explicate the demand of the divine as given in

sacred law. Yet these communities do reflect upon the nature
of faith and the meaning of the divine in a manner somewhat
analogous to Christian thought.

Hoping to include the orthopractic (and other) traditions in
a world religious discourse, Smith offers a general definition
of theology: '. . . a critical intellectualization of (and for) faith,
and of the world as known in faith . .'.[5] One notes that here
theology is not confused with faith; for faith is the richer
reality, with the theologian standing in relation to it much as
an art critic stands in relation to his or her subject matter.[6]
Elsewhere Smith similarly speaks of theology as an honest
attempt to conceptualize one's faith.[7] Understood in this
broad fashion, the theological act occurs wherever rational
conversation about religious consciousness and the reality it
illuminates is found. So defined, Buddhists and others, such
as the Jains, who do not believe in a creator God, qualify as
theologians. They too speak of an encounter with truth/reality
that entails conceptual explication. However, the question
remains whether the term 'theology' can be accepted in this
expanded sense by members of other religions. The answer
will need to be decided by an inter-cultural body of scholars.
Problems await. For Buddhists may naturally feel that the *theos*
in 'theology' has irredeemable theistic connotations and may
prefer a more technically correct term such as 'buddhalogy' or
'dharmalogy'.

In earlier times theologians (in the broad sense) reflected on
religious existence as manifest in their communities. On
occasion this reflection took into account a variety of paths, as
in China and India. But such reflection never attained to a
universal level.[8] The consequence of this limitation is fundamental in that the entirety of previous theological activity must
be judged as partial, inadequate and unintentionally parochial.
This situation takes us to the centre of the problem of pluralism
in which various models of reality, some derived from non-
Western cultures, others from humanist and scientific modes
of thought, compete for allegiance. The devotees of these
separate paths scarcely attempt to integrate their perspectives

with those of other models. To remedy this Smith calls for the
development of a world-view that seeks to attain a harmony
of 'multicultural values, of religious pluralism in tight
collaboration'.[9]

Smith is not suggesting that the strife of theological schools
be settled by unanimity or conformity. He prizes the richness
of diversity and does not wish to remove difference for
the sake of concord. However, he does suppose that the
theologian, as a servant of truth, ought to respond to truth as
it appears in a plurality of contexts. Since religious truth is
universally present and since each prior formulation of
religious insight is theologically inadequate, the task of finding
a coherence to humankind's partial apprehensions of reality
falls upon the shoulders of theologians in the twentieth century.
Smith invites scholars to move towards a pluralist vision of
truth that is larger than any one religion's perception. This is
the challenge of forming a world or global theology.

In rejecting a particularist notion of *Heilsgeschichte* Smith's
programme constitutes a departure from the dominant exclusivism of Christian history. Though some universal
approaches appear in the Gospel of John and in Hellenistic
theologians, the exclusive hypothesis has been prevalent.[10]
Smith therefore asks Christians to revise their understanding
of salvation. He suggests that a salvific process is discernible
wherever faith has emerged. The true record of God's saving
acts is to be found in world history, not in the Judaeo-
Christian or the Judaeo-Christian-Islamic strand of history.
Comparative religion, the study of the totality of religious
consciousness, offers a truer version of *Heilsgeschichte* than the
church's prior formulations. If this is so, world history,
understood as the record of humankind's experiment with
faith, becomes foundational for theology. The consequence is
that 'henceforth the data for theology must be the data of the
history of religion'.[11]

One common criticism of Smith's inclusive approach to
salvation is that it appears more Hindu than Christian.[12] This
is partly correct, for Smith will use a Hindu analysis of religion

if it sheds light on religious activity elsewhere. A comparativist will use knowledge from one culture and apply it to another. For example, the Hindu concept of faith, *sraddha*, is helpful in understanding faith elsewhere. If, however, one means that Smith is a Hindu because he accepts the legitimacy of multiple ways to the Real, it must be remembered that the West has also had universalists. But the charge that Smith is a Hindu usually involves the belief that he is a relativist concerning spiritual truth. This, however, is not the case if by being a relativist one means that there is no way of distinguishing the more from the less true. Since Smith recognizes that all major religious societies encounter religious truth and provide ways of dividing the more from the less true, it is more correct to say that Smith is a relationalist rather than a relativist. When a Christian exclaims that God is Love, he or she means that God is Love for him- or herself. This is a confession of a personal relation to the Real. The Buddhist, on the other hand, may experience Reality as cosmic law. For Smith, both are most probably correct in what they confess and incomplete in what they fail to see. This approach has led some authors to object that Smith offers no standard by which to evaluate religious or moral truth. This is a correct observation; but its correctness is due to our present imperfect understanding of the standards by which other traditions divide the less true or moral from the more so. I also made this objection in a paper presented to Wilfred Smith.[13] His reply was that the programme of critical corporate self-consciousness provides a route to achieve norms, but that such norms do not exist today since they must be the product of a community of scholars who have attained a high degree of critical corporate self-consciousness. Smith does not see it as a weakness that univeral norms are non-existent; instead, he is more concerned with the readiness of Western scholars to judge other religions. Norms cannot be imposed by a single tradition. They remain a future achievement. At present our obligation is to judge the adequacy of the tradition in which we are personally engaged and for which we are personally responsible.

Smith acknowledges that he has a number of guiding norms, such as: the loving nature of God; the principle of non-exclusivism; the importance of a unified humankind, etc. These he brings to the table of colloquy, knowing that they may be enriched, altered or challenged in the ongoing conversation. It is only when the context of religious wisdom becomes universal that relative and partial insights into religious truth can be overcome.

Smith does not deny that he finds elements of Hindu inclusivism attractive. He states that: 'It is only by becoming in part Hindu that a Westerner is enabled to be both Christian and Muslim at the same time, one may aphorize.'[14] Yet this statement is insufficient for labelling Smith a Hindu. One should recall that he has also internalized insights from the Islamic and humanist traditions. He recommends that truth be appropriated whatever its source. Despite his use of Hindu motifs, Smith's concerns, style and attitudes remain profoundly Western and Christian.

> . . . let no one imagine . . . that my analysis of religious reality can be characterized unsophisticatedly . . . as being Hindu or oriental rather than Christian, which would be absurd . . . fewer . . . will appreciate as deeply as Christendom either the scientific, historical, dynamic, quality of the proferred analysis, or the global concern.[15]

Once aware that the world-view(s) present in Christian theology is but one of several legitimate responses to truth/ reality, the theologian is required to explain the fact of God's universal salvific activity. More personally, he or she is constrained to incorporate whatever appears true in non-Christian traditions. To refuse to acknowledge that which appears illuminating, helpful or morally excellent is to discount theology as a serious intellectual enterprise and to brand theologians as personally inauthentic. Whenever Christian theologians have refused to learn from truth in the past, whatever its source – be it the truth of science, philosophy, psychology, or the history of religions – theology has become defensive and trivial. Honest scholars must have their vision of reality as wide as possible.

One may refuse the task of expanding one's theological horizon and prefer to view cultural and religious differences in terms of conflict. Rather than develop novel forms of co-operation, Christian thinkers may opt for the prize of theological hegemony. However, that which appears to threaten may in fact suggest the promise of a larger version of truth. It is often the case that persons affirm the truth they understand and deny what they are not sensitized to recognize. Because of this, Smith prefers to explain the preconditions for recognition rather than engage in premature judgments. He comes near to holding that persons are correct in what they assert and wrong in what they deny.[16] For example, the fact that Buddhists do not encounter a personal deity in their meditations does not require Christians who do to pronounce Buddhists in error. The mystery of Being is large and there may be a variety of forms of legitimate response to the Real. Disagreement does not require charges of error. Traditions seemingly at variance may, upon deeper study, be seen to reinforce each other.

Smith's call for a universal theology has stirred the imagination of some theologians and with good reason. For if he is prophetic about theology's future mission, the theological enterprise will be restored to the forefront of creative disciplines. One enthusiast has written:

> . . . I also agree that Smith's vision has captured the future of theology. At a time when that old queen of the sciences is mired down in the cognitive confusion bred by competing world-views and cowers beneath the might of secular rationalism, he clears the air and grants theology a new power. This book should be required reading for every seminarian, every scholar of religion and every thoughtful Christian.[17]

It is interesting that at the Eleventh International Congress for the History of Religions (1965) Asian scholars supported Smith's dialogic method, agreeing that religious insight is more likely to be transmitted if shared and studied in personal encounter with representatives.[18] Asian scholars also found the so-called 'objective' approach to the study of religions sterile. The practical purpose of realizing a deeper unity with the rest of humankind rang strong in their statements. One wonders if Christian scholars will also share their expansive concern.

If theologians are to appropriate the truths of other communities they must rely on personal interaction with colleagues from other traditions. The doing of global theology requires non-Christian partners for validating Christian perceptions of other versions of reality, and vice versa. Though corporate validation has been realized in some measure by the international activity of comparative religion, it has not produced a global theology.[19] Students of comparative religion have often avoided the normative issues of theological truth. This has led to a situation in which theologians narrowly speak of reality from within a single tradition while comparative religionists present the world-views of other peoples but fail to reflect upon the truth that they proclaim.[20]

Critical corporate self-consciousness requires theologians to rethink the question of whom they experience as their peers. This involves a re-self-imaging. The result is an expansion of collegiality that includes thinkers from each faith position. The most significant clue that an individual is ready to think in global fashion is revealed in who he/she includes in the use of the pronoun 'we'. Many of these thoughts may already be familiar to readers acquainted with the burgeoning literature on dialogue. However, it is important to acknowledge Smith as one of the earliest voices to propose the necessity of interpersonal exchange among faith participants. By the late 1950s Smith already predicted that the Christian churches' next great challenge would consist in the acceptance of non-Western religious truth.[21]

Despite his accord with much of the dialogical movement which has supervened upon centuries of monologue Smith nonetheless objects to the use of the term 'dialogue' and prefers instead 'colloquy'.[22] He finds in the connotations of 'dialogue' a sense that meetings for inter-faith exchange are to be special and occasional. 'Colloquy', on the other hand, carries a sense of a more enduring interaction and co-operation between communities. In addition, 'dialogue' is a bi-lateral term that intimates something of polarization between persons, while 'colloquy' suggests a broader inclusiveness – a multi-lateral position that refers not so much to a confrontation but to a corporate involvement with shared problems.[23] Once participants have learned from one another in the dialogical process, a new movement will emerge towards synthesis. Smith therefore puts forth the slogan 'from dialogue to colloquy' to indicate the next phase in the church's relationship to other communities.[24]

Though Smith is normally concerned about personal faith-sharing between members of different paths, that which is shared at this level becomes gradually circulated within the larger communities. Personal interactions have corporate effects. And once the benefits of colloquy are understood by the larger church, institutional commitments will be necessary for continuing the process. Unlike comparative religion, which has a global network in universities, the church has no adequate institutional base to ensure development in critical corporate self-consciousness. To further this end it is recommended that: 'Every contemporary Christian theological seminary . . . should have a chair for a visiting professor from some other community; or perhaps two, one Jewish and one other.'[25]

Dialogue as normally understood refers to a transitional stage of learning that is necesary but must be passed beyond. And beyond dialogue lies the task of absorbing insight into the larger communities. It thus implies an enlargement and transformation of traditions. When Christians find valuable elements in Buddhist tradition, Christian theology must to that extent be Buddhized.[26] Conversely, one may speak of Buddhist tradition becoming Christianized, and also Judaized, Islamicized and so on. Critical corporate self-consciousness eventuates in mutual transformation among religious communities.

A theology founded on critical corporate self-consciousness will eventually become a world theology, which is for Smith the ultimate, though at present distant, goal of religious thought. To formulate a global theology it is necessary to advance beyond confessional forms of theology to a universal, truth-centred position. A major difficulty in developing theology of this sort lies in our undeveloped ability to enter the various world-views as personal sources of insight. Smith states:

> The theology of comparative religion . . . must be the product of thinkers who see . . . and feel . . . know men and women of all religious groups and all centuries, as members of one community, one in which they themselves also participate. And this situation, is just beginning but *very* incipiently – to emerge.[27]

Given the incompleteness of an emerging corporate community, conditions do not exist as yet that would enable Smith to propose a concrete theology of comparative religion. As an alternative he focuses upon the prerequisites that future theologians must meet if they aspire to think from a world perspective.

The practice of global theology

Global theology as an intellectual reflection upon faith in its many forms attempts theoretically to understand ultimate reality as it has appeared in religious consciousness. Global theology is faith seeking understanding in inter-cultural partnership as it synthesizes various perceptions of the infinite into a unified whole. Smith realizes, of course, that such a task is in some ways unrealistic, perhaps even an eschatological hope.[28] Within just a single tradition, such as the Christian, theologians are unable to agree upon a summary statement of faith that would cover all Christians and all denominations.

Yet, ideally, Christian theologians endeavour to express the foundational insights of Christian experience. In a parallel way, world theologians would attempt to reflect upon the basic experiences of all or, at least, most of the major world religions. Summarizing, Smith explains: ' . . . we aspire to a statement of God and his diverse involvements with mankind'.[29]

Because the task of a world theology is novel Smith is concerned that it should not be confused with prior understandings. A world theology should not be conceived of as a theology of religions. For it is not about religions when these are understood as merely the data of external traditions. In Smith's words a global theology is not 'an objective genitive'.[30] It cannot be written by those understanding religions from the outside but must be created by persons who apprehend the faith of others from within.

The foremost requirement of critical corporate self-consciousness is that the researcher perceive as does the adherent. A portion of the world of the other is thus experienced as a portion of the researcher's own self-consciousness. Since the wisdom of a foreign tradition is transformative, the Christian theologian is not engaged in merely objective learning when he/she grasps the import of an alien faith.

A global theology is not, moreover, a Christian theology about other religions.[31] It is not a 'subjective genitive', where either Christians or members of other communities form the subject. For that would imply that a particular vision of the world has an internationally acknowledged right to judge other traditions by its own canons. If a Christian theology maintains a critical and distant posture towards other paths, then it has succumbed to the objective fallacy. In this instance, the theologian is most probably fearful that an encounter with another tradition might alter his or her inherited vision of reality.

Faith understood as ultimate valuation cannot be objectified since it is the organizing centre of each of life's dimensions. Because of this a theologian can create a Christian theology of marriage, of political action, of work, etc., but not a Christian theology of another faith.[32] A unique centre is able to organize the peripheries of its own existence but cannot incorporate another centre into itself. When Christian theology evaluates the significance of another vision from its own perspective it becomes a form of imposition and disqualifies itself as a candidate for a genuine world theology. The faith of another must be experienced to some degree so that its power as an ongoing centre of value is grasped.

Since a world theology must reveal what is valuable in each religion, no single community can stand as its sole author. Such a theology is in some sense a subjective gentive, but the subject is extended to consist of 'a global and verifiable self-consciousness of religious diversity'.[33] Because this sort of consciousness is incipient, one can only begin to form the necessary conditions. For theologians this means being responsive to the value of other types of religious consciousness. The degree to which this is achieved determines the degree to which a world theology is feasible.

There is one way in which it is correct to speak of a world theology as being a Christian theology. It must be at least a Christian theology, but one that is Christian plus, and similarly at least a Buddhist theology, but one that is Buddhist plus.[34] An analogy to what Smith envisages can be found in recent ecumenical formulations.

> There is clearly a difference between an ecumenical (Christian) theology, and a specifically Presbyterian theology of ecumenism; even though the former would not be valid if it were not in some sense Presbyterian, yet not merely Presbyterian.[35]

This example suggests that Smith perceives the relationship between religious communities in the future as analogous to the current relationship between Christian denominations. In the present ecumenical atmosphere Catholics have come to value Luther while Protestants take eagerly to the writing of Hans Küng. This mutual regard, scarcely thinkable thirty years ago, presages the type of co-operation Smith foresees amongst the great religions.

A world theology will necessarily be the work of persons rooted in a particular tradition. It will not be the creation of abstract universalists who have not experienced conviction in a specific religious culture. Further, it is not to be viewed as the formation of a new religion, nor as a philosophy pretending to stand outside and above the perceptions of the great traditions. World theologizing is a process in which participants enlarge their perception of religious truth through acts of critical corporate self-consciousness. This process is seen as a necessary extension of the integral thought of each particular religion.[36]

In approaching religious insight, one commences with the wisdom of one's community and extends it to grasp the similarities and differences of foreign insight. For Christians the nature of Buddhist compassion is grasped by a sympathetic comparison with Christian agape. The same procedure applies to all participants. And this entails that each formulation of global theology will bear the imprint of the culture of its author. Paticularity will inevitably remain.[37] A Christian contribution to a world theology will be readily recognized as displaying a Christian ambience by those outside the Christian community.

Since genuine religious knowledge always transforms, the recognition of a depth-dimension in the symbols of another's faith leads to the development of a secondary faith within one's self.[38] This is required by the logic of authenticity which demands that one instil into oneself that which is true. To appreciate the faith of another is to enter in some degree into community with that other, since community is constituted by participating in shared symbols. Smith has himself entered this larger community of secondary faith through his own practice of critical corporate self-consciousness in Islamic studies. Concerning his ability to perceive Islamically, Richard H. Robinson observes:

I have never been able to listen to Professor Smith talk about
Islam without feeling that he shares the faith of Muslims in
some way without compromising his Christian
commitment.[39]

The phrase 'without compromising his Christian commitment' is consistent with Smith's insistence that an absorption of
religious truth, regardless of its source, leads to an enlargement
rather than denial of one's inheritance.

A programme for enlarging the Christian tradition with the
insight of other cultures is consistent with the intention of
classical Christian theology. Aquinas, for instance, attempted,
though not without charges of heresy, to unify three modes
of reflection on the Divine – the Greek via Aristotle, the
Christian via the New Testament and Catholic tradition, and
the Islamic via Averroes (Ibn Rushd).[40] This sort of effort
has been abandoned by contemporary confessional theology.
Compared to the daring of an Aquinas, modern theologians
appear timid. To correct this, Smith invites Christian scholars
to respond to a more international range of ideas; for too
frequently Christian intellectuals have been responsive solely
to Western secular critics while remaining ignorant of non-
Christian thinkers of world status. Plato, Aristotle and Plotinus
have already been pervasively active in Christian theology. Is
it not perverse that Shankara, Nagarjuna, Iqbal and Aurobindo
are persistently ignored – a situation that indicates that commitment to the Western tradition has been placed above commitment to truth?[41]

One may perhaps object to the hope that critical corporate
self-consciousness, when applied to theology, will create a
friendly inter-mix of cultural sharing. Will not irreconcilable
beliefs remain even after it has become established? Christians
will presumably continue to revere Christ as the second Person
of the Trinity, while Muslims continue steadfastly to regard
him as a significant prophet. Buddhists might attend to him
as a manifestation of the Dharma, though not the Son of God
– there being no creator God.[42] Yet even if these doctrinal

dilemmas are not surmounted one can hope for a growth in
tolerance appreciation. Having passed through critical
corporate self-consciousness the reasonableness of the various
theological positions would be clear. One would, for example,
see why the above interpretations of Christ would be intelligent
and consistent in their respective frameworks.

Even this meagre gain would herald an important intercom-
munal sensitivity. However, Smith is more sanguine about
the application of critical corporate self-consciousness. For he
trusts that its practitioners will be profoundly modified in their
exchanges. Though they might maintain traditional doctrine,
the hard edges of dogmatic separation would be softened.
Exclusivist Christians would notice that something analogous
to the fruit of the Spirit appears to be operative elsewhere.
Being empirical and inductive (essential pre-conditions for
critical corporate self-consciousness) these practitioners would
necessarily expand their soteriology. Other absolutist claims
would likewise alter. Muslims, understanding that early
Christian experience was formulated in a Greek rather than
Semitic horizon, would perceive that Christians are (were) not
inescapably ignorant or wilful in their deification of Jesus.
Hindus of the Advaitic persuasion might become less eager to
embrace other religions as less mature versions of their own,
and come to deal more honestly with them.

One might criticize Smith's collaborative scheme as a
dangerous incentive to eclecticism. This term, however, with
its history of negative associations, requires reconsideration.
It often connotes an unsystematic pastiche of items taken from
disparate systems and thrown together into an arbitrary whole.
Smith thinks of eclecticism more positively. He would certainly reject the pastiche approach; his research on Islam has
taught him how difficult it is to establish clear analogies
between systems. But in an age when science and pluralism
have shattered the coherence of traditional societies, it is no
longer as clear as it once was that the insights of one civilization
are incompatible with those of another. In the twentieth
century we have inherited a vocation to assimilate that which

is valuable from a cluster of sources. And to this end Smith affirms the necessity of eclecticism.[43]

Borrowing between traditions is not eclectic in the sense of unengaged. A Protestant minister practicing yoga does so, one might surmise, because he finds it vital for his self-definition. It offers him a spiritual discipline of the body not available within his own tradition. Thus his practice forms part of a living whole. His historical context includes yoga, which was probably not available as a real option to his father. Though rigidities and hostilities remain between religious communities, a richer and more interfused context for faith has emerged. Ingredients that once awakened a sense of the exotic have become effective forces in contemporary culture.

The situation is somewhat analogous to the time of the late Roman Empire, when theologians attempted to assimilate what they perceived as philosophically and spiritually apt in neo-Platonism, Stoicism and the mystery religions. At present no empire exists that is able to embrace the totality of the earth's religious positions. But a symbolic empire may be seen in the image of our globe as newly discovered from space. A new sense of finitude exists. Unknown seas no longer beckon and rumours of strange civilizations have expired. Humankind is accounted for; and now theologians are challenged with a synthetic task that dwarfs the projects of Augustine and the Fathers.

The concept of a religion as a bounded community, coupled with exclusivism, has retarded the Christian ability to recognize and emphasize the interconnectedness of the earth's religions. But if the church is to develop a world-wide perspective it will need to surpass the limitations of past scholarship which could barely acknowledge the presence of non-Jewish or non-Christian elements in scripture or tradition. When research uncovered the fact that the Book of Proverbs reflected a generous borrowing from an earlier Egyptian wisdom or that the Psalms included ideas of kingship adapted from Canaanite people, scholars hurriedly apologized for the existence of pagan material by explaining how Jewish thought profoundly altered the appropriated material and expressed the unique world-view of the chosen people. Though this explanation is accurate enough – for all peoples re-adapt borrowed material – the tone of the argument is highly defensive. But guarded behaviour is not unusual for Christian scholars who work within a limited concept of *Heilsgeschichte*. The contributions of non-Jews and non-Christians are but slightly acknowledged and are generally minimized. As Smith suggests:

> The unity of humankind's religious history is obvious, once one sees it. We have, however, been assiduously trained not to see it. Even more strongly, we have been pressured not to think it; and not to feel it. [44]

A different focus is more consistent with a world theology. Rather than accent the uniqueness and otherness of one's own tradition, it is possible to acknowledge indebtedness and to proffer thanks for all contributions to one's patrimony. In Christendom this has been accomplished by acknowledging the New Testament's debt to the thought of the Old. This was psychologically palatable for Christians because the Jewish people had been and perhaps still were included in the plan of salvation. But once the plan of salvation is increasingly recognized as global in scope, borrowings from foreign sources are more readily acknowledged. A more generous appreciation of the religious accomplishments of other peoples results in a correspondingly more adequate scholarship. It also coincides with a posture of friendship.

A unity of interrelatedness

Though unity of doctrine is not discernible amidst the traditions, a unity of interrelationship can be traced. A world theology recognizes that faith emerges in multi-cultural contexts. In Christian history we readily observe that our tradition is not autonomous. The ingredients of Christianity have in significant part come from outside. The theologian finds it impossible to understand the Christian world-view in isolation. The major religions have all interacted with other streams of ideas and practices. They have directly interacted with, grown out of, or been influenced by the others.

A single tradition cannot be understood in itself, but rather is a formation out of the religious past. Smith sees the various religions as strands in a global whole that interweave in multiple and often hidden ways. He underlines the fact that this interdependence is newly discovered. The various strands have interacted for centuries, and in some instances millennia, without this exchange being observed. Such monumental blindness can be attributed to an undeveloped state of historical science and to exclusivism that leads one to ignore interconnectedness for the sake of venerating an us/them dichotomy.

Examples of interconnectedness are legion in the history of religions. One might begin with the widespread custom taken from our palaeolithic heritage (and still vital today) of burying the dead.[45] Nearer in time, we note the presence of Zoroastrian motifs in early Christian writings, initially borrowed by exilic Jews. The New Testament is pervaded with Persian imagery in its drama of cosmic dualism, angelology, eschatological portraits of hell and towering personifications of evil. If one turns to religious practice one discovers that Roman Catholics are indebted to Islamic influence for their use of prayer beads, while Muslims in turn are indebted to Hindu tradition, as are Buddhists. In a striking illustration of inter-cultural linkage, Smith describes a visit to California in which he unexpectedly observed that Catholics arriving from Europe and Buddhists arriving from Japan both shared the discipline of prayer beads. The custom had become global with participants unaware that they took part in a common inheritance.[46]

Many fundamental concepts, symbols and practices found in the earth's religions are trans-cultural. Though they are always appropriated in a unique manner, they cannot be said to belong to a single tradition. Christians cannot claim the symbol of God, or Satan, or the concept of scripture, or the idea of prophecy, or the practice of prayer, or the ritual of baptism, as singularly their own. Each of these items belongs to the earth's storehouse of religious elements. Therefore Smith asks scholars to rethink the meaning of all of these items in world historical terms. If Christian intellectuals viewed their church's handling of the symbol 'God' as but one of many participations in the evolution of a widespread symbol, they would arrive at a more total perception of humankind's experience of personal divinity. To reflect on the way each culture reworks transcultural concepts like 'God', 'grace' or 'prayer' would lower psychological barriers beween communities.

One of Smith's concerns in describing the hidden inter-lacings of religious history is to demonstrate that the context in which persons come to salvation has in large measure been bequeathed us by those very others who in old-line soteriology were referred to as the damned! Freed to think in more universal ways, Christian scholars can re-vision religious boundaries as more porous, and thus become sensitized to the facts of interconnectedness rather than the myths of separateness.

Though a unity of interconnectedness can be illustrated, less obvious unities are also apparent. Pervasive forms of unity larger than specific traditions also exist. For religious communities often participate in overarching cultural attitudes that are simultaneously shared by several traditions. One might think of the spiritual mood and intellectual style that Jews, Muslims and Christians shared in, known as mediaeval scholasticism.[47] One can trace a milieu in the mood of asceticism that religiously stirred the earth for millennia. Those under its spell sought salvation in withdrawal from material concerns.[48] Yet this perspective is not found in the period of Abraham or the early Vedas. It is likewise scarce today, and not readily understood by the this-worldly wisdom of the present. For a new mood has penetrated all traditional societies that is earth affirming and earth transforming.

In order to promote an awareness in which theologians 'know men and women of all religious groups and all centuries as one community', Smith hopes to write a world history of faith century by century rather than system by system, as is customary, to portray our hidden interconnectedness.[49] He also asks that a global history of faith be prepared by scholars from all religions, and monitored by an international society of scholarship. This would insure the existence of a confirmed apprehension of the faith heritage of the earth.

Another task lies in forging an international vocabulary to describe religious existence, so that scholars can think together in shared terms and enter into dialogue with the surety that their positions are understood.[50] Such a venture will require an expansion of familiar Christian terms such as God, theology, salvation, etc. Each word of Western origin will be enlarged to bear multi-cultural freight. 'Salvation', for example, with its Christian connotations, will be amended in order to describe a variety of spiritual transformations from self- to reality-centred existence.[51] 'Theology' itself may prove an unworthy candidate for global thought. The Christian goal of under-standing (*logos*) God (*theos*) may appear presumptuous to orthopractic theists. Jews and Muslims may prefer to compose a morality of comparative religion rather than a theology.[52] Non-theists, humanists and Buddhists may not recognize their way of grasping truth in 'theology', even though they may applaud the direction in which it points. Since 'theology' may prove too culture-specific, Smith submits 'transcendentology' – which he hopes is an acceptable cipher for discussions about multiple apprehensions of truth/reality.[53]

Each of Smith's proposals – to reflect generically, to write global histories of faith century by century, to have histories of religious consciousness monitored by cross-cultural teams of scholars, to generate new terminologies – presupposes an acceptance that one's religious culture is but one of many paths to the Divine. In all his publications since *The Faith of Other Men* (1960), one discerns an intellectual and moral challenge to advance beyond parochial absorption in a segment of religious history (one's religion) to a larger view of that segment's relation to the whole. In the modern age when all communities are minorities, no culture can pretend to glorify itself as the Middle Kingdom. The West can no longer in good faith evaluate world history in terms of its antecedent value for Western civilizations. De-centring is necessary to create an identification with 'the only community there is, the one to which I know that I truly belong . . . the community world-wide and history-long of humankind'.[54]

Though Smith's universalism is unabashedly idealistic, it is not fanciful. In the West students in high schools and universities have for the first time access to the religious teachings of the race. Many have come to experience themselves as heirs of a global religious treasure. The time when Greece, Rome and Palestine constituted the West's sole value foundation is past. The reality of a universal consciousness in which the parts, the members of the faith communities, are awakening to an awareness of the entire religious process is becoming increasingly apparent. 'The process of each is becoming conscious of the process of all'; Smith continues in Hegelian terms: 'the ongoing process is becoming self-conscious'.[55]

This evolution will proceed as an academic study of comparative religion advances, as international scholarship increases, as insights and spiritual practices are increasingly shared and as each religious community rightly insists that others represent them fairly. Cross-cultural borrowings will likewise persist, whether in small matters like the Muslims' adoption of the West's Christmas card custom for their own 'Id festival or the Buddhist adoption of a Western institution in the setting up of YMBAs.[56] More profoundly, Catholic priests will continue in their practice of zazen and Protestant ministers will experiment with techniques of yoga.

Though Smith does not describe in detail the effects that critical corporate self-consciousness will have on the trans-formation of Christianity, he does realize that a church engaged in authentic dialogue inevitably acquires an enlarged self-definition. When theologians embrace critical corporate self-consciousness as representatives of a church, their findings gradually enter the mainstream of Christianity. This process has occurred unconsciously in the past. Gautama, for example, was active in Christendom as a symbol of sanctity for a thousand years under the guise of St Josaphat, a young prince who renounced wealth to seek truth through ascetic discipline in the wilderness.[57] Nineteenth-century scholars, discovering the Buddha in mediaeval legend, exorcised it immediately. Smith prefers that we legitimize the church's earlier wisdom in revering the Buddha. For mediaeval piety correctly sensed the value of Gautama's quest. If today the church is to prove its coming of age in a pluralist world, it will move beyond unconscious borrowing to conscious assimilation. A fully awake incorporation now challenges the Christian scholar.

In 1941 H. R. Niebuhr argued that the Catholic/Protestant division could only be superseded when Protestants claimed Thomas Aquinas as their own and Catholics canonized Luther and Calvin.[58] Today Niebuhr's prescription for unity, which seemed fantastic in 1941, has largely come to pass. On the Catholic side we have seen Vatican II, and on the Protestant side we have a friendlier and more accurate portrait of both Aquinas and Catholic tradition. A still larger dream of unity exists in Smith's project. Like Niebuhr's fantasy it, too, appears improbable. And genuinely greater obstacles await it. For unlike Niebuhr's hope, it has its unifying focus in transcendent reality rather than in the shared memory of Christ. Yet despite this, theologians are beginning to respond to the task. A recent writer in the field of Buddhist/Christian dialogue has described what an expanded historical memory that included elements of Buddhism would mean for the church.

Gautama . . . is a figure of human history revered also by many Christians. But that is just a beginning. The story of the Buddhist saints and the expansion of Buddhism throughout East Asia is not yet a part of the effective historical memory of Christians. And the history of what took place in Palestine remains outside the effective historical memory of Buddhists. If Buddhism and Christianity are to grow together, both must cultivate a global memory.[59]

Exclusivism and revelation

Exclusivists will naturally object to placing Christian truth on the same plane as that of non-Christian religions. A popular objection has it that extra-Christian world-views are the handiwork of men, while Christian faith is a response to the specific revelatory act of God. This describes the Neo-Orthodox position inspired by Karl Barth, who made much of the distinction between revelation as the divine Self-disclosure and religions as idolatrous creations.[60] Smith takes a less dogmatic, more empirical position, and finds revelation, like faith, to be a universal phenomenon, of which Christian revelation is one significant form.

Revelation for Smith is a humane rather than objective concept; that is, revelation does not refer to a body of objective revealed truth existing apart from the interpretative activity of human receivers. He rejects an understanding of revelation as the communication of divine propositional truths. For Smith, God does not disclose propositions; rather He/She/It discloses Himself/Herself/Itself.

Revelation is best understood in bi-polar terms. It is insepar-able from finite perceptions of the Real. An analogy exists between understanding revelation and understanding the aesthetic act. In aesthetics a perennial question is whether the work of art is beautiful in itself or whether beauty is a subjective projection. In a bi-polar aesthetic genuine artistic perception occurs in the interaction of the work of art with the sensitivity of an individual properly educated to respond to a particular form of beauty.[61]

Revelation can also be thought of as requiring both objective and subjective poles, with reality (God) as the objective pole (experienced frequently as a transcendent subject), and a receiver, conditioned by the symbols of a tradition, as the subjective pole. Apart from this interaction, revelation does not occur. This view is consistent with Smith's overall under-standing of knowledge, which exists not in books or external symbols but in acts of thought. Each generation must discover the living message in their religious inheritance. Revelation cannot be passed on in the form of objective statements, though such statements have potential for becoming revelatory in each generation.

Revelation cannot be whittled down to human interpretation. The infinite confronts the finite subject in the revelatory act and does not yield to human manipulation. The Qur'an given to Muhammad is instructive in this regard. Smith argues that the divine Word made available to Muhammad was limited in expression and comprehension by the capacities of Arabian culture and the personality of the Prophet. The divine reality is both revealed and veiled in the Qur'an, which may be thought of as 'the closest approximation to the Eternal Word that Muhammad could rise to'.[62] If the language about Muhammad 'rising' sounds excessively voluntaristic, one should note that Smith would accept the alternative reading: the closest approximation that Muhammad could be raised to.

Smith appears to understand the prophetic experience of Muhammad and other prophets as an inbreaking of creative perception from imaginative depths that are in contact with, or are contacted by the divine.[63] It follows that a similar account applies to Christian revelation. Smith does not directly comment on the implications of this position for christology, but it would suggest that Jesus' awareness of God was also formed by his religious ambience. The case is somewhat different in that incarnational revelation is not primarily a revealed speech, as in Islam, but a revealed exemplary life. Yet whether revelation has its locus in words or in persons, the principle remains the same – that which is human and finite is incapable of fully revealing the divine.

One may be disturbed by Smith's position that denies revealed propositions; for if this is the case, how can theologians speak at all of the truths of Christianity? Is not theology's purpose to speak rationally, and therefore in propositions, about Christian revelation? Smith is not recommending that theologians be reduced to silence. Nor does he deny that something true about the universe is given in the Gospel. It is more true to say that God is love than to say that God is hate. But the nature of love must be understood analogically, for it is dangerously incomplete to assert unqualifiedly that God is love. The divine is often experienced as the Holy One whose presence is frightening and partially annihilating to those in the grasp of self-centred existence. But the God of Love and the God of Holiness cannot be known apart from human involvement. Theologians can speak of such involvements and compare them with other types of experience. They can compare religious utterances with other forms of speech. In this activity it is possible to say that there are truths that are more adequate than not. It is truer to say that God is Holy than that God is Polluted. But such truths are problematic when wrested from the rich symbols of personal encounter. Lastly, it is not propositions that are true for Smith but the meaning they have for those who use them. Therefore Smith holds that religious truths should not be accepted unless they have been personally apprehended.[64]

It is significant that Smith calls himself a rationalist.[65] The meaning of 'rationalist', however, is not at first apparent. It means several things, such as: (a) that he is an intellectual dedicated to a reasonable and a consistent analysis of religious issues; (b) that he places himself under the ideal of reason and recognizes its legitimate demands; and (c) that religious experience is about the truth of value, and that this can be unified with, and does not deny, the truth of facts. Smith is not a rationalist in the popular sense of one who rationalizes away or subjectivizes experience of the Divine. His rationalism is further qualified in that he does not find the tools of reason adequate to encompass the Real. When applied to revelation, Smith's rationalism means that supernatural knowledge can not be inserted into history. Revelation is a creative modification of the religious patrimony. The Qur'an, the Bible, the Bhagavad Gita are creative elaborations of past religious insight.

Smith conceives of revelation as a continuous process in the

life of a culture; he is critical of the over-emphasis on the part
of the reformers concerning the primacy of original revelation.
He names this focus the 'big bang theory of revelation'.[66] For
Smith the reformers' preoccupation with origins has had
negative consequences. Western scholarship has continuously
explored original revelations, assuming them to be the real or
essential meaning of a religion. In so doing they have by-passed
or minimized the significance of the developing communities'
later interpretations. The 'big bang' approach in scholarship is
in actuality a reflection of the Protestant rejection of the
Catholic principle of doctrinal development in time, of the
legitimacy of ongoing revelation. Yet, to be alive, revelation
must occur in the present tense. It is what the community
realizes in the now, not what it thinks about the past, that
constitutes the life of a community. In Christianity the Good
News is not something past but the divine as currently active.[67]
Smith is concerned that when excessive interest is placed on
prior revelations, individuals become detached from the more
urgent task of uncovering their ultimate concern today.

> . . . Western thought . . . tended to lose hold of those
> important facets of the earlier Christian tradition that stress
> the continuing contemporaneity of revelation; and gradually
> got pushed into a corner from which God's and even Christ's
> revelation seemed personally and historically remote. . .
> Muslim thinkers have been pushed in the same direction
> . . . Hindus almost not at all.[68]

As we have seen, Smith is critical of Christian exclusivism.
Though this position is rejected by a growing number of
Protestant and Catholic thinkers, it yet remains invincibly
embedded in the minds of millions of Christians. The Neo-
Orthodox position which dogmatically asserts that non-
Christian religions are devoid of revelation is deductive,
circular and non-empirical. It implicitly denies the importance
of observation and the possibility of verification. It has the
effect of inviting Christians to judge the religious life of
others without proper investigation. If one is acquainted with

spiritually evolved persons from non-Christian communities, the exclusivist asks one to deny one's perceptions. Such an approach minimizes the need for familiarity with the data of other religions, for such material is thought to be either spiritually valueless or perhaps even evil. Smith wonders whether this attitude is adopted by Christians towards friends in other communities or whether it is possible only by non-acquaintance and unconcern. If the latter, the exclusivist position objectivizes persons and implicitly recommends that Christians avoid any inter-cultural friendship that jointly explores the religious dimension.

The exclusivist argument is structurally similar to that of creationists in the last century. Then Christians 'knew' without investigation that the age of the earth must be 6,000 years, for geological empiricism must yield to the inspired propositions of scripture.[69] Most thoughtful persons in the church have rejected this form of science. Yet a substantial number of Christians continue to embrace a theory that dehumanizes the majority of the earth's population. In rejecting the evidence, millions remain in a position that is intellectually embarrassing and inter-personally alienating.

Smith is also forthright in his rejection of the exclusivism of St Paul. He insists that Paul was in error.[70] Further, Paul must be understood as one unfamiliar with religious thought outside the Roman world. It may also be doubted whether he was acquainted in any depth with the religio/philosophical life of the Empire. If revelation is non-propositional, Paul's exclusivism needs to be interpreted in a personal manner, either as a zealous error, or as a statement about his disenchantment with legalism.

If Christians are asked why they find their own revelation true, most probably they would answer that it works in their lives or that they have been grasped by its message. If they are mystically inclined, they will perhaps speak of an encounter with the Holy. Finding the recommended life of grace and love effective, they will speak of a journey from self to God-centredness. Personally, Christians 'know', though not with logical certainty, nor with the comfort of the knowledge of an external fact, that the God witnessed to in the life of Jesus is the God they encounter. There is nothing in this confession of lived truth that excludes the possibility of a similar verification in other communities. In fact there appears to be nothing in the nature of Christian experience that would require an exclusivist world-view.

A modified version of exclusivism has it that aside from the Christian tradition persons know God partially, whereas it is only in Christian revelation that one discovers the fullness of revelation. This standpoint is inextricably joined to a christology which affirms that God is (or was) fully revealed in Jesus Christ. Such a position conflicts with Smith's appraisal of the nature of revelation. For if revelation always entails a finite perception of Reality, it is not possible to speak of the full revelation of God in Christ. Because of this difficulty Smith states: 'God is not revealed fully in Jesus Christ to me, nor indeed to anyone that I have met; or that my historical studies have uncovered.'[71] This quotation perhaps marks Smith's most controversial departure from the majority Christian position. For he finds the traditional focus on salvation through Christ a stumbling-block in recognizing God's more universal saving activity. Christ is therefore not central in Smith's global theological vision. It would appear that Smith is espousing a totally pluralist view in which ontological claims for the finality of a unique savour cannot be made. Since revelation cannot offer proof of such a claim, Smith is content with the empirical observation that each religion has resources that point the faithful in the direction of the Real.

Smith is naturally aware of the seriousness of Christian commitment to the ultimacy of Christ.[72] Nevertheless, his pluralist concern points in the direction of a community of non-ultimate revelations, the revelation in Christ being one. From this standpoint Christ may be confessionally witnessed to as a personal ultimate, but this does not entail an absolute ontological claim. Loyalty to a particular path no longer requires the possession of a superior revelation. This does not mean that all revelations are of equal value. It does suggest that revelation be viewed in a more sociological manner, for it may be the case that certain forms of revelation are more adequate to the spiritual needs of particular cultures. Just as one might maintain one's Irish or French heritage in the ethnic mix of the United States, so too one might participate in global religious life in a Christian, Buddhist, Islamic, etc., fashion.

It is difficult for members of one religion to prove the superiority of its values to those of other communities. This is because members have been formed by, and appreciate, the very values they hope to convince the other of. Persons in a specific religion are therefore in a superior position to sense the excellence of their legacy. On the other hand, those outside the community will tend to miss its spiritual depth. At present no criteria exist to gauge the superiority of a given religion. Indeed the arrival of more adequate criteria await the future results of critical corporate self-consciousness and the formation of individuals sensitive to the excellence of many paths. Until critical corporate self-consciousness is firmly established, the question of merit cannot be adequately addressed.

One might with some justification object to Smith's understanding of the way Christ is mediated to Christians. Though it is correct in what it says, it nevertheless omits much. For Smith, Christ exists as a shifting image in the life of the church, a figure in history whose changing visage permits Christians to find a Messiah they can relate to.[73] Every generation reinterprets the Christ-image in large or minor ways, and through him finds ultimate meaning. Christians, however, who experience Christ in a Pauline manner and who apprehend him as a living and luminous Lord, will not find their faith represented in Smith's picture of the way Christ is active in Christian history. Though it is proper to delinate the changing face of Christ in Christian history, this sort of exercise does not leave space for an encounter with an actual resurrected person.

Smith's position is consistent with his rejection of the possibility of knowing supernatural realities other than the presence of God and transcendent value.[74] This, I believe, is a major difficulty in his writings; for his position implies that Paul did not encounter a resurrected Christ on the road to Damascus, but either was deluded or mistakenly perceived the general presence of God as a specific presence. Note that I am not pleading here for a special hearing for Christian mystical knowing alone. I know of few mystics who would be satisfied with Smith's minimalist interpretation of religious experience. Although Smith's classification has merit, the spiritual life is more complex than his representations. The New Testament, as one among many spiritual writings, is a storehouse of mystical and paranormal phenomena – numinous dreams, waking visions, apparitions, clairvoyance, spiritual healing, etc. Though Smith, I believe correctly, rejects the exaggerated Hindu belief about the omniscience of the *jivanmukta*, his minimalist account will not satisfy those accustomed to the rich phenomena of the spiritual life. This is perhaps another facet of his rationalism.

It is conceivable that we have not heard Smith's last word on the issue of revelation. He has acknowledged that his definition of revelation as the divine Self-disclosure has been set forth 'rather arbitrarily' and that it would require a lengthy discussion for its justification.[75] Should Smith decide to proceed with such a justification he will need to clarify a major question concerning the foundation of Christian revelation. Is the Christian tradition primarily constituted by the early community's recognition of undying value in the life of Jesus? Or is it more supernaturally constituted by the inbreaking of the exalted Christ into the awareness of his followers?

If the tradition is interpreted in the first manner, my objection concerning limiting the activity of Christ to a changing image in history stands. If the second alternative is chosen, it would seem that the religious mind is not limited to experiencing a divine presence and transcendent value, but is instead able to encounter specific transcendent facts – in this instance a risen Lord, in other traditions perhaps a bodhisattva.

A further objection to Smith's notion of revelation is that it ultimately leads to a severing of concern with the historical Jesus. Though I concur with Smith's concern for correcting the 'big bang' concept of revelation, so that the study of origins does not prevent us from attending to the developing drama of faith, I fear that his emphasis upon the existential meaning of faith might lead to a severing of symbol from history. The primitive church witnessed to the fact that the historical Jesus and the resurrected Christ were one. Yet in Smith's model of revelation it would seem to follow that if some future manuscript unearthed the fact that Jesus was an imposter or rogue, the Christian tradition would nonetheless remain intact. For the symbol rather than the historical reality of Jesus would continue to inspire religious individuals. The gospel story would be retained for its poetic truth as long as it remained sufficiently attractive to awaken faith. Without questioning the revelatory quality of poetry or myth, it would seem that a demonstration of the unworthiness of the historical Jesus would rupture the tradition so radically that it is doubtful whether the Christian strand of religious history could continue as a viable path of salvation.

Smith and christology

Smith correctly identifies the core of Christian exclusivism in christology. If the Christ event is viewed as unique in securing salvation or in revealing God's saving intent, then those outside the Christian community are either outside God's saving work or participate in the divine life in an inferior manner. This dilemma is at the centre of Smith's assertion that 'we [Christians] have had or are having our Copernican Revolution, but not our Newton'.[76] Just as Copernicus upset mankind's perception of the unique status of the earth by recognizing it as one of several planets moving round the sun, so too Christians have recently realized that their form of faith represents but one legitimate apprehension of the Real. With Christianity no longer at the centre of the religious world, each religion can be recognized as having a partial perspective on the divine. Unfortunately, Christian theology has not seriously considered the practical and theoretical consequences of this reconceptualization. Nor has it arrived at a convincing theology that integrates the new information about global religious faith in a way comparable to Newton's organization of the data of astronomy in the formulation of universal gravitation.

To hold Christ as the absolute revelation of God theoretically blocks other communities from having independent access to the divine. This difficulty is reflected in the World Council of Churches' inability to formulate a unified policy concerning the soteriological significance of non-Christian traditions.[76] Some members of the Council continue to hold to the Barthian distinction between faith and religion, finding in non-Christian traditions only the efforts of sinful man. This position, though denying God's activity in non-Christian communities, should not be conceived of as a radical exclusivism. Barth himself was a universalist who viewed the Christ event as sufficient for the saving of humankind. Nevertheless, Barth refers to the Christ event as the sole sufficient source of salvation and denies a soteriological role to other religions. However, signs of a more generous attitude towards foreign traditions are apparent even within the evolving Neo-Orthodox movement. Jürgen Moltmann has affirmed the importance of inter-religious dialogue and has rejected the previous Neo-Orthodox premise that the faiths of non-Christian communities are necessarily the 'self-assertion of man'.[77]

Within Catholicism, John Paul II in his inaugural address *Redemptor Hominis* insisted that salvation occurs beyond the church.

> The human person – every person without exception – has been redeemed by Christ; because Christ is united to the human person . . . even if the individual may not realize this fact.[78]

Hans Küng has further argued that God in Christ works through the world's religions to execute salvation, even though

Christianity remains the sign of what they are eventually to become.[79] Karl Rahner has coined the phrase 'anonymous Christian' to refer to those who unwittingly receive the grace of Christ outside the church.[80]

The difficulty with each of these positions lies in its insistence that spiritual transformation comes only from Christ and is made available only through the Christ event. For Buddhists, for Jews, for Jains, for all, Christ remains the guarantor of their salvation. In each case the church alone knows the origin of grace. If salvation is thought to take place in other communities, this is because spiritual reality conforms to the message of the church. A Christian one-upmanship is thus always near the surface. Smith's position in contrast does not have this difficulty since he does not share the classical understanding of the Christ event in which an objective estrangement between humanity and God was bridged through the work of Christ. For Smith, Christ has a revealing rather than an atoning significance. He says: 'For me God is not dead, and the miracle of the Son is that He has shown the glory of the Father – and has enabled me to see and to receive it and to live in it through grace.'[81]

Contemporary Catholic statements on the saving significance of non-Christian religions are no doubt improvements over earlier and cruder forms of exclusivism. They ensure that at least second-class status is granted to non-Christian views of religious truth. The danger of the new position lies in the fact that other communities can never share an equal spiritual status with Christianity. These communities can never have anything as important to offer to Christians as Christians have to offer to them.

For this reason Smith is critical of christological approaches to a theology of world religions. Christology operates as the central prop in Christian absolutism. Yet any form of absolutism prevents the Christian community from becoming a democratic member of the earth's religions. Smith advises theologians wishing to work with a pluralist model of religious truth to move away from a christocentric to a theocentric orientation. He accuses the World Council of Churches of having become 'unitarian of the Son' and protests that 'if Christians insist that Christ is the centre of their lives, it is time that we rediscover that God is the centre of the universe'.[82]

In his article 'The Christian in a Religiously Plural World' Smith asks that the doctrine of the Trinity be reinterpreted to ensure a recognition that other paths have access to the divine.[83] In so doing Smith wants Christians to remember that God is not only the Son, but also the Father, and thus Creator and Spirit, and therefore universal spiritual power.[84] One must, however, ask if it is necessary to de-emphasize the Second Person in order to move toward an appreciation of God's universal saving activity. Smith appears not to distinguish between Jesus of Nazareth, understood as the human actualization of the Logos, and the Logos understood as God in his universal revealing and saving activity. For the operation of the Logos need not be limited to, nor exclusively contained within, Jesus of Nazareth.[85]

This Logos christology has received a recent bold depiction in John Cobb's *Beyond Dialogue*, where the author affirms that the saving activity that Christians name Christ (Logos) is the same activity which Amida Buddhists name Amida.[86] In this christology, loyalty to Christ as the immanent soteriological principle is not dogmatic, parochial or static. It refers comprehensively to a loyalty to the transforming work of God in the earth – a loyalty that is necessary for all dialogue partners if they are to grow beyond traditional view-points. The Christ impulse is here seen as creatively pressuring members of each religion towards greater mutual acceptance.

Though I object to elements of Smith's rationalism and to his minimizing of christology, I agree with his concern to enlarge the Christian world-view with insight from other paths.[87] When Smith speaks of the necessity of viewing revelation as 'continuing contemporaneity' he makes known his opposition to a static concept of revelation.[88] He challenges the Christian community to hear the gospel in fresh ways appropriate to a pluralist vision. In this his concern is identical to those advocating a universalist Logos theology.[89]

The function of missions

A revision of christology has practical consequences for missions, and in this area Smith is more than a theorist, having spent a number of years as a missionary in what is today Pakistan. Much of his ire against exclusivism arose from his experience of friendship with a variety of persons from non-Christian traditions. His writings on missions have had weighty significance for the United Church of Canada. The article 'The Christian in a Religiously Plural World' was first presented as an address in 1961 to a joint meeting of the Canadian Theological Society, the Canadian Society of Church History, and the Canadian Society of Biblical Studies. It included a repudiation of exclusivism on empirical and moral grounds, and was directed against the then official position of the United Church's commission on faith which held: 'Without the particular knowledge of God and Jesus Christ men do not really know God at all.'[90] Smith's essay was soon to become a catalyst for a new church position that emerged in *World Mission: Report of the Commission on World Missions* (1966). Reversing earlier opinion, the report concluded that the creative and redemptive operations of the divine are to be found throughout the earth's religious traditions.[91]

If Smith has been effective in producing change in the official position of his own church, he has also proved correct in foreseeing the shape of a new theological mind-set in regard to non-Christian religions. As early as 1961 he accurately predicted that:

> . . . a time will come, perhaps fairly soon, when men will see that if the Christian Revelation is valid, then it follows from this very fact that other men's faith is genuine, is the form through which God encounters those other men, and saves them.[92]

By emphasizing that God is the type of God witnessed to in the ministry of Christ, Smith convincingly articulated a developing mood in the church which feels that the divine concern for humankind must indeed be global if it is to be worthy of a benevolent Deity. This evaluation can be found in the writing of later theologians such as Küng, Rahner, Hick and Cobb, and has come to pervade the atmosphere of dialogical studies.

Smith does not urge the abandonment of missionary activity. He would find objectionable fashionable denunciations of missionary work which hold that missionaries have merely been the instruments of colonialism and/or triumphalism. Instead, his evaluation of the missionary adventure is cautiously mixed. He strenuously criticizes the often crude attempts at proselytizing which failed to consider the sociological, psychological, institutional and economic effects of conversion.[93] The habit of snatching human beings from their inherited contexts has proved both naive and disastrous. However, on the positive side, Smith applauds much of the medical and educational work of the missions. Yet despite this acknowledgment of achievement he fears that the majority of Christians remain dangerously uninstructed about the darker side of missionary activity. There is also the difficulty that the average Christian has invested missionary work with an aura of sanctity that has prevented a critical evaluation of the degrees of missionary complicity in the mercenary faith of imperialism.[94]

One acquainted solely with Smith's writing on comparative religion and unaware of his attitudes towards missions might conclude that Smith's allegiance to pluralism would eventuate in a complete rejection of Christian missions. Such a conclusion would prove wide of the mark. Smith does not renounce the benefits missions have wrought. One of these is the resurgence of regenerated Asian communities which arose in response to the colonial and missionary assault. Ironically, the leaders of this resurgence were often aided by a solid training at missionary colleges. Nor does Smith renounce the wider

Christian concern to spread its perception of religious truth. Rather, he calls upon Christians, and indeed all persons, to sensitize themselves to religious truth wherever it appears. In this context the Christian message is seen as an aspect of world religious insight that needs, along with other messages of faith, to be made known.

A genuinely pluralist approach to the problem of missions requires a rethinking of missionary activity. One fundamental alteration consists in revising the primary theological goal of conversion – a goal that has been embarrassingly elusive. An instance of this failure may be seen in Smith's remark about his experience in a missionary college in Lahore.

> No one doubted that the community and goodwill created by the college were of outstanding value, as was the educational service provided. On the other hand, there apparently had not been a conversion within the missionary college at any time during the present century, and none seemed likely.[95]

One might inquire why conversions had not taken place. Missionaries had preached the good news with diligence, had evidenced their ideals in faithful service, and had received the grateful respect of a benefited community. Nonetheless, their efforts had minimal effect on conversions. The missionaries had experienced at first hand a phenomenon readily observable in the modern world. It appears that wherever the world religions interact, conversions are rare. Perhaps conversion is unnecessary because the indigenous people are already adequately related to the divine via their own culture. This conclusion does not imply that non-Christians have nothing of significance to learn from Christians. But it does suggest that Christians likewise have much to learn from the very persons they seek to convert.

Smith expects few conversions to Christianity in the twentieth century.[96] More generally, he expects few conversions from any community to another. He does happily note that missionary activity has turned out to be a global affair and is multi-cultural rather than merely Western. For while Christians continue to dispatch their missionaries, Hindus, Muslims and Buddhists likewise send representatives to the West.[97] In this situation Smith urges a new understanding of the purpose of missionary work, an understanding in which proselytizing plays no part.[98] Once exclusivism has been disclaimed, the urgency of making converts falls away. In lieu of the older goal, Smith calls upon the Christian community to consider a new vocation of recognizing the message of salvation in a variety of religious paths.[99]

This challenge requires Christians to renounce their well-publicized arrogance towards their counterparts in other communities. Such a reununciation should not merely be understood as spiritual hygiene. It also has the more specific purpose of releasing Christians from the assumption that if the Christian form of faith is true, all others must be false. The converse of this logic is that if the faith of a non-Christian is valid, then the Christian form of faith must be false. Since truth and falsity in the religious domain have ultimate consequences, this results in a vested interest in the damnation of other peoples. This fearful attitude, whether subconscious or deliberate, is diluted in the instance of Christians who, while not damning their peers, assume that they nevertheless have an inferior form of faith and are spiritually inadequate. On the other hand, if the faith of others is recognized as adequate, the Christian is liable to feel that his own form of faith is inferior. Recognizing that the emotional consequences of this pattern of thought are spiritually unworthy, Smith holds that the fitting response to the salvation of non-Christians is joy in the multi-faceted activity of divine love.[100]

Smith sees polite disagreement continuing in the future over the respective excellence of the various paths. Yet in a pluralist future such disagreement will be sublimated and redeemed. Competitive impulses still remaining may be resolved in more neighbourly ways. The church for instance may compete to outdistance other communities in an accurate appreciation and fair representation of other traditions, or some may wish to engage in a rivalry of reconciliation.[101]

Mutuality will require a language reform similar to that proposed for women and minorities. Smith suggests we discard the term 'non-Christian' when speaking of, and especially when speaking to, persons from a different faith community. He finds the phrase 'non-Christian' self-centred. It suggests that the earth is inhabited by two groups, namely Christians and others.[102] In an age when each religious group is a minority the church is called to rectify its language to find its realistic place in the scheme of salvation.

A church re-imaged by the demands of pluralism will see itself as one of many groups dedicated to preaching their forms of good news. The new missionary will no longer inquire how he or she can save the lost, but rather how he or she may contribute in the building of a world community. Such changes will considerably alter the missionary's self-image; and in this spirit Smith has redefined the contemporary missionary.

> The missionary, if he is to escape from being a slightly absurd and slightly pathetic proselytizer, must be a man who feels that his religious community has caught a certain vision of God, has seen an aspect of ultimate truth, which he wants to contribute to the general search for God and truth in which men of other communities are also engaged.[103]

A supplementary definition has it that a missionary is a 'man who deliberately participates in the history of another faith'.[104]

In earlier days, when cultures were less involved, a missionary crossed oceans to work in exotic lands. Now the exotic is ordinary, or at least familiar to many. In fact, many people are today partial missionaries. Those who sympathetically discuss the religious visions of those outside the West take part, however slightly, in another culture. Of such involvement there are many degrees, for cultural convergence occurs at different rates for different persons. The participation is multilateral and escalating.

One might consider the many Christians seized by the

teachings of Mahatma Gandhi, who himself exhibited a partial involvement in the Christian tradition. Consider that prior to the current (1983–1985) resurgence of interest in Gandhi, the Mahatma was shaking the heart of American civilization through his Christian disciple Martin Luther King. A growing confluence of world thought exists today in which Muslims write their reactions to Karl Barth, while borrowing concepts from Paul Tillich, and in which Christians are stimulated by Ramanuja. The result is the creation of conditions in which each culture participates in all cultures. As this occurs, the methods, thoughts and concerns of those interacting will be mutually interiorized (in part), and will come to form a portion of one another's world picture.

The new missionary is historically unusual in that he or she is an invited guest rather than a trespasser in the house of another civilization. Smith holds that the modern missionary must be a welcome participant in the host culture, just as Tillich was in Tokyo, as Aurobindo was at Oxford, and as Radhakrishnan was at Harvard.[105] But Smith selects Martin Buber as his nominee for model missionary. For Buber did not understand his purpose as the conversion of Christians to Judaism, yet benefited his Christian readers with writings that drew deeply from Jewish wisdom.[106] Buber is also an exceptional candidate in being unusually prepared to speak to his audience as an expert in both New Testament and Christian mystical studies. He bore the mark of missionary excellence in his ability to understand and represent the tradition he addressed.[107] He further made apparent his respect for the unique form of salvation witnessed to in Christian tradition. Though few will be able to approach Buber's scholastic attainments they will be able, one hopes, to emulate his sensitivity to the faith of others.

The guest principle requires recognition that Christians do not have the moral authority to send missionaries to lands where they are undesired. It also implies that Christians (or devotees of any path) who aspire to share in a converging world forfeit their integrity if they are not prepared to invite

missionaries from the countries to which their own missionaries are sent. Conventional missionary commissioning was
strictly unilateral. But Smith proposes that mission boards
plan their activities with an equal number of representatives
from host countries in order to arrive at a collaborative decision
as to what needs the missionaries might meet. Those who wish
to serve are asked not to impose their version of the good upon
others. This position seriously defends the notion that the
divine is to be heard in the needs of others; the importance of
practising the art of listening is apparent.

Smith's recommendations are appropriate to the realistic
prediction that no world religion is likely to conquer another.
The great religions have proved themselves in their collisions.
They have met each other, sometimes furiously, and have not
failed. In past ages conflict between the gods was one of
humankind's ways of sifting the more profound, more moral
and more true from the less. The fact that the great traditions
have clashed and not collapsed leads one to suspect that in each
case abiding worth is present. Yet one wonders if Smith's
recommendations apply as easily to smaller tribal cultures.
Though he writes primarily for members of the great
traditions, containing the earth's majority, it would be interesting to hear his thoughts on proselytizing among animists.
For it does appear that in the historical process the gods and
the ways of tribal cultures fall to or become absorbed within
the larger and more complex world tradition. One wonders if
Smith would find this type of thinking too Hegelian, élitist or
impersonalist.

One might doubt whether Smith's pacific approach to
the religions is in all instances the best one for solidifying
relationships between members of the religions. Simple
psychological observation indicates that love and struggle are
not foreign to each other. Quarrels often appear when persons
are emotionally near and affect is strong. There is not only a
truth that is born of compassion but one that is hewn out of
struggle. But Smith may have already implicitly included this
reflection in his thought. His programme for the religious

communities to incorporate multi-cultural insight would have the effect of drawing persons into a closer family of shared vision. Perhaps he hesitates to speak of the benefits of honest conflict, finding that the networks of colloquy are still too fragile for the intensity of family quarrelling.

Smith's argument against the continuation of proselytism is appropriate in the light of Christianity's arrogance towards alternative forms of salvation, and in the face of the gospel's inability to convince the majority of the earth. But there may still be the need for a certain form of proselytizing that Smith does not explicitly mention. In the cities of the world there are hundreds of thousands of spiritually homeless persons. Is it not urgent, and would it not be compassionate, for the various religions to continue to preach their good news to the hopeless and faithless? In the future of missions the Christian response to a conversion to Buddhism, by one grasped in the sickness of anomie, should be one of gladness. For he or she who was lost has been found.

There is still one other form of proselytizing that will not cease. Given the nature of critical corporate self-consciousness, that which is true or excellent or good in each community, will continue to speak with the authority of an integrated life.

CONCLUSION

If we look back on the last five chapters we see the heart of Wilfred Cantwell Smith's thought. Faith is a human quality that must be grasped by a combination of objective scholarship and disciplined sympathy. Belief is not faith, and what passes for belief in modern times has never been the central concern of prior religions. Truth is a personalist category and must be understood contextually. Critical corporate self-consciousness is the means to guarantee that one has seen the faith of another and has encountered in some degree his or her personal truth. The future of theology lies in the creation of a global theology that will be the product of truly cosmopolitan minds. We have met these ideas in some detail and have realized that they contain more than academic significance. I therefore think it fitting to end this work by summarizing the practical consequences of Smith's thought. In each instance a challenge is offered to the way in which scholars interact with persons from other cultures. In each instance institutional changes are involved.

In religious studies the participant is to be included as a partner in verification. In seminary and college planning, chairs are to be established for scholar-representatives of other religions. In the field of theology, theologizing itself is to become an inter-cultural operation. In the social sciences the inward and ideal elements of a culture are to be studied as being as significant as the hard data of economics or politics. As in religious studies, courses dealing with foreign traditions are to be taught by or with scholars from those cultures. A mixture of students from the West and from the cultures studied is encouraged. In matters of church organization, mission boards are to plan their activities with members of the communities they seek to serve. The goal of conversion is to be replaced with that of service and mutual understanding. Western philosophers are called to expand their community by including the philosophers of the rest of the earth, thereby raising the level of reflection to a global scale. The entrance fee for all members is a patient study of the multiple ways of perceiving truth. And in the field of library science Smith has written about the need to re-write classification systems for each culture, since other cultures divide reality in different ways than the categories of Western librarianship. [108]

The implications of these suggestions have political importance and will press the members of nation states to think in world terms. The future seems caught up in Smith's project and only the future will tell if his programme is prophetic.

NOTES

Introduction and 1 An Understanding of Faith

1. Wilfred Cantwell Smith, *Islam in Modern History*, Princeton: University Press 1957; *The Meaning and End of Religion*, with a Foreword by John Hick, New York: Harper and Row, and London: SPCK, paperback ed. 1978.

2. Wilfred Cantwell Smith, *Faith and Belief*, Princeton: Princeton University Press 1979.

3. Daud Rahbar, review of *The Meaning and End of Religion*, by Wilfred Cantwell Smith, in *Journal of Bible and Religion* 32, July 1964, p. 277.

4. Wilfred Cantwell Smith, *The Meaning and End of Religion*, p. 183.

5. Wilfred Cantwell Smith, 'The Christian in a Religiously Plural World', in *Religious Diversity*, ed. Willard G. Oxtoby, New York: Harper and Row, 1976, p. 11.

6. Smith is primarily concerned with living traditions, rather than small or pre-historical groups of interest to anthropologists, and with traditions that contain the earth's majority of religious persons. As illustrations of his focus upon the major religious traditions, see: Wilfred Cantwell Smith, 'Comparative Religon: Whither – and Why?', in *Religious Diversity*, pp. 144–5; 'Religously Divided History Approaches Self-Consciousness', in *Religious Diversity*, p. 101.

7. Wilfred Cantwell Smith, 'Participation, The Changing Christian Role in Other Cultures', in *Religious Diversity*, p. 137.

8. Smith, *The Meaning and End of Religion*, p. 49.

9. Ibid., pp. 156–7. For a clear presentation of the relationship between faith and tradition, consult Antonio Robert Gualtieri, 'Faith, Tradition, and Transcendence: A Study of Wilfred Cantwell Smith', *Canadian Journal of Theology* 15, April 1969. This article was described in 1973 as 'the only treatment of Smith's thought more extensive than a book review' by Gordon E. Pruett, 'History, Transcendence,

and World Community in the work of Wilfred Cantwell Smith',
Journal of the American Academy of Religion 41, December 1973, p. 578.
Though a handful of articles have appeared since this remark, the
amount of serious material on Smith's thought remains small.

10. John Hick, Foreword to *The Meaning and End of Religion*,
p. xvii.

11. The actual variety within the Christian tradition is often
overlooked by those who are comforted by the idea of a doctrinally
unified church. For a more realistic presentation of the plurality of
Christianities as viewed by an historian of religion, the reader may
wish to consult Ninian Smart, *In Search of Christianity*, New York:
Harper and Row 1979.

12. Emmanuel Rackman, review of *The Meaning and End of
Religion*, by Wilfred Cantwell Smith, in *Jewish Social Studies* 27,
October 1965, pp. 273–4.

13. This early publication (1963) predates the intense contemporary
concern with sexist language. In later works such as *Faith and Belief*
(1979), *Belief and History* (1977), *Towards a World Theology* (1981),
Smith consistently refers to male and female individuals as persons.
His methodological approach to the study of persons (critical
corporate self-consciousness) is consonant with feminist concerns.
See *Towards a World Theology*, London: Macmillan and Philadelphia:
The Westminster Press 1981, pp. 69–72, for his discussion of the
inadequacy of white male social researchers in understanding both
women and black subjects. Further, Smith has long been concerned
with women's rights. See *Modern Islam in India: A Social Analysis*,
rev. ed. London: V. Gollancz, 1946; reprinted New York: Russell
and Russell 1972, pp. 74–84, for a trenchant analysis of male domination in Islamic India.

14. Smith, *The Meaning and End of Religion*, pp. 44, 47. It is not
accidental that an excellent summary of Smith's distinctions between
faith and belief can be found in an important psychological study of
faith by James W. Fowler, *Stages of Faith: The Psychology of Human
Development and the Quest for Meaning*, New York: Harper and Row
1981, pp. 9–15. Both Fowler and Smith are interested in separating
vital faith from propositional belief. Both combine therapeutic and
intellectual concerns.

15. Smith, 'Traditional Religions and Modern Culture', in *Religious
Diversity*, pp. 72–5.

16. Wilfred Cantwell Smith, 'Religious Atheism? Early Buddhist
and Recent American', in *Comparative Religion: The Charles Strong
Trust Lectures*, ed. John Bowman, Leiden: E. J. Brill 1972, p. 74;
'Secularity and the History of Religion', in *The Spirit and Power of*

Christian Secularity, ed. Albert Schlitzer, Notre Dame: University of Notre Dame Press 1969, p. 48.

17. For illustrations of the significance of 'through' see Wilfred Cantwell Smith, *Belief and History*, Charlottesville: University Press of Virginia, 1977, p. 93; 'Religious Atheism? Early Buddhist and Recent American', pp. 68–9.

18. Wilfred Cantwell Smith, 'The Finger That Points to the Moon': Reply to Per Kvaerne', *Temenos*. Helsinki, 9, 1973, p. 172.

19. Ibid. For further elaborations of 'the shape of faith' see Smith, *Belief and History*, pp. 127–8, n. 44.

20. Smith, 'Religious Atheism', pp. 83–4.

21. Smith, *Faith and Belief*, p. 12.

22. See Smith, *Islam in Modern History*, pp. 8–9, 210–19, for an analysis of the effects of unobservable factors in human behaviour.

23. Smith, *Faith and Belief*, p. 3. See also Wilfred Cantwell Smith, 'Non-Western Studies: The Religious Approach', in *A Report on an Invitational Conference on the Study of Religion in the State University, Held October 23–25, 1964 at Indiana University Medical Center*, New Haven: The Society for Religion in Higher Education 1965, p. 58.

24. Smith, *Belief and History*, p. 25.

25. Smith, 'Traditional Religions and Modern Culture', p. 72. See also: Smith, 'Secularity and the History of Religion', pp. 42–44; 'The Islamic Near East: Intellectual Role of Librarianship', *Library Quarterly* 35, 1965, p. 287; 'Non-Western Studies: The Religious Approach', p. 67; *The Faith of Other Men*, p. 17.

26. Smith, *Faith and Belief*, p. 139.

27. Ibid., p. 137.

28. Ibid., p. 142.

29. Ibid., p. 138.

30. Ibid., p. 330, n. 3. Smith's conception of the essentially cultural nature of man, wherein human 'nature' may be described as the capacity to be formed in terms of a culture, parallels, but was arrived at independently from a similar understanding found in Clifford Geertz, 'The Impact of the Concept of Culture on the Concept of Man', in *New Views of the Nature of Man*, ed. John R. Platt, Chicago: University Press 1965, pp. 93–118.

31. Ibid., p. 70.

32. Wilfred Cantwell Smith, 'The Study of Religion and the Study of the Bible', in *Religious Diversity*, p. 55.

33. Per Kvaerne, ' "Comparative Religion: Whither – and Why?" A Reply to Wilfred Cantwell Smith', *Temenos*, Helsinki, 9, 1973, pp. 162–3.

34. Ibid., p. 161.

35. Ibid., p. 165.

36. Smith, ' "The Finger That Points to the Moon": Reply to Per Kvaerne', p. 170.

37. Ibid.

38. Wilfred Cantwell Smith, *Questions of Religious Truth*, New York: Charles Scribner's Sons 1967, p. 107.

39. Ibid, p. 101.

40. Smith, *Towards a World Theology*, p. 168.

41. Smith, 'Comparative Religions: Whither – Why?', p. 35; *The Meaning and End of Religion*, pp. 187–8. A clear article analysing Smith's understanding of how it is possible to know the faith of others is available. See: Antonio Roberto Gualtieri, 'Can We Know the Religious Faith of Others?', *Religion and Society* 20, September 1973, pp. 6–17.

42. A notable exception to Smith's analysis of Western scholarship's obsession with objective data at the expense of the meaning dimension and living faith of participants is Huston Smith's *The Religions of Man* (New York 1958). Smith states: 'This last (*The Religions of Man*) is a luminous example of the treatment of religion as the faith of *persons*: note the opening paragraphs, which present people worshipping, the book moving on from this to portray their religion as the substance of their worshipping. . . This book is perhaps the first adequate textbook in world religions, precisely because it treats religions as human', 'Comparative Religion: Whither – and Why?', p. 38.

43. 'Religion as Symbolism', introduction to Propaedia, part 8, 'Religion', *Encyclopedia Britannica*, 15th ed, Chicago: Encyclopedia Britannica 1974, 1:500

44. Ibid., p. 68.

45. Ibid., p. 17.

46. Ibid., p. 15.

47. Smith, *Faith and Belief*, p. 131.

48. Smith, *The Meaning and End of Religion*, p. 190.

49. Cited in Smith, *Faith and Belief*, p. 180.

50. Ibid., pp. 131–2.

51. Ibid., p. 328, n. 1.

52. Ibid.

53. Ibid.

54. Smith, 'Traditional Religions and Modern Culture', p. 75.

55. This view has been presented by Langdon Gilkey in 'A Theological Voyage with Wilfred Cantwell Smith', a multiple review of *The Meaning and End of Religion, Belief and History, Faith and Belief*

and *Towards a World Theology*, by Wilfred Cantwell Smith, in *Religious Studies Review* 7, October 1981, pp. 303–4.

56. Smith, *Towards a World Theology*, p. 169.

57. Ibid., p. 171.

58. Wilfred Cantwell Smith, 'University Studies in Religion in a Global Context', in *Study of Religion in Indian Universities: A Report of the Consultation Held in Bangalore in September 1967*, Bangalore: Bangalore Press 1970, p. 68.

59. There are exceptions to Smith's criticism. He mentions McGill, Chicago and Harvard Universities as equipping scholars of comparative religion with the capacity to serve as mediators between two religions, 'Comparative Religon: Whither – and Why?' p. 51.

60. Smith, 'Religiously Divided History Approaches Self-Consciouness', in *Religious Diversity*, p. 113.

61. Ibid., p. 111.

62. For the fullest discussion of Smith's rejection of essentialism, see his McGill Inaugural Lecture, 'The Comparative Study of Religion: Reflections on the Possibility and Purpose of a Religious Science', in *McGill University, Faculty of Divinity, Inaugural Lectures*, Montreal: McGill University 1950, pp. 49–55.

63. Smith, *The Faith of Other Men*, pp. 15–16.

64. Ibid., p. 20.

65. Smith, *Faith and Belief*, p. 53.

66. Smith, *The Faith of Other Men*, p. 89.

67. Smith, *Towards a World Theology*, p. 182.

68. Ninian Smart, 'Truth and Religions', in *Truth and Dialogue in World Religions: Conflicting Truth Claims*, ed. John Hick, Philadelphia: The Westminster Press 1974, p. 45.

69. Ibid., p. 46.

70. Huston Smith, 'Faith and Its Study: What Wilfred Smith's Against and For', a multiple review of *The Meaning and End of Religion, Belief and History, Faith and Belief*, and *Towards a World Theology*, by Wilfred Cantwell Smith, *Religious Studies Review* 7, October 1981, p. 307. Other reviewers have likewise opted to accept Smith's criticisms of the concept of religion while nevertheless retaining the term. See: John B. Noss, review of *The Meaning and End of Religion*, by Wilfred Cantwell Smith, in *The Muslim World* 54, April 1964, p. 137; C. Douglas Jay, review of *The Meaning and End of Religion* and *The Faith of Other Men*, by Wilfred Cantwell Smith, in the *Canadian Journal of Theology* 13, January 1967, p. 73.

71. Ibid., pp. 307–8.

72. John A. Hutchison, 'Faith and Belief–Some Critical Reflections on the Thought of W. C. Smith', paper presented at the Claremont

Graduate School, at a conference entitled 'Toward a Philosophy of Religious Diversity', Claremont, California, January 1981, p. 2. See also: John Hick, Foreword to *The Meaning and End of Religion*, p. xiv.

73. Smart, 'Truth and Religions', p. 46.

74. Ninian Smart, *The Phenomenon of Religion*, New York: Herder and Herder, 1973, Ch. 1, passim.

75. Smith, *The Meaning and End of Religion*, pp. 49–50.

76. Smart, 'Truth and Religions', p. 46.

77. Ibid. In offering evidence for his position, Smart quotes Smith as saying: 'This is not the place to enter on a systematic study of faith's expressions.' This quotation from *The Meaning and End of Religion*, p. 155, however, offers inadequate evidence. On the contrary, it supports the fact that Smith does not speak of 'faith' in the plural. Faith remains a unitary capacity.

78. John Cobb, 'Smith's World Theology: An Appreciative Critique', paper presented at the Claremont Graduate School, at a conference entitled: 'Toward a Philosophy of Religious Diversity', Claremont, California, January 1981.

79. Ibid., p. 14.

80. Wilfred Cantwell Smith, 'On "Dialogue and Faith": A Rejoinder', *Religion* 3, 1976, p. 113.

81. For an illustration of Smith's linkage of the Neoplatonic One with the God of Semitic traditions, see *Towards a World Theology*, p. 188.

82. Cobb, 'Smith's World Theology: An Appreciative Critique', p. 15–16.

83. Ibid., p. 16.

84. Ibid., p. 13.

85. Smith, *Towards a World Theology*, p. 114.

86. Willard G. Oxtoby, Introduction to *Religious Diversity*, p. xx.

87. Wilfred Cantwell Smith, ' "The Finger that Points to the Moon": Reply to Per Kvaerne', p. 171. A similar error is to be found in Mac Linscott Ricketts' belief that Smith insists upon the reality of God for those doing religious research. Instead, Smith merely insists on an accurate phenomenology of religious life. See: Ricketts, review of *The Faith of Other Men* and *The Meaning and End of Religion*, by Wilfred Cantwell Smith, in *Journal of Asian Studies* 76, May 1979, p. 745.

88. Smith, 'On "Dialogue and Faith": A Rejoinder', p. 109.

89. Ibid.

90. Ibid.

91. Hutchison, 'Faith and Belief – Some Critical Reflections on the Thought of W. C. Smith', p. 4.

92. Ibid., p. 5.

93. Smith, *The Meaning and End of Religion*, p. 195.

94. Cobb, 'Smith's World Theology: An Appreciative Critique', pp. 8–9.

95. Smith, *Islam in Modern History*, p. 239.

96. Smith, *Modern Islam in India: A Social Analysis*, p. 307. See also Preface, p. 9.

97. Ibid., p. 308.

98. Ibid., p. 307.

99. Smith, *Islam in Modern History*, pp. 210–11 n. 5.

100. Smith, *Islam in Modern History*, p. 211.

101. Wilfred Cantwell Smith, 'The Crystallization of Religious Communities in Mughul India', in: *Yad Name ye Irani ye Minorsky*, eds. Mojtaba Minovi and Iraj Afshar, Ganjine-ye Tahqiqat-e Irani, no. 57, Publications of Tehran University, no. 1241, Tehran: Instisharat Daneshgah 1969, p. 212. For a similar analysis of this period, coupled with a similar rejection of Marxist critique see: Smith, 'The "Ulama" in Indian Politics', in: *Politics and Society in India*, ed. C. H. Phillips, London: George Allen and Unwin Ltd 1963, p. 45.

102. Smith, 'The Meaning of Modernization', in *Religious Diversity*, pp. 79–80.

103. Smith, *Islam in Modern History*, p. 183.

104. Smith, *The Faith of Other Men*, pp. 13, 73.

105. Willard G. Oxtoby, Introduction to *Religious Diversity*, pp. xii–xiii.

106. Ibid., p. 91

2   The Voyage of Belief

1. Smith, *Faith and Belief*, p. 158.

2. Ibid., p. 125.

3. Ibid., p. 12.

4. Ibid., p. 48.

5. Smith, *Belief and History*, pp. 54–5. Note that I am not referring to a Kantian theory in which one would have to say that certain forms of perception must be presupposed in order to structure a world.

6. Ibid., p. 120.

7. Wilfred Cantwell Smith, 'Is the Qur'an the Word of God?', in *Religious Diversity*, pp. 28–32.

8. Smith, *The Faith of Other Men*, p. 59.

9. Smith, *Islam in Modern History*, p. 103.

10. Ibid., p. 104.

11. Smith, *The Meaning and End of Religion*, pp. 327–8, n.6. Smith

here refers to Itrat Husain, *The Dogmatic and Mystical Theology of John Donne*, London 1938, and *The Mystical Element in the Metaphysical Poets of the Seventeenth Century*, London and Edinburgh 1948; and more recently, Muhammad Kamil Husayn, *Qaryah Zalimah,* Cairo 1957, translated *City of Wrong: A Friday in Jerusalem*, by Kenneth Craig, Amsterdam 1959.

12. Smith, *Faith and Belief,* pp. 80–1.

13. Ibid., p. 213.

14. Smith, *Belief and History*, p. 27.

15. Smith, 'University Studies of Religion in a Global Context', pp. 81–3.

16. Smith, *Faith and Belief*, p. 56.

17. For a discussion of these developments, see John Hick, *Death and Eternal Life,* London: Collins and New York: Harper and Row 1976, Chs. 16–19. See especially Ch. 16, pp. 297–8; Ch. 18, pp. 358–60; Ch. 19, pp. 374–5.

18. Smith, *Faith and Belief*, p. 52.

19. Ibid., pp. 43–44.

20. See: Smith, *Faith and Belief*, Ch. 6, passim, and *Belief and History*, Ch. 2. passim.

21. Smith, *Belief and History*, p. 96, and *Faith and Belief*, p. 46.

22. Smith, *Faith and Belief*, p. 127.

23. Ibid., p. 77.

24. Ibid., pp. 105–6.

25. Ibid., p. 106.

26. Ibid., p. 107.

27. Ibid.

28. Ibid., p. 112.

29. Quoted in Smith, *Faith and Belief*, p. 116.

30. Smith, *Belief and History*, p. 72.

31. Smith, *Faith and Belief*, pp. 116–17.

32. Cited in Smith, *Belief and History*, p. 65. For the entire entry, see *The Random House Dictionary of the English Language,* 1966, s.v. 'belief'.

33. Smith, *Faith and Belief*, p. 120.

34. Ibid., *Belief and History*, p. 46.

35. Quoted in Smith, ibid., p. 47.

36. Quoted in Smith, ibid., p. 48.

37. Ibid., p. 48.

38. Quoted in Smith, ibid., p. 50.

39. Ibid., p. 51.

40. Ibid., pp. 62–3.

41. Quoted in Smith, ibid., p. 51.

42. Ibid., p. 52.

43. Ibid.

44. Smith notes in *Belief and History*, p. 52, that the ratio of first and second person, 'I or you believe' to third person 'he/she/they believe(s)' has decreased since the fifteenth century. Ordinary language depersonalizes more slowly, but academic usage has taken the lead away from the first and second person, towards the impersonal.

45. Ibid., p. 53.

46. Ibid., p. 57. One might object that the assertion sign (H) implies a verb. Yet this is the case only in some logical operations and implies an anonymous asserter.

47. Ibid., p. 53.

48. Ibid., p. 68.

49. Ibid., p. 60.

50. Smith, *Faith and Belief*, p. 39.

51. Ibid., p. 47.

52. Ibid., pp. 42–3.

53. Ibid., p. 54.

54. Ibid., p. 58.

55. Ibid., pp. 61, 223, n. 45.

56. Ibid., p. 62.

57. Ibid., pp. 65–6. See also p. 241, n. 73 where Smith espies a firm linkage between faith (*sraddha*) and truth (*satyam*) within the Hindu tradition.

58. Smith, *The Meaning and End of Religion*, pp. 180–1.

59. Ibid.

60. Smith, *Belief and History*, p. 39.

61. Smith, *Faith and Belief*, p. 28.

62. Ibid., p. 127.

63. Smith, *Belief and History*, pp. 70–1.

64. Ibid., p. 71.

65. Smith, *Faith and Belief*, pp. 116–17.

66. Smith, *Belief and History*, p. 72.

67. Ibid.

68. Ibid., p. 73.

69. Ibid., p. 89.

70. Ibid., pp. 89–90.

71. Ibid., p. 91.

72. Ibid., p. 126.

73. Ibid., p. 85.

74. Ibid., p. 83.

75. Ibid., pp. 81–4.

76. Ibid., p. 82.
77. Smith, *Faith and Belief*, pp. 76–7.
78. Ibid., p. 76.
79. Ibid., p. 77.
80. Ibid.
81. Ibid., p. 258.
82. Ibid., p. 78.
83. Ibid., p. 255.
84. Ibid., p. 257.
85. Ibid., p. 84.
86. Ibid., p. 85.
87. Ibid.
88. Ibid., p. 84.
89. Ibid., p. 87.
90. Ibid.
91. Ibid.
92. Ibid., p. 90.
93. Ibid., pp. 91–100.
94. Ibid., p. 103.
95. Ibid.
96. Ibid.
97. Ibid.
98. Ibid., p. 52.
99. Ibid., pp. 121–2.
100. Ibid., p. 125.

3   An Understanding of Truth

1. Wilfred Cantwell Smith, 'Methodology and the Study of Religion: Some Misgivings', in: Robert D. Baird (ed.), *Methodological Issues in Religious Studies*, Chico, California: New Horizons Press 1975, p. 19.
2. Smith, *Towards a World Theology*, p. 86.
3. See Smith, 'Comparative Religion: Whither – and Why?', p. 35, for his suggestion to 'recall the once lucid and important notion that there may be gradations of reality'. See also Wilfred Cantwell Smith, 'Thinking About Persons', *Humanitas* 15, 1979, p. 49, in which he discusses the metaphor of a 'level of reality . . . higher than ourselves'.
4. Smith, 'Methodology and the Study of Religion: Some Misgivings', p. 20. For a similar analysis see also: 'Secularity and the History of Religion', p. 34.
5. Smith, 'Methodology and the Study of Religion', p. 21.
6. Ibid., p. 20.
7. Ibid., p. 14.

8. Ibid., pp. 16–17.

9. See Wilfred Cantwell Smith, *Faith and Belief*, p. 331, n. 3.

10. Ibid.

11. Ibid., pp. 289–30 n. 75.

12. Smith, *The Faith of Other Men*, p. 34.

13. Ibid., p. 36.

14. See Smith, *Towards a World Theology*, p. 185, where he acknowledges his 'Neo-Platonist tendencies'.

15. Wilfred Cantwell Smith, 'A Human View of Truth', in *Truth and Dialogue in World Religions: Conflicting Truth-Claims*, ed. John Hick, Philadelphia: Westminster Press 1974, p. 34.

16. Smith, *Faith and Belief*, pp. 87, 125.

17. Wilfred Cantwell Smith, 'The Intellectuals in the Modern Development of the Islamic World', in: Sydney Nettleton Fisher (ed.), *Social Forces in the Middle East*, Ithaca: Cornell University Press 1955, pp. 191–3.

18. Smith, 'Methodology and the Study of Religion', p. 10.

19. Smith, *Faith and Belief*, p. 160.

20. Smith, 'A Human View of Truth', p. 21.

21. Ibid.

22. Wilfred Cantwell Smith, *Orientalism and Truth: A Public Lecture in Honor of T. Cuyler Young, Horatio Whitridge Garrett Professor of Persian Language and History, Chairman of the Department of Oriental Studies*, Princeton: Program in Near Eastern Studies, Princeton University 1969, p. 11.

23. Smith, *Belief and History*, p. 51.

24. Terence Penelhum, review of *Belief and History*, by Wilfred Cantwell Smith, in *Sciences religieuses/Studies in Religion* 7, July 1978, pp. 453–4.

25. Smith, *Faith and Belief*, p. vii.

26. Smith, *Belief and History*, p. 4.

27. Ninian Smart, *The Phenomenon of Religion,* pp. 2–3.

28. Penelhum, review of *Belief and History*, p. 453.

29. Smith, *Belief and History*, p. 103, n. 3.

30. Ibid., pp. 4–5.

31. See Malcolm L. Diamond, 'The Challenge of Contemporary Empiricism', in *The Logic of God: Theology and Verification*, ed. Malcolm L. Diamond and Thomas V. Litzenburg, Jr, Indianapolis: The Bobbs-Merrill Company 1975, pp. 3–54, for a summary exposition of the contemporary evolution of verification theory and its application to religious language.

32. Smith, *Belief and History*, pp. 12–13.

33. Huston Smith, 'Faith and Its Study: What Wilfred Smith's Against, and For', p. 308.

34. Ibid.

35. See Smith, *The Faith of Other Men*, Chapter 3, passim.

36. Smith, *Faith and Belief*, p. 153.

37. Ibid., p. 154.

38. Ibid.

39. Ibid., p. 332, n. 10.

40. Smith, 'A Human View of Truth', p. 22.

41. Ibid., p. 40.

42. Irwin M. Copi, *Introduction to Logic*, 4th ed., New York: Macmillan Company 1972, p. 6.

43. Smith, *Faith and Belief*, p. 333, n. 12. See also *Belief and History*, p. 105.

44. Smith, *Faith and Belief*, p. 17.

45. Ibid., pp. 20–1.

46. Gilkey, 'A Theological Voyage with Wilfred Cantwell Smith', p. 302.

47. Wilfred Cantwell Smith, 'Conflicting Truth-Claims: A Rejoinder', in: *Truth and Dialogue in World Religions: Conflicting Truth Claims*, ed. John Hick, Philadelphia: The Westminster Press 1974, p. 158.

48. Ibid., p. 160.

49. Ibid., pp. 158–9

50. Ibid., p. 208, n. 41.

51. Ibid., p. 148.

52. See Ian Ramsey, *Religious Language*, London: SCM Press Ltd 1957, pp. 19–23.

53. Smith, *Faith and Belief*, p. 329, n. 1.

54. Quoted in Eric H. Pyle, 'Diagnosis of Religion', in: *Prospect for Theology: Essays in Honor of H. H. Farmer*, Welwyn Garden City: James Nisbet 1966, p. 226.

55. Smith, *Faith and Belief*, pp. 325–6, n. 65.

56. Ibid., p. 99.

57. Herbert Henry Farmer, *Revelation and Religion*, Welwyn Garden City: James Nisbet 1954, passim.

58. For Nanak as a personalist, see Wilfred Cantwell Smith, 'The Crystallization of Religious Communities in Mughal India', pp. 199–200. Here personalism is understood as the enemy of formalism. Also: Smith, *Faith and Belief*, p. 326, n. 65, for an understanding of Jesus as an I/Thou personalist and *Belief and History*, pp. 70–99 passim, for a non-propositionalist analysis of New

Testament thought; also p. 39 for a reference to the Qur'an as a personalist document.

59. One hesitates to use the word 'influence', since Smith finds the word imprecise, astrological and misleading – misleading because it confers a passive role on those who are 'influenced'. See Wilfred Cantwell Smith, 'Interpreting Religious Interrelations: An Historian's View of Christian and Muslim', in *Studies in Religion/ Sciences religiuses* 6, 1976–77; 'Participation: The Changing Christian Role in Other Cultures', p. 126; *Towards a World Theology*, pp. 39–40.

60. Smith, *Towards a World Theology*, p. 61.

61. Smith, 'Thinking About Persons', p. 148.

62. Smith, *Towards a World Theology*, pp. 65, 69.

63. Ibid., p. 62. See also: Smith, 'Comparative Religion: Whither – and Why?' pp. 31–4.

64. One thinks of the massive and as yet untranslated work of Joachim Wach on the nature of understanding: Joachim Wach, *Das Verstehen*, 3 vols., Tübingen: Siebeck 1926–32.

65. Kees Bolle finds Smith to be without a 'good grounding' in hermeneutical and epistemological issues, in a review of *The Meaning and End of Religion, Journal of Religion* 44:2, April 1964, pp. 170–2.

66. Pruett, 'History, Transcendence, and World Community in the Works of Wilfred Cantwell Smith', pp. 588–9.

67. Smith, *Towards a World Theology*, p. 84. A similar pragmatic approach to understanding the religious existence of others may be found in Ninian Smart who observes that ordinary speech indicates that understanding is of degrees and that a sympathetic entering into the world of another is a common day affair. It happens regularly in the reading of literature. See: *The Phenomenon of Religion*, p. 72, and *The Philosophy of Religion*, New York: Oxford University Press 1979, pp. 24–5.

68. Oxtoby, Introduction to 'Participation: The Changing Christian Role in Other Cultures', in *Religious Diversity*, pp. 117–18.

69. Smith, *Belief and History*, p. 85; see also pp. 122–5 for a summary view of the use of 'person' in Western history.

70. Smith, 'Thinking About Persons', p. 148.

71. Ibid., p. 21.

72. Ibid.

73. Ibid., p. 33.

74. Ibid., pp. 21–2.

75. Ibid., p. 22.

76. Ibid.

77. Ibid., pp. 22–5.

78. Ibid., p. 24.
79. Ibid., pp. 24–5.
80. Ibid., p. 25.
81. Ibid.
82. Ibid.
83. Ibid., p. 26.
84. Ibid., p. 27.
85. Ibid.
86. Ibid.
87. Ibid.
88. Ibid.
89. Ibid., p. 34.
90. Ibid.
91. Ibid.
92. Ibid.
93. Ibid., p. 35.

4   A New Method: Critical Corporate Self-Consciousness

1. Smith, *Towards a World Theology*, pp. 124–5.
2. Ibid., pp. 127, 186.
3. Ibid., p. 124.
4. Ibid., p. 124.
5. Smith, 'The Comparative Study of Religion', p. 46.
6. Smith, 'Comparative Religion: Whither – and Why?', p. 51.
7. Ninian Smart refers to connotations of exclusivity in the history of the use of 'comparative religion' in *Worldviews*, New York: Charles Scribner's Sons 1983, p. 20. John A. Hutchison also rejects 'comparative religion' for its connotations of normative religion. For Hutchison the term has been too associated with attempts to discover the 'best' religion or to abstract and uncover the common essence of religion. Hutchison, *Paths of Faith*, 3rd ed., New York: McGraw Hill 1975, p. xii.
8. See Hutchison, *Paths of Faith*, pp. xiii-xv, for the use of 'path', and Ninian Smart, *Worldviews*, pp. 1–8, for discussion of the term 'world-view'.
9. Smith, 'Religion as Symbolism', pp. 498–500.
10. Smith, *Towards a World Theology*, p. 78.
11. Ibid., p. 10.
12. Ibid., p. 9.
13. Wilfred Cantwell Smith, 'Objectivity and the Humane Sciences', p. 174.
14. Ibid.
15. Ibid., p. 175.

16. Ibid.

17. Smith, 'Methodology and the Study of Religion', p. 12.

18. Ibid., p. 19. For an excellent appreciation of, and amplification on, Smith's concern for recognizing the necessary human qualities that a researcher requires, see Ninian Smart, 'Scientific Phenomenology and Wilfred Cantwell Smith's Misgivings', in an unpublished *Festschrift* for Wilfred Cantwell Smith, 1984, pp. 8–13.

19. Smith, *Towards a World Theology*, p. 56.

20. Smith, 'The Comparative Study of Religion', p. 42.

21. Smith, 'Objectivity and the Humane Sciences', p. 163.

22. Ibid., p. 164.

23. Ibid., p. 163.

24. Smith, *Towards a World Theology*, p. 64.

25. Ibid., p. 87.

26. Ibid., p. 64.

27. Ibid.

28. Ibid.

29. Ibid., p. 164.

30. Ibid., pp. 101–2.

31. Ibid., p. 69.

32. There is no indication that Smith is familiar with Carl Roger's classic *On Becoming a Person*, Boston: Houghton Mifflin 1961.

33. Smith, *Towards a World Theology*, pp. 90–1.

34. Ibid., p. 103.

35. Smith, 'Objectivity and the Humane Sciences', pp. 178–9.

36. The entire movement of identification is expressed in the statement that: 'Students would do well to ask themselves, concerning any account or any project that they meet, in which category it falls; impersonals/it, impersonal/they, we/they, we/you, we-both, or we-all. A writer should clarify in his own mind which kind of book or article he is proposing to write; and an organizer, which kind of university department, or conference, or journal, he is proposing to run', 'Compartive Religion: Whither – and Why?', p. 57.

37. Wilfred Cantwell Smith, 'Divisiveness and Unity', in *Food/Energy and the Major Faiths*, ed. Joseph Gremillion, Maryknoll: Orbis Books 1978, p. 79.

38. Ibid., pp. 79–80.

39. These remarks were made on 23 January 1981, at a conference at the Claremont Graduate School, entitled 'Toward a Philosophy of Religious Diversity'.

40. Gilkey, 'A Theological Voyage with Wilfred Cantwell Smith', p. 304.

5 The Search for a Global Theology and Conclusion

1. Smith, 'The Christian in a Religiously Plural World', pp. 7–8.
2. Ibid., p. 21.
3. Smith, *The Faith of Other Men*, p. 122.
4. Smith, *Towards a World Theology*, pp. 1, 179.
5. Ibid., p. 125.
6. Smith, *The Faith of Other Men*, p. 81.
7. Smith, *Belief and History*, p. 91.
8. Smith notes that Hindus, Sufis and members of the Chinese religious complex have dealt with pluralism in a generous and thoughtful manner not generally present in the West. These traditions, however, produced theories of pluralism that are today inadequate, since based on a limited portion of the earth's religious life. *Towards a World Theology*, p. 180.
9. Smith, *The Faith of Other Men*, p. 107.
10. Smith explicitly refers to Clement of Alexandria, ibid., p. 90.
11. Smith, *Towards a World Theology*, p. 126.
12. Charges of having a Hindu orientation have appeared in: Martin Conway, review of *Questions of Religious Truth*, by Wilfred Cantwell Smith, in *Student World* 6:4, 1967, p. 359; Victor E. Hayward, review of *Questions of Religious Truth*, by Wilfred Cantwell Smith, in *International Review of Missions* 57, July 1968, p. 374; Per Kvaerne, in ' "Comparative Religion: Whither – and Why?" ' A Reply to Wilfred Cantwell Smith', p. 168.
13. Edward J. Hughes, 'The Understanding of Truth and Faith in the Writings of Wilfred Cantwell Smith', paper presented at the Claremont Graduate School, at a conference entitled 'Toward a Philosophy of Religious Diversity', Claremont, California, January 1981, p. 6.
14. Smith, *Faith and Belief*, p. 247 n. 2.
15. Smith, *The Meaning and End of Religion*, pp. 328–9, n. 9.
16. Smith, 'Secularity and the History of Religion', p. 65; *Towards a World Theology*, p. 161.
17. Mark Juergensmeyer, review of *Towards a World Theology*, by Wilfred Cantwell Smith, in *America* 145, December 1981, p. 407.
18. Guilford Dudley III, *Religion on Trial: Mircea Eliade and his Critics*, Philadelphia: Temple University Press 1971, p. 26.
19. Smith sees this situation ameliorating as departments of religious studies move in a collaborative direction. But he hopes that theologians will not leave these issues totally in the hands of comparative religionists. *Towards a World Theology*, pp. 151, 193.
20. Smith does not ask the scholar to discard the practice of the *epoche* in his or her descriptive work. It remains necessary to 'bracket'

one's preconceptions to enter into an alien world-view. He does challenge the student of comparative religion to move beyond scholarly objectivity and engage in the task of discerning truth in that which they study. *Towards a World Theology*, p. 151.

21. This challenge first appears in 'The Christian and the Religions of Asia'. In: *Changing Asia: Report of the Twenty-Eighth Annual Couchiching Conference: A Joint Project of the Canadian Institute on Public Affairs and the Canadian Broadcasting Corporation*, Toronto: Canadian Institute on Public Affairs 1959, pp. 9–16. A more accessible reprint can be found: 'Christianity's Third Great Challenge', *The Christian Century*, 77:17, 27 April 1960, pp. 505–08.

22. Wilfred Cantwell Smith, 'The Mission of the Church and the Future of Missions', in: George Johnston and Wolfgang Roth (eds), *The Church in the Modern World: Essays in Honour of James Sutherland Thomson*, Toronto: The Ryerson Press 1967, p. 179; *Towards a World Theology*, p. 193: 'On Dialogue and Faith': A Rejoinder', p. 107.

23. Smith, *Towards a World Theology*, p. 193.

24. Ibid.

25. Ibid., p. 194.

26. For an independent but parallel development of the theme of mutual transformation, see: John B. Cobb, Jr, *Beyond Dialogue: Towards a Mutual Transformation of Christianity and Buddhism*, Philadelphia: Fortress Press 1982, pp. 48, 142.

27. Smith, *Towards a World Theology*, p. 125.

28. Ibid., p. 126.

29. Ibid.

30. Ibid., pp. 110, 124.

31. Ibid., p. 110.

32. Ibid.

33. Ibid., p. 124.

34. Ibid., p. 125.

35. Ibid.

36. Ibid., pp. 153–4.

37. Cobb acknowledges that Smith intends to expand the Christian heritage by incorporating elements from other traditions, but argues that Smith is not a syncretist 'in the sense of failing to recognize specific roots and ties in the Christian heritage'. *Beyond Dialogue*, p. 38.

38. Note that the phrase 'secondary faith' is not a Smith usage. Instead, it belongs to Richard H. Robinson in the discussion that is appended to 'Non-Western Studies: The Religious Approach', p. 65.

39. Ibid.

40. For Smith's avowal that his programme for greater theological

inclusiveness is consistent with classical Christian theology see: *Towards a World Theology*, p. 17; *Faith and Belief*, p. 161.

41. Smith, *Towards a World Theology*, pp. 190–1.

42. John Hick, 'Comparative Perspectives in Theology', paper presented at the Pacific Coast Theological Society, Berkeley, California, 23 April 1982, pp. 4–5.

43. Smith, 'Religious Atheism? Early Buddhist and Recent American', p. 80; *The Faith of Other Men*, p. 80. For a similar analysis of 'syncretism', see: 'Participation: The Changing Christian Role', p. 126; see also: *The Meaning and End of Religion*, p. 316. Smith argues that all religious traditions borrow foreign elements and integrate them into their particular vision. In this sense, each religious tradition is syncretistic.

44. Smith, *Towards a World Theology*, p. 6.

45. Ibid., p. 16.

46. Ibid., pp. 11–12.

47. Ibid., p. 17.

48. Smith draws approvingly on the overview of religious historical development given in Robert N. Bellah's 'Religious Evolution', *American Sociological Review* 39, 1964, and the same author's *Beyond Belief: Essays on Religion in a Post-Traditional World*, New York: Harper and Row 1970. Cf. Smith, *Towards a World Theology*, pp. 18, 199.

49. Smith, *Towards a World Theology*, p. 125.

50. Ibid., p. 181.

51. Smith does not explicitly speak of a movement from self to reality-centred existence. This sort of depiction does, however, follow from his discussion of faith. See *Towards a World Theology*, pp. 181–2. This form of language is found in John H. Hick, *Philosophy of Religion*, 3rd. ed., Englewood Cliffs: Prentice-Hall, Inc. 1983, p. 3.

52. Smith, *Towards a World Theology*, pp. 144–45.

53. Ibid., p. 183.

54. Ibid., p. 44.

55. Smith is not a Hegelian in the espousal of the primacy of fact over concept. A major difference between Hegel's and Smith's understanding of religious evolution lies in Smith's more adequate understanding of non-Western religious life. One should also mention that Smith does not share in the deification of Western thought or in the idea of Christianity. Ibid., p. 37.

56. Ibid., p. 14.

57. The term 'Boddhisattva' (Guatama's title prior to Enlightenment) mutated first into 'Bodisof' in Manichaean traditions, then

'Yudasof' in the Georgian tongue, becoming 'Ioasoph' in Greek, and finally taking the Latin 'Josaphat', ibid., pp. 7–11.

58. Cited in Cobb, *Beyond Dialogue*, p. 54.

59. Ibid., p. 52.

60. Smith, *The Meaning and End of Religion*, pp. 304–5.

61. An analogy with aesthetic perception presupposes a relational theory of value that sees value as emerging from the relation between subjective interest and objective presentation. 'A good painting that is satisfying no one's interest at the moment possesses only potential value. A good painting possesses properties that under proper conditions are likely to stimulate the interests of a valuer', F. David Martin and Lee A. Jacobus, *The Humanities Through the Arts*, 2nd ed., New York: McGraw-Hill 1978, p. 446.

62. Smith, 'Can Religions be True or False?', in *Questions of Religious Truth*, p. 93.

63. Smith suggests that the Romantics may have been correct in holding that elevated imagination can apprehend realities unreachable by other means. For Smith, God uses imagination to 'save . . . through awareness of truth', *Belief and History*, p. 89. This is not to say that imagination is the primary mode of revelation, for God can reveal himself through all aspects of a tradition, *Towards a World Theology*, p. 165.

64. Smith, *Belief and History*, p. 72.

65. Ibid., pp. vi, 38.

66. Smith, *Towards a World Theology*, p. 154.

67. Ibid., p. 176.

68. Ibid., p. 173.

69. Smith, 'The Christian in a Religiously Plural World', pp. 17–18.

70. Smith, *Towards a World Theology*, p. 171.

71. Ibid., p. 175.

72. Smith, *The Faith of Other Men*, p. 93; 'Christianity's Third Great Challenge', p. 506.

73. Smith, *Towards a World Theology*, p. 175.

74. Smith, *Faith and Belief*, pp. 328–9, n. 1.

75. Smith, *Towards a World Theology*, p. 173.

76. For a summary report on the history of the World Council of Churches' attitude towards non-Christian tradition see Cobb, *Beyond Dialogue*, pp. 17–22.

77. Quoted in Cobb, *Beyond Dialogue*, p. 35.

78. Ibid., p. 24.

79. Ibid., pp. 22–3.

80. Ibid.

81. Smith, *Towards a World Theology*, p. 177.

82. Ibid., p. 171.

83. Smith, 'The Christian in a Religiously Plural World', p. 19.

84. Ibid., p. 137.

85. Cobb, *Beyond Dialogue*, p. 45.

86. Ibid., p. 128.

87. A number of critics have expressed concern over Smith's deabsolutized christology. Victor Hayward, review of *Questions of Religious Truth*, p. 374; Langdon Gilkey, 'A Theological Voyage with Wilfred Cantwell Smith', p. 303; William M. Thompson, review of *Towards a World Theology*, by Wilfred Cantwell Smith, in *Horizons* 9, Spring 1982, p. 180; John N. Jonsson, review of *Towards a World Theology*, by Wilfred Cantwell Smith, in *Review and Exposition* 80, Winter 1983, p. 153.

88. Smith, *Towards a World Theology*, p. 173.

89. Note that I am not suggesting that Smith would reject this type of christology, only that he has not presented it formally. At the Claremont Conference, in January 1981, entitled 'Toward a Philosophy of Religious Diversity', Smith spoke in a manner congruent with a universal Logos theology, saying that when Jesus exclaims that no man can come to the Father save by the Son he is speaking as the Logos, the perfect way of love. Smith agrees that those who would come to God must pass through the way of love.

90. Smith, 'The Christian in a Religiously Plural World', pp. 13–14.

91. Willard G. Oxtoby (ed.), *Religious Diversity*, p. 4.

92. Smith, *The Faith of Other Men*, p. 92.

93. Smith, 'Participation: The Changing Christian Role', pp. 129–30.

94. Smith, 'The Christian in a Religiously Plural World', pp. 5–6.

95. Smith, 'Christianity's Third Great Challenge', p. 505.

96. Smith, 'Participation: The Changing Christian Role', p. 130.

97. Ibid., p. 127.

98. Smith, 'Comparative Religion: Whither – and Why', p. 50.

99. Smith, *Towards a World Theology*, p. 178.

100. Smith, 'Christianity's Third Great Challenge', p. 507.

101. Smith, 'Orientalism and Truth', p. 6; 'The Christian in a Religiously Plural World', p. 13.

102. Smith, 'Christianity's Third Great Challenge', p. 507.

103. Smith, 'The Comparative Study of Religion', p. 58.

104. Smith, 'Participation: The Changing Christian Role', pp. 127–8.

105. Ibid., p. 131.

106. Ibid., p. 132.
107. Ibid., p. 134.
108. Smith, 'The Islamic Near East: Intellectual Role of Librarianship', pp. 287, 93.

APPENDIX

Descriptions of Faith

1. 'By faith I mean in part a way of looking at the world' (*Faith of Other Men*, p. 76.)

2. 'One of the things needed in a comparative study of religion is an ability to see the divine, which I call faith. Another is an ability to see it in new and different ways' (*Faith of Other Men*, p. 87).

3. 'A man of faith is a man whose vision goes beyond his immediate environment, but whose life is lived within it; so that his task, as a man of faith, is to apply that vision to the immediate environment, in all its specific actuality' (*Faith of Other Men*, pp. 105–6).

4. 'By "faith" I mean personal faith. . . . For the moment let it stand for an inner religious experience or involvement of a particular person; the impingement on him of the transcendent, putative or real' (*Meaning and End of Religion*, p. 156).

5. 'Yet suppose one proffers an operational definition, such as that religious faith is what happens to or in a man when he responds to the universe in a way that has been made available to him by the or a cumulative tradition' (*Meaning and End of Religion*, p. 330).

6. 'Rather, faith is the name that we give to the fact that one is in pursuit of something (or Someone) else' (*Meaning and End of Religion*, p. 331).

7. 'Faith, therefore, is not an entity. It is, rather, the adjectival quality of a person's living in terms of transcendence' (*Meaning and End of Religion*, p. 331).

8. 'Faith is nourished and patterned by the tradition, is formed and in some sense sustained by it – yet faith precedes and transcends the tradition, and in turn sustains it' (*Faith and Belief*, p. 5).

9. 'Faith, then, is an engagement: the involvement of the Christian with God and with Christ and with the sacraments and with the moral imperatives and with the community; the involvement of the Hindu with caste and with the law of retributive justice and the *maya* - quality of this mundane world and with the vision of a final liberation;

the involvement of the Buddhist with the image of the Buddha and with the moral law and with an institutionalized monastic order and with the dream of a further shore beyond this sea of sorrow; the involvment of the primitive animist with the world perceived in poetic, if bizarre, vitality and responsiveness' (*Faith and Belief*, pp. 5–6).

10. 'Since it is an *engagement*, to know faith authentically is to become oneself involved, to know it in personal committed fashion in one or another of its varied forms' (*Faith and Belief*, p. 6).

11. 'Faith', then I propose, shall signify that human quality that has been expressed in, has been elicited, nurtured, and shaped by the religious traditions of the world. This leaves faith unspecified, while designating its locus. We do not yet say what it is, but indicate where we are to look in order to find out. Thus an inquiry becomes possible, historical and empirical' (*Faith and Belief*, p. 6).

12. 'Faith, the historian reports, is the fundamental religious category; even, the fundamental human category. The theologian – Christian, Islamic, or other – may hardly dissent' (*Faith and Belief*, p. 7).

13. 'It is an orientation of the personality, to oneself, to one's neighbor, to the universe; a total response; a way of seeing whatever one sees and of handling whatever one handles; a capacity to live at a more than mundane level; to see, to feel, to act in terms of, a transcendent dimension' (*Faith and Belief*, p. 12).

14. 'Faith, then, is a quality of human living. At its best it has taken the form of serenity and courage and loyalty and service; a quiet confidence and joy which enable one to feel at home in the universe, and to find meaning in the world and in one's own life, a meaning that is profound and ultimate, and is stable no matter what may happen to oneself at the level of immediate event' (*Faith and Belief*, p. 12).

15 'Some might wish perhaps to make a pass at it, by suggesting, for instance, that his or her faith has traditionally been a commitment that the life of the mind is worthwhile and reliable, that the universe is (at least in part) intelligible or at least that the striving to render it intelligible is valid or obligatory or rewarding or humanly proper – or, more etymologically, by suggesting that his or her faith is a love of wisdom' (*Faith and Belief*, p. 16).

16. 'A comparativist looking out over the religious history of mankind is liable to hold that faith cannot be defined; and yet he or she might be attracted to a characterizing of it as the capacity of human beings to devote themselves to transcendence' (*Faith and Belief*, p. 103).

17. 'Faith is not to be subordinated to belief, nor to anything else mundane. To it, all religious forms are to be seen as at best strictly secondary – as faith itself is secondary to, derivative from, answerable to, transcendent reality and final truth' (*Faith and Belief*, p. 125).

18. 'One might argue that it is *the* essential human quality: that it is constitutive of man as human; that personality is constituted by our universal ability, or invitation, to live in terms of a transcendent dimension, and in response to it. Certainly the human everywhere is, and from the beginning has been open to a quality of life in oneself, in one's neighbor, and in the universe that lifts one above the merely mundane and the immediate, and means that one may be always in part but is never totally simply a product or a victim of circumstance' (*Faith and Belief*, p. 129).

19. 'Faith varies. Some have faith that is large, rich, strong, serene, and that renders them generous, courageous, compassionate, patient, nobel, creative' (*Faith and Belief*, p. 131).

20. 'A less limited vision, however, offering a comprehensive and fairly demonstrable assessment, is that in each particular case faith has been the confluence of both time and what one may wish to call eternity; it is the locus of man's transcendence, a channel of particularized shape by which man has reached, been reached by, a truth that transcends those and all particulars' (*Faith and Belief*, p. 132.)

21. 'Faith is man's participation in that *Heilsgeschichte*. Faith, as a global human characteristic, is – or shall we say, keeping to our more strictly historical approach, faith has been – man's responsive involvement in the activity of God's dealing with humankind: that on-going and multifaceted activity. By modern eyes, unless they wear blinkers, that divine activity can be seen as having Hindu and Greek, Buddhist and Jewish, Islamic and Christian, and many another sector' (*Faith and Belief*, p. 140).

22. 'Faith is man's participation in God's dealing with human kind. The aphorism is inadequate: granted, I still have no desire to put aside my joyous contention that all formulations of faith fail to do it justice – to do justice either to its depth of substance, or to its variety of form' (*Faith and Belief*, p. 140).

23. 'Faith is neither rare nor automatic. Rather, it is ubiquitously astonishing. It is the prodigious hallmark of being human' (*Faith and Belief*, p. 142).

24. 'Faith is beyond apprehension because it is the human potentiality for being human. It is our strange dynamic towards becoming our true selves, or becoming divine. Those who have said traditionally that faith is supernatural may in our century be heard by some

as affirming that persons are, that personality is, non-reducible, more than mundane; faith is that quality of or available to humankind by which we are characterized as transcending, or are enabled to transcend, the natural order – an order both in and beyond which, simultaneously, it has been normal, we may observe, for men and women to live' (*Faith and Belief*, p. 142).

25. 'Faith is a virtue. Believing is not' (*Faith and Belief*, p. 142).

26. 'Moreover, faith is a quality of the whole person. It has, therefore, as many dimensions as has personhood. Accordingly, it has an intellectual dimension' (*Faith and Belief*, p. 158).

27. 'Taking these components one by one, one may aver the history of faith to be a history of insight. There is a difference between knowing that something is true and knowing its truth, recognizing it' (*Faith and Belief*, p. 159).

28. 'To recognize, at least in part, the justice of what is in fact just, the cogency of a logical argument, the goodness of a cup of cold water given in love or the horrendous evil of Auschwitz, the glory of a sunset or of a cherry blossom – these are insights. These are faith' (*Faith and Belief*, p. 160).

29. 'For faith, too, intellectually, is insight. It is so on a potentially grander scale, at its best, than any of these; yet it is continuous with them. For the follower, as distinct from the leader, religious faith intellectually is first of all the ability to see the point of a tradition. At the propositional level, religious or otherwise, it concerns an ability that formulations potentially have: that of allowing or inducing those who hear them to move beyond them to the truth with which the person who framed them was in touch' (*Faith and Belief*, p. 160).

30. 'Faith is a saying 'Yes!' to truth; and it would not do to minimize the truth that Christians, or that Muslims, or that any of the others did in fact see and to which in their lives they responded, and in terms of which they and their fellows reared and sustained a civilization' (*Faith and Belief*, p. 163).

31. 'Faith is not a belief in a doctrine. It is not even belief in the truth as such, whatever it be. It is "assent" to the truth as such, in the dynamic and personal sense of rallying to it with delight and engagement. It is the exclamation mark in saying not merely "yes" but "Yes!" to the truth when one sees it. It is the ability to see and to respond' (*Faith and Belief*, p. 168).

32. 'Faith is, among other things, an attitude; and for intellectuals, an attitude to truth. It involves, among other matters, the will; and for intellectuals, the will to know and to understand. It requires – or

confers – among other virtues, integrity; and for intellectuals, the utmost intellectual honesty' (*Faith and Belief*, p. 168).

33. 'It is the capacity to see for oneself the loveliness of what is lovely; to see the difference between justice and injustice; to see the stupendous importance of truth; to see the point of a cup of cold water given in love, or the point of a man dying on a cross. If we see what is there waiting to be seen in our life and in this strange world of ours, waiting not necessarily on the surface but just beyond it, and then more beyond that, then we have faith. If we see even a little, we soon find that there is more and more. If we do not see, if we see nothing beyond the surface at all, which is life's supreme tragedy, then we do not have faith' (*Belief and History*, p. 79).

34. 'If one does not realize, has not recognized, that the universe that we live in has coherent transcendent qualities in it which have been called divine, and that these are more worthwhile, more rewarding than anything else that one can pursue, then one will not get close to the reality of those qualities. This is faith: the recognition of worth' (*Belief and History*, p. 80).

35. 'If faith be primarily a quality of the person, then we err in underplaying this. Even if it be, as many would hold, a relationship – "faith is man's relation to transcendence", for example – still, both sides of the relation are involved; and "faith" is primarily the name for the human side – which alone is available for study' (*Belief and History*, p. 92).

36. 'I am insisting that faith is one of the human virtues, like courage and loyalty; and that if we are to understand human religious life we should re-learn to see it so' (*Belief and History*, p. 92).

37. 'If faith is the name of a relationship between the human person and God (which has certainly been one powerful way of approximating in words to expressing its mystery), then we do well to recognize how much of an innovation it is to conceive that relation as one between a subject and an object. If one is to use theist language of this sort, then is it not better to conceive it as a relation between the two in which, rather, God is the subject? It would be a mistake, however, to think that the human person, in turn, then becomes the object. Rather, he or she, in faith, becomes co-subject' (*Belief and History*, p. 95).

BIBLIOGRAPHY

Abe, Masao, 'Faith and Self-Awakening: A Search for the Fundamental Category of Covering All Religious Life'. Paper presented at the Claremont Graduate School, at a conference entitled 'Toward a Philosophy of Religious Diversity', Claremont, California, 23–24 September 1981.

Bolle, Kees, review of *The Meaning and End of Religion*, by Wilfred Cantwell Smith, *Journal of Religion* 44, April 1964, pp. 170–2.

Cobb, John B., Jr, 'Smith's World Theology: An Appreciative Critique'. Paper presented at the Claremont Graduate School, at a conference entitled 'Toward a Philosophy of Religious Diversity', Claremont, California, 23–24 September 1981.

—, *Beyond Dialogue: Toward a Mutual Transformation of Christianity and Buddhism*, Philadelphia: Fortress Press 1982.

Conway, Martin, review of *Questions of Religious Truth*, by Wilfred Cantwell Smith, *Student World* 61, 1967, pp. 357–9

Copi, Irving M., *Introduction to Logic*, 4th ed., New York: Macmillan Company 1976.

Diamond, Malcolm L., 'The Challenge of Contemporary Empiricism', in *The Logic of God: Theology and Verification*, pp. 3–53, by Malcolm L. Diamond and Thomas V. Litzenburg, Jr., Indianpolis: The Bobbs-Merril Company 1975.

Dudley, Guilford, III, *Religion on Trial: Mircea Eliade and His Critics*, Philadelphia: Temple University Press 1977.

Fowler, James W., *Stages of Faith: The Psychology of Human Development and the Quest for Meaning*, New York: Harper and Row 1981

Gilkey, Langdon, 'A Theological Voyage with Wilfred Cantwell Smith', review of *The Meaning and End of Religion, Belief and History, Faith and Belief, Towards a World Theology*, by Wilfred Cantwell Smith, *Religious Studies Review* 7, October 1981, pp. 293–306.

Gualtieri, Antonio Roberto, 'Faith, Tradition, and Transcendence:

A Study of Wilfred Cantwell Smith', *Canadian Journal of Theology* 15, April 1969, pp. 102–11.

—, 'Can We Know the Religious Faith of Others?: Some Light from Wilfred Cantwell Smith', *Religion and Society* 20, September 1973, pp. 6–17.

Hayward, Victor E., review of *Questions of Religious Truth*, by Wilfred Cantwell Smith, *International Review of Missions* 57, July 1968, pp. 372–5.

Hick, John H., *Death and Eternal Life*, London: New York: Harper and Row 1976

—, Comparative Perspectives in Theology'. Paper presented at the Pacific Coast Theological Society, Berkeley, California, 23 April 1982.

—, *Philosophy of Religion*, 3rd ed., Englewood Cliffs: Prentice-Hall 1983.

Hutchison, John A., *Paths of Faith*, 2nd ed., New York: McGraw-Hill 1975.

—, 'Faith and Belief – Some Critical Reflections on the Thought of W. C. Smith'. Paper presented at the Claremont Graduate School, at a conference entitled 'Toward a Philosophy of Religious Diversity', Claremont, California, 23–24 September 1981.

Jay, C. Douglas, review of *The Faith of Other Men* and *The Meaning and End of Religion*, by Wilfred Cantwell Smith, *Canadian Journal of Theology* 13, January 1967, pp. 72–4.

Johnsson, John N., review of *Towards a World Theology*, by Wilfred Cantwell Smith, *Review and Expositor* 80, Winter 1983, pp. 151–2.

Juergensmeyer, Mark, review of *Towards a World Theology*, by Wilfred Cantwell Smith, *America* 145, December 1981, p. 407.

Kvaerne, Per, ' "Comparative Religion: Whither – and Why?" A Reply to Wilfred Cantwell Smith', *Temenos* 9, 1973, pp. 166–8.

Martin, F. David, and Jacobus, Lee A., *The Humanities Through the Arts*, 2nd ed., New York: McGraw-Hill 1978.

Noss, John G., Review of *The Meaning and End of Religion*, by Wilfred Cantwell Smith, *The Muslim World* 54, April 1964, pp. 136–7.

Penelhum, Terence, Review of *Belief and History*, by Wilfred Cantwell Smith, *Studies in Religion/Sciences religieuses* 7, July 1978, pp. 452–4.

Pruett, Gordon E., 'History, Transcendence, and World Community in the Work of Wilfred Cantwell Smith,' *Journal of the American Academy of Religion* 41, December 1973, pp. 573–90.

Pyle, Eric H., 'Diagnosis of Religion', in *Prospect for Theology: Essays in Honour of H. H. Farmer*, Welwyn Garden City: James Nisbet 1966, pp. 201–7.

Rackman, Emmanuel, review of *The Meaning and End of Religion*, by Wilfred Cantwell Smith, *Jewish Social Studies* 27, October 1965, pp. 273–4.

Rahbar, Daud, review of *The Meaning and End of Religion*, by Wilfred Cantwell Smith, *Journal of Bible and Religion* 32, July 1964, pp. 275–77.

Ramsey, Ian T. *Religous Language*, London: SCM Press 1957.

Ricketts, Mac Linscott, review of *The Faith of Other Men* and *The Meaning and End of Religion*, by Wilfred Cantwell Smith, *Journal of Asian Studies* 25, August 1966, pp. 774–5.

Smart, Ninian, *The Phenomenon of Religion*, New York: Oxford University Press 1979.

—, 'Truth and Religions', in *Truth and Dialogue in World Religions: Conflicting Truth Claims*, ed. John Hick, Philadelphia: The Westminster Press 1974.

—, *The Philosophy of Religion*, New York: Oxford University Press 1979.

—, *In Search of Christianity*, New York: Harper and Row 1979

—, *Worldviews*, New York: Charles Scribner's Sons 1983.

—, 'Scientific Phenomenology and Wilfred Cantwell Smith's Misgivings', unpublished manuscript for a *Festschrift* for Wilfred Cantwell Smith, 1984.

Smith, Huston, 'Faith and Its Study: What Wilfred Cantwell Smith's Against, and For', Review of *The Meaning and End of Religion, Belief and History, Faith and Belief* and *Towards a World Theology*, by Wilfred Cantwell Smith, *Religious Studies Review* 7, October 1981, pp. 306–10.

Smith, Wilfred Cantwell, *Modern Islam in India: A Social Analysis*, Lahore: Minerva 1943. Revised ed: London: Gollancz '1946' (sc. 1947). Reissued Lahore: Sh. M. Ashraf 1963, 1969; New York: Russell and Russell 1972, and pirated edition, Lahore, Ripon, 1947 (with a spurious chapter 'Towards Pakistan' by an unknown other hand).

—, *Pakistan as an Islamic State*, Lahore: Sh. M. Ashraf '1951' (sc. 1954).

—, *Islam in Modern History*, Princeton: Princeton University Press 1957. Reissued: London: Oxford University Press 1958; New York: New American Library (Mentor Books) 1965; Princeton and London: Princeton University Press (Princeton Paperback) 1977.

—, *The Faith of Other Men*, Toronto: Canadian Broadcasting Corporation, 1962. Enlarged edition: New York, New American Library 1963. Reissued: New York: New American Library (Mentor

Books) 1965; London: New English Library (Mentor Books) 1965; New York and London: Harper and Row (Torchbook) 1972. Part II ('The Christian in a Religiously Plural World') reprinted in *Religious Diversity* (infra) in slightly abridged form; also in John Hick and Brian Hebblethwaite (eds.) *Christianity and Other Religions*, London: Collins (Fount Paperbacks) 1980, pp. 87–107.

—, *The Meaning and End of Religion: A New Approach to the Religious Traditions of Mankind*, New York: Macmillan 1963. Reissued New York: New American Library (Mentor Books), 1964; London: New English Library (Mentor Books) 1965; New York: Harper and Row, and London: SPCK 1978.

—, *Modernization of a Traditional Society*, Bombay, Calcutta, etc.: Asia Publishing House 1965. Chapter 1, reprinted in slightly abridged form in *Religious Diversity* (infra).

—, *Questions of Religious Truth*, New York: Charles Scribner's Sons; and London: Gollancz 1967. Second chapter ('Is the Qur'an the Word of God?') reprinted in slightly abridged form in *Religious Diversity* (infra).

—, *Religious Diversity*, ed. Willard G. Oxtoby, New York and London: Harper and Row 1976.

—, *Belief and History*, Charlottesville: University Press of Virginia 1977.

—, *Faith and Belief*, Princeton: Princeton University Press 1979.

—, *Towards a World Theology*, London: Macmillan and Philadelphia: Westminster 1981.

—, *On Understanding Islam*, Religion and Reason Series: No. 19, The Hague: Mouton Publishers, 1981.

—, *Islam dawr-i hazir men (muntakhab-i mazamin)*, ed. Mushiru-l-Haqq, Delhi: Maktabah'-i Jami'ah 1984 (a collection of WCC published articles, translated into Urdu, with an introduction by the editor).

Articles on Religion Generally

—, 'The Comparative Study of Religon: Reflections on the Possibility and Purpose of a Religious Science', *McGill University, Faculty of Divinity, Inaugural Lectures*, Montreal: McGill University 1950, pp. 39–60.

—, 'The Christian and the Religions of Asia', in: *Changing Asia: Report of the Twenty-Eighth Annual Couchiching Conference: A Joint Project of the Canadian Institute on Public Affairs and the Canadian Broadcasting Corportion*, Toronto: Canadian Institute on Public Affairs 1959, pp. 9–16. Reprinted: *Occasional Papers*, Department of Missionary Studies, International Missionary Council (World Council of Churches), London, no. 5, April 1960; also as 'Christianity's Third Great Challenge', *The Christian Century* 77:17, 17 April 1960, pp. 505–8; also abridged, *The Beacon*, London, 39, 1962, pp. 337–40.

—, 'Comparative Religion: Whither – and Why?', in : Mircea Eliade and Joseph M. Kitagawa (eds.) *The History of Religions: Essays in Methodology*, Chicago: The University of Chicago Press 1959, pp. 31–58. Reprinted in abridged form in *Religious Diversity* (supra).

—, 'Mankind's Religiously Divided History Approaches Self-Consciousness', *Harvard Divinity Bulletin* 29:1, 1964, pp. 1–17. Reprinted in slightly abridged form in *Religious Diversity* (supra)

—, 'Secularism: The Problem Posed', *Seminar*, New Delhi 67, 1965, pp. 10–12.

—, 'Religious Atheism? Early Buddhist and Recent American', *Milla wa-Milla,* Melbourne 6, 1966, pp. 5–30. Reprinted: John Bowman (ed.), *Comparative Religion: The Charles Strong Trust Lectures 1961–70*, Leiden: E. J. Brill 1972, pp. 53–81.

—, 'The Mission of the Church and the Future of Missions', in: George Johnston and Wolfgang Roth (eds.), *The Church in the Modern World: Essays in Honor of James Sutherland Thomson*, Toronto: The Ryerson Press 1967, pp. 154–70.

—, 'Traditional Religions and Modern Culture', in: *Proceedings of the XIth International Congress of the International Association for the History of Religions*, Vol. 1. *The Impact of Modern Culture on Traditional Religions*, Leiden: E. J. Brill 1968, pp. 55–72. Reprinted in slightly abridged from in *Religious Diversity* (supra).

—, 'Secularity and the History of Religion', in: Albert Schiltzer (ed.), *The Spirit and Power of Christian Secularity*, Notre Dame and London: University of Notre Dame Press 1969, pp. 35–38. Discussion follows, pp. 59–70.

—, 'University Studies of Religion in a Global Context', in: *Study of Religion in Indian Universities: A Report of the Consultation Held in Bangalore in September 1967*, Bangalore: Bangalore Press, nd (1970), pp. 74–87.

—, 'Participation: The Changing Christian Role in Other Cultures', *Occasional Bulletin*, Missionary Research Library, New York, 20:4, 1969, pp. 1–13. Reprinted: *Religion and Society*, Bangalore, 17:1, 1970, pp. 56–47; in abridged form in Gerald H. Anderson and Thomas F. Stransky (eds.), *Mission Trends No. 2*, New York: Paulist Press, and Grand Rapids: Eerdmans 1975, pp. 218–19; and in *Religious Diversity* (supra).

—, 'The Study of Religion and the Study of the Bible', *Journal of the*

American Academy of Religion 39, 1971, pp. 131–40. Reprinted with minor alterations in *Religious Diversity* (supra).

—, 'A Human View of Truth', *SR: Studies in Religion/Sciences religieuses* 1, 1971, pp. 6–24. Reprinted: John Hick (ed.) *Truth and Dialogue: The Relationship between World Religions*, London: Sheldon Press 1974; *Truth and Dialogue in World Religions: Conflicting Truth Claims*, Philadelphia: Westminster Press 1974, pp. 20–44, with a new addendum, 'Conflicting Truth Claims: A Rejoinder', ibid., pp. 156–62.

—, 'On "Dialogue and Faith": A Rejoinder' (to Eric J. Sharpe, 'Dialogue and Faith', in the same issue), *Religion* 3, 1973, pp. 106–144.

—, ' "The Finger That Points to the Moon": Reply to Per Kvaerne', (Kvaerne, ' "Comparative Religion: Whither and Why?" A Reply to Wilfred Cantwell Smith', in the same issue), *Temenos*, Helsinki 9, 1973, pp. 169–72.

—, 'Religion as Symbolism'. Introduction to Propaedia, part 8, 'Religion', *Encyclopedia Britannica*, 15th ed., Chicago, Encyclopedia Britannica, 1974, vol. 1, pp. 498–500.

—, 'Methodology and the Study of Religion: Some Misgivings', in: Robert D. Baird (ed.), *Methodological Issues in Religious Studies*, Chico, California: New Horizons Press 1979, pp. 1–25. ('Discussion', pp. 25–30); 'Is the Comparative Study of Religion Possible? Panel Discussion', with Jacob Neusner, Hans H. Penner, ibid., pp. 95–109; 'Rejoinder', pp. 123–4.

—, 'An Historian of Faith Reflects on What We are Doing Here', in: Donald G. Dawe and John B. Carman (eds.), *Christian Faith: A Religiously Plural World*, Maryknoll, New York: Orbis 1978, pp. 139–48

—'Divisiveness and Unity', in: Gremillion, Joseph (ed.), *Food/Energy and the Major Faiths*, Maryknoll, New York: Orbis 1978, pp. 71–85.

—, 'The Modern West in the History of Religion', *Journal of the American Academy of Religion* 52, 1984, pp. 3–18.

—, 'Philosophia, as One of the Religious Traditions of Humankind: the Greek Legacy in Western Civilization, viewed by a Comparativist', in: Jean-Claude Galey (ed.), *Différences, valeurs, hiérarchie: Textes offerts à Louis Dumont*, Paris: Éditions de l'École des Hautes Études en Sciences Sociales, pp. 253–79.

—, 'The World Church and the World History of Religion: the theological issue', *Catholic Theological Society of America: Proceedings* 39, 1984, pp. 52–68.

Articles on Education, Area Studies, and Social Concern Generally

—, 'The Place of Oriental Studies in a Western University', *Diogenes*, no. 16, 1956, pp. 104–11.

—, 'Non-Western Studies: The Religious Approach', in: *A Report on an Invitational Conference on the Study of Religion in the State University, Held October 23–25, 1964 at Indiana University Medical Center*, New Haven, The Society for Religion in Higher Education (1965), pp. 50–62. Comments and discussion follow, pp. 62–7.

—, 'Objectivity and the Humane Sciences: A New Proposal', *Transactions of the Royal Society of Canada*, Ottawa: Royal Society of Canada 1975, 4/12, 1974, pp. 81–102. Reprinted in abridged form in *Religious Diversity* (supra). Reprinted in: Claude Fortier et al., *Symposium on the Frontiers and Limitations of Knowledge/Colloque sur les frontières et limites du savoir*, Ottawa: Royal Society of Canada 1975, pp. 81–102.

—, *The Role of Asian Studies in the American University*, the plenary address of the New York State Conference for Asian Studies, Colgate University (1976), (Pamphlet).

—, 'The University', review article of: Murray Ross, *The University: The Anatomy of Academe*, New York 1976, in *Dalhousie Review* 57, 1977–78, pp. 540–9.

—, 'Thinking About Persons', *Humanitas* 15, 1979, pp. 147–52.

—, 'Responsibility', in: Eugene Combs (ed.), *Modernity and Responsibility: Essays for George Grant*, Toronto: University of Toronto Press 1983, pp. 74–84.

—, 'On Mistranslated Booktitles', *Religious Studies* 20, 1984, pp. 27–42.

Articles on Islamic Subjects

—, 'Islam Confronted by Western Secularism, (A): Revolutionary Reaction', in: Dorothea Seelye Franck (ed.), *Islam in the Modern World: A Series of Addresses Presented at the Fifth Annual Conference on Middle East Affairs, Sponsored by the Middle East Institute*, Washington, Middle East Institute 1951, pp. 19–30.

—, 'The Intellectuals in the Modern Development of the Islamic World', in: Sydney Nettleton Fisher (ed.), *Social Forces in the Middle East*, Ithaca: Cornell University Press 1956, pp. 190–204.

—, 'Some Similarities and Differences between Christianity and Islam: An Essay in Comparative Religion', in: James Kritzeck and R. Bayley Winer (eds.), *The World of Islam: Studies in Honour of Philip K. Hitti*, London: Macmillan and New York: St. Martin's Press 1959, pp. 47–59.

—, 'The Comparative Study of Religion in General and the Study of

Islam as a Religion in Particular', in: *Colloque sur la sociologie musulmane: Actes, 11–14 September 1961*, Correspondence d' Orient 5, Bruxelles: Publications du Centre pour l'étude du monde musulman contemporain (1962), pp. 217–31.

—, 'The Historical Development in Islam of the Concept of Islam as an Historical Development', in: Bernard Lewis and P. M. Holt (eds.), *Historians of the Middle East*, Historical Writing on the Peoples of Asia 4, London: Oxford University Press 1962, pp. 484–502.

—, 'The "Ulama" in Indian Politics', in: C. H. Philips (ed.), *Politics and Society in India*, London: George Allen and Unwin 1963, pp. 39–51.

—, 'The Islamic Near East: Intellectual Role of Librarianship', *Library Quarterly* 35, 1965, pp. 283–294. Discussion follows, pp. 279–97. Reprinted: Tsuen-Hsuin Tsien and Howard W. Winger (eds.), *Area Studies and the Library*, Chicago and London: The University of Chicago Press 1966, pp. 81–92 (92–95).

—, 'The Crystallization of Religious Communities in Mughul India', in: Mojtaba Minovi and Iraj Afshar (eds.), *Yad-Name-ye Irani [sic]-ye-Minorsky*, Ganjine-ye Tahqiqat-e Irani, no. 57; Publications of Teheran University, no. 124, Tehran: Intisharat Daneshgah 1969, pp. 197–220.

—, *Orientalism and Truth: A Public Lecture in Honor of T. Culyer Young, Horatio Whitridge Garrett Professor of Persian Language and History, Chairman of the Department of Oriental Studies*, Princeton, Program in Near Eastern Studies, Princeton University 1969, 16 pp. (pamphlet).

—, 'Interpreting Religious Interrelations: An Historian's View of Christian and Muslim'. in: *SR Studies in Religion/Sciences religieuses* 6, 1976–77, pp. 515–26.

Thompson, William M., *Review of Towards a World Theology*, by Wilfred Cantwell Smith, *Horizons* 9, Spring 1982, pp. 179–80.

Whaling, Frank (ed.), *The World's Religious Traditions: current perspectives in religious studies – essays in honour of Wilfred Cantwell Smith*, Edinburgh: T. & T. Clark 1984.

Wiebe, Donald, 'The Role of "Belief" in the Study of Religion: A Response to W. C. Smith', review of *Belief and History*, by Wilfred Cantwell Smith, *Numen* 26, December 1979, pp. 234–48.